THE HOUSE
OF GOD

EDWARD NORMAN

THE HOUSE OF GOD

CHURCH ARCHITECTURE, STYLE AND HISTORY

With 387 illustrations, 80 in colour

THAMES AND HUDSON

For the members of Christ Church College, Canterbury:

Hospes eram, et collegistis me

It is a great advantage to the author of a book like this to have had the opportunity of visiting nearly all the places whose features and histories are discussed. For many years I have had the privilege, as a lecturer for Swan Hellenic Cruises, of introducing many travellers to the churches of Mediterranean countries. I am also indebted to the BBC for allowing me, in the course of extensive journeying for programme research, the chance to see churches throughout the rest of the world. Academic colleagues in Canada and the United States have generously given their time to enable me to sample the extraordinary and enriching diversity of Christianity in North America.

E.R.N.
Christ Church College, Canterbury, 1990

Frontispiece: the Romanesque cathedral of Peterborough, under construction during most of the twelfth century, looking south-west from the crossing.

© 1990 Thames and Hudson Ltd, London

Printed and bound in Singapore by C.S. Graphics

CONTENTS

Introduction

St Elizabeth holds a model of the church dedicated to her at Marburg, Germany, a polychrome statue of about 1480.

THE CHURCH BUILDINGS which Christian believers have provided for themselves are not merely assembly halls for worship. They have always, from the very beginning, expressed, either in their structures or in the choice of their location, transcendent associations and spiritual insight. Churches have been raised upon sites particularly associated with the miraculous works of saints; they have been placed upon hills and mountains in honour of the heavenly hosts; and they have enclosed the earthly remains of revered men and women.

Church buildings have thus acquired symbolical significance. Partly as a consequence, they have sometimes been too heavily invested with detailed theological meaning. The cruciform shape of the Latin cross plan for church design, for example, evolved from the *porticus*, or small chambers, the one for the priest and the other for the remains of the dead, which were added to each side of the nave of the basilicas of the late Roman period. But the cruciform design was very early given mystical significance. Eusebius, the great fourth-century ecclesiastical historian, was already describing the material form of church buildings in terms of the Persons of the Trinity, and by the time of the Gothic cathedrals of medieval Europe the cruciform shape was always taken to represent the Cross of Christ. Symbolism has indeed been important in the development of church designs, but all interpretations of structural symbolism are controversial, on both historical and liturgical grounds. It is surprising how little is really known about liturgical practices and requirements until the late Middle Ages, both in the West and in the Byzantine East, and assumptions about the exact relationships between church forms and the performance of the worship and the rites of Christianity must usually be regarded with reserve.

The account which follows is not a work of architectural history, nor is it intended as a guide to the history of the Church as an institution mirrored in its physical remains. Correlations are not exact enough for that. There would be, for example, little point in providing short narrative essays summarizing the leading features of the ecclesiastical history of each age, only then to point out that the church buildings of each show little correspondence, in terms of style, to the predominant historical characteristics. What this study attempts is a survey of how church styles came to be adopted, how variations occurred, and how geographical distribution produced both similarities and further variations. It is intended for visitors to churches, that they may be assisted in their interpretation of the rich tradition of building whose surviving remnants are plentiful in the present world. Where it is possible, of course, an attempt *is* made to reflect aspects of the history of the Church in its buildings; but what must most impress the observer, in the largest perspective, is the priority of architectural and decorative *style*.

The adoption of a style is invariably the work of an élite – where there is evidence to know at all. The Byzantine world was covered with churches which echoed the form of Justinian's church of the Holy Wisdom in Constantinople; but that great building was an invention of genius, it did not derive from any popular mode of church building. The Gothic cathedrals of the medieval Latin

West, similarly, were ordered by patrons, ecclesiastical and lay, who sought to emulate the grandeur of other buildings they had seen in the style. It was a later species of romanticism, encouraged by Pugin and Ruskin, to suppose that they were thrown up by the spiritual imagination of folk culture. For all that, it must also be said that many churches, in all periods, were built according to existing styles simply because no one could envisage any other way of building them. In Rome architects may have been very self-conscious about building methods from the Renaissance onwards, but throughout the Christian world local patrons had no name for the various designs of buildings until the eighteenth century, and therefore lacked the screens of learned interpretation through which to categorize them. For centuries the Gothic style had no name: it was simply the shape churches were.

'Material edifices are no part of religion,' Cardinal Newman once remarked, 'but you cannot have religious services without them.' In point of fact you can: some of the most expansive and vital of the independent Black Christian sects and churches of present-day Africa meet for worship under trees or upon the banks of rivers which, to them, have cultic significance as the place of purification rites. The contemporary spread of the 'house church' movement within Western Christianity has also dispensed with the concept of sacred buildings for religious services. But Newman's essential contention stands; Christians believe that 'the Church' is the corporate existence of God in the world, and the Divine resides within all men if they will only bring their minds and wills into correspondence with what can be known of his purposes.

'The Church' is a condition of things, not a building. To examine a church structure, therefore – as in the pages which follow – is to contemplate the material evidence of a reality which is invisibly present. It is to see the imperfect description of faith, not its substance. But it is, nevertheless, to sense something of the spiritual splendour which the world anticipates and which, Christians believe, eternity delivers.

Two dedication scenes which show the lay patrons rather than the titular saints presenting their churches. Top: Enrico Scrovegno with his chapel at Padua, painted by Giotto about 1310. Bottom: Giangaleozzo Visconti presenting the Certosa of Pavia, 1488–90.

1 The footsteps of Jesus: the Holy Land and the Early Christians

UNTIL THE FOURTH CENTURY, Christian worship took place wherever space and safety could be found – in private rooms or the underground chambers of catacombs. Congregations were small. Meetings had often to be in secret. There were no churches.

The earliest Christian buildings were shrines rather than churches. First came the places associated with the life and death of Jesus – the 'upper room' of the Last Supper, the sites where various miracles had taken place, and those of the Crucifixion and burial. When St Helena, the mother of Constantine, came to the Holy Land three hundred years later, she found local tradition still strong. The churches built over these sacred spots have been repaired and rebuilt many times but are still among the most evocative of Christian buildings. In other parts of the Eastern Mediterranean and in Italy the places associated with the death and burial of martyrs and the preservation of their relics also came to be commemorated by buildings, often modelled on Roman tombs and mausolea.

The reign of Constantine marks the beginning of Christian architecture. Suddenly, without previous experiment or evolution, a major new building type was invented. Its closest predecessor was the Roman basilica: a large open hall used for civic meetings or legal affairs, consisting of two rows of columns with a flat entablature. The walls above the columns were pierced by windows (the clerestory), and outside them ran covered passages (aisles): an arrangement that is still called 'basilican', and which has remained widely used ever since. The altar was in an apsed space at the end opposite the entrance (conventionally, though not invariably, the east end), and between the nave and the apse there were often deeper spaces (transepts) transforming the plan into a cross.

The biggest of Constantine's basilicas was Old St Peter's in Rome. This was demolished in the sixteenth century, but others very like it still survive in S. Paolo fuori le Mura and Sta Maria Maggiore. Similar churches were built at Constantinople, Jerusalem, Bethlehem and elsewhere. Their architectural vocabulary was purely Roman. Very often they were made of reused Roman materials. But their function and the whole spiritual dimension that they embodied distinguished them sharply from every previous type of building. In their layout, furnishing, decoration and iconography they were completely new. Conditioned as they were by liturgical demands – the Eucharist, the sermon, choral singing and communal prayer – that are essentially unchanged, Early Christian churches are recognizably the ancestors of those still being built today.

For captions to colour plates 1–8, see p. 17

2,3

4,5

Colour plates 1–8

1 *The cross, enigmatically emerging in this aerial view from the rocky landscape of Ethiopia, is the roof of one of the oldest and strangest churches in the world. Christianity was introduced into the country about 330, but with the rise of Islam it was effectively isolated from Europe for a thousand years, retaining its traditions untouched. A unique feature of these churches is that they are not built but hollowed out of the rock.*

2 *As Christian doctrine was hammered out at the early Church councils, ideas that were often highly abstract and intellectual needed to be expressed symbolically for the comprehension of the laity. This fifth-century mosaic from the baptistry of Albenga, Italy, gives visible form to several interconnected concepts: the Chi-Rho (XP), the first letters of the Greek 'Christos', stand for Christ: repeated in a threefold circle they represent the three Persons of the Trinity, since baptism was pronounced in the name of the Father, the Son and the Holy Ghost. The letters alpha and omega, the first and the last, similarly repeated, carry the same message, while the doves symbolize the twelve Apostles.*

3 *The wall-painting of* The Good Shepherd *in the catacombs of Sta Priscilla illustrates the transition from paganism to Christianity. The classical figure of the shepherd carrying a lamb became one of the archetypes of Christ.*

4 *The dedication of churches to particular saints seems to be as old as churches themselves. The patron often represented himself literally handing the building to its spiritual owner. Here, in a mosaic of about 625, Pope Honorius I holds his church of S. Agnese fuori le Mura ('outside the walls') in Rome.*

5 *Sta Maria in Cosmedin, Rome, was built in the fifth century to serve members of the Greek community in Rome. The columns are reused from classical buildings. The church still possesses its ancient marble pavement and screen enclosing the choir.*

6 *A church to commemorate the Nativity in Bethlehem was built first by Constantine and then by the Crusaders in the twelfth century. These steps lead down to the underground room where a silver star marks the traditional site of Christ's birth.*

7 *The site of the Holy Sepulchre in Jerusalem was confidently established by St Helena, the mother of Constantine. The present church over it dates from the eleventh and twelfth centuries, but, inside the Greek chapel of the Anastasis, one of the rock surfaces of the original tomb can still be seen.*

8 *The present Moslem Dome of the Rock marks the site where Abraham prepared to sacrifice Isaac. It is all that is left of the Jewish Temple, destroyed by the Romans in 70 AD. This photograph was taken from the chapel of Dominus Flevit ('The Lord Wept') on the Mount of Olives, from which Jesus gazed at Jerusalem and pronounced his prophecy of its destruction.*

18

The footsteps of Jesus

IN THE CHRISTIAN VIEW of the world the presence and attributes of God were first known through experience of the natural order. This was a universal phenomenon: men and women everywhere, in enormously varying cultural developments and in diverse material circumstances, came to have some intimation of a creator who was involved with the work of his hands. The world which God had made was the physical representation of a divine scheme whose purposes somehow paralleled the immediate perceptions of the human senses and declared the existence of an unseen world of transcendent values. It was neither arbitrary in its demands upon men nor formless in the structures it provided for the mutual association of living things. Through seemingly countless ages the human understanding of the natural order evolved a series of necessarily crude religious responses, each sucessively related to survival, to interpretation of natural events, to making human emotions sacred, and finally to images of an existence beyond death.

From these leading elements, and from many other lateral developments, the religions of the ancient world emerged, each comprehending aspects of authentic divinity and in some sense being, therefore, of God. With an increasingly sophisticated and articulated consciousness of the divine presence there came also explanations of human frailty; the reverse of the anticipation of God's glory was the reality of men's sin. What was wrong with humanity, furthermore, seemed out of all proportion to available earthly means of correction: the problem was not one of ordinary moral lapse, making, as it did, for insensitive dealings within society, but of the much more basic and encompassing inability of men to trust in the God whose presence their cultural consciousness had identified and formalized. Even when God revealed himself as a person and as One – as he did progressively to the Jewish people – the instincts of men managed to convert this special dispensation to wrong purposes. But the Jewish understanding of God was in itself sound: Christ, in the Christian understanding, did not come into the world to overturn it, but to fulfil it. This was the great turning-point, the dynamic of Revealed religion, and the completion of the divine scheme first disclosed in the natural order. The Jews had understood the nature of God correctly, but had corrupted their covenant with him, principally by failing to allow it to evolve from the collective to the personal. The other religions of the ancient world had incorporated some sense of God's presence but it remained latent and descriptive. Christ came among men with a simple ministry of teaching whose main purpose was to confirm that the kinds of ways in which God had been understood in Natural religion, and the very language used to express those insights, were broadly right. Yet he came also – and this was the unique gift of Revealed religion – to redeem men and the world which was their home and the place from which they derived and tested their values. Hence the Incarnation. God literally became a man in order that the human categories of spirituality could be recognized as truly divine, and not the mere invention of a frightened race seeking some means of converting a miserable and ephemeral existence into a dignified and permanent purchase upon the existence of the universe. God also

The Cross and the Lamb, both symbols of Christ's sacrifice, with a dove bearing the martyr's crown: this detail from an Early Christian sarcophagus at Ravenna is an iconographic summary of the Church's message.

Opposite: in the apse mosaic of Sta Pudenziana, Rome, Christ sits enthroned like a Roman senator dispensing the Law. It was made in the early fifth century, when the classical style still prevailed, but has been very heavily restored.

The site of the Last Supper is traditionally associated with the 'upper room' of a building that contains the so-called 'Tomb of King David'. The lower level seems at one time to have been made into a church, of which one battered and smoke-blackened niche survives. The room over it (above), known as the Cenacle or Hall of the Last Supper, was entirely rebuilt in the fourteenth century.

became a man in order to forgive men for their sins through the great act of expiation which has, ever since, formed the central rite of Christian worship.

The final distillation of Christian experience of God is personal: God is a person, in the form of a man, who was known and loved in his short earthly life, and who, Christians believe, was still truly a man in his Resurrected body and not a spirit or phantasm. Almost nothing is known of his appearance or human dispositions, but he left behind him, among his first disciples, such fragrance of personality and such a sense of the great love of God, that the new religion – or fulfilled older one, to be more precise – was from the start the cult of a person. And that is why any study of Christian churches should begin with Christ himself, for it was in order to be near the most closely remembered scenes of his earthly life that the first Christians resorted to the places where he had been, and established their first sanctuaries there.

After the Resurrection, and until the descent of the Holy Spirit at Pentecost, the disciples continued to meet in the 'upper room' where Jesus had appeared in his risen form among them. That is recorded in two of the Gospels. Tradition has always placed this house on Mount Zion in Jerusalem, but the present Cenacle building, to which pilgrims have gone since the Crusades in order to venerate the scene of the Last Supper and the Resurrection appearances, dates only from the fourteenth century. Beneath it, however, is the chamber containing the 'Tomb of King David', with its large and almost certainly inauthentic sarcophagus. The Tomb of David was known in Herodian times – in the period of the life of Christ – but with the subsequent expulsion of the Jews from the Holy City in 70 AD, and

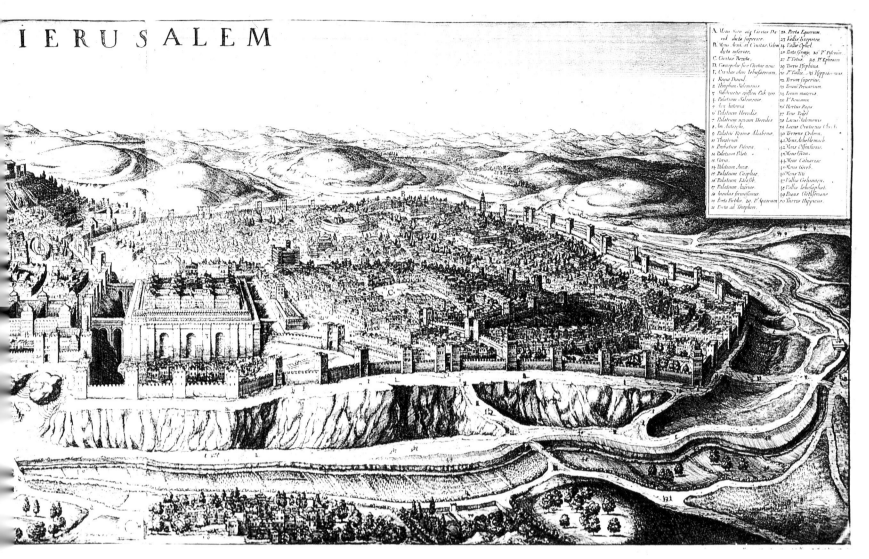

IERUSALEM

with the destruction of the shrines in Jerusalem by the Persian invaders in 614, the location of the site had been lost. The existing chamber is certainly ancient, and there are Herodian remains in the immediate area; probably none of the stones of the chamber itself actually date to the time of Christ, but there is another important clue to the true nature of this place. Behind the Tomb of David, in the north wall of the chamber, is a rounded niche, the stones blackened by fire. It is thought by some scholars that this is the last fragment of the 'Church of Holy Zion', built in the fourth century, and burned down by the Persians. This church had been built to enshrine the site of the original 'upper room'; and the apse-like niche in the Tomb of King David may thus be the only surviving trace of the first Christian church in the world.

Early church structures also covered most of the scenes of the life of Christ. In 326 St Helena, the mother of the first Christian emperor, Constantine, is said to have visited the Holy Land, and afterwards the imperial commissioners began to identify the holy places and to supervise the construction of basilicas in each of them. There were, in the end, over two hundred churches of this period in Palestine, whose ruins, where they have been uncovered, may now be recognized by characteristic mosaic floors, sometimes of extraordinary richness of decoration, and rounded apses. They are the best clue to the authenticity of the sites. Modern Christians are sometimes confused by the duplication of shrines in the Holy Land: there are two Holy Sepulchres, one in the famous basilica, and one, discovered by General Gordon in the 1880s, and known as the 'Garden Tomb'; there are two Emmauses, one at El Quebeibh, and one at Abu Ghosh; there are

In the seventeenth century the artist Wenceslaus Hollar attempted this reconstruction of Jerusalem as it was in the time of Jesus. He relied more on Renaissance hearsay than on topographical knowledge, but his bird's-eye view does contain all the holy places in roughly their real relation to each other.

It was not uncommon for pagan temples to be converted into Christian churches. The most famous is the Pantheon, erected by the Emperor Hadrian as a shrine to 'All the Gods' and rededicated to St Mary and All Saints in 608. This eighteenth-century etching is by Piranesi.

two Canas of Galilee, one at Kefar Kanna and another at Kh. Quana. There are even two sets of 'Shepherds' Fields' near Bethlehem. But there is also a great measure of agreement about which sites correspond to ancient tradition, and this has inevitably been confirmed by the discovery of early basilica foundations indicating particular veneration of the places at least as early as the fourth century. Oral tradition had a persistence and accuracy in the ancient world which modern people, with the easy availability of retrieval systems, find hard to imagine; and the Christians at the time of St Helena in 326 explained how their predecessors had visited the holy places to say their prayers, and sense again the mysterious presence of the remembered Christ, from the very beginning. This custom seems to have continued right through the periods of first Jewish, and then Roman, official hostility until the conversion of Constantine.

Of Christian church buildings before these fourth-century structures it is impossible to be precise, but Christian temples are recognized in the edicts of the era of Diocletian, and they were known to have existed even before then. There is almost no way, however, of knowing what the earliest places of worship were like. Religious bodies afflicted with persistent persecution leave faith, not buildings, behind them as the evidence of their vitality. Most were doubtless 'house churches', meetings for worship held in the home of a local leader of the new cult. Some were converted buildings of modest scale and used originally for commercial or other purposes. At Old Corinth, redolent of associations with St

Paul, for example, a row of shops was built in the third century, of which the central one, now partially restored by excavators of the site, was converted into a Christian church. Traces of mural paintings, with Christian symbols, have been found in the interior of the shop. The triumphalist assertion of Christianity after the Edict of Milan in 313, which gave Christianity social legitimacy, and the conversion of Constantine meant that the redeployment of buildings for Christian worship could proceed on a more ambitious scale.

In some places the existing pagan temples were made into Christian churches, and in others they were pulled down. It is interesting to seek to discover what determined their fate. Christianity sometimes recognized the authentic religiosity of the cults of the ancient world, and had some measure of respect for the immanence of the Divine represented in aspects of non-Christian worship. Pagan sites which were taken over were not really evidence of a kind of syncretism, however, like the survival of pre-Christian rites within the sometimes thinly veiled official Catholicism of the early Spanish colonial empire. Nor was a temple left standing and adapted to Christian use simply in order to avoid giving offence to local sensibilities. The matter is more complicated than that. It is as well to remember that the first Christians were Hellenized Jews, and that the Church extended in the first few centuries was heavily Greek in culture and personnel. Cultural continuity, not religious syncretism, accounts for the adaptation of pagan sanctuaries. At Delphi, the most sacred place in Greek religion, a Christian basilica was constructed on the first terrace: its traces may still be seen in the carved stone slabs that line the site. The mosaic floor is now in front of the museum. The decline of Delphi was not due to Christian hostility; it had already occurred under the Romans, when the temples were frequently plundered. The place has evident numinous qualities, and the Emperors Constantine and Theodosius carried off some of the pagan memorials to decorate the new Christian city of Constantinople. The great shrine of Delos had also declined under the Romans; here, too, however, a Christian presence was established, and there was a bishop on the island in the third century. The basilica of Agios Kyrikos, in the harbour area and near the slave-markets, had a classic rounded apse.

Where a pagan site was more characteristically associated with a famous idol, on the other hand, or where religious controversy was pursued with particular relish, as at Alexandria, the treatment meted out to pagan sanctuaries could be very different. The cult of Serapis at Alexandria was an invention of the Ptolemaic dynasty: an Egyptian religion in a Greek cultural form. The great temple of the cult, the Serapeion, was the centre of a religion whose adherents were mostly Greek settlers, and the cult spread among Greek populations of the Mediterranean coastline. Since Christianity appealed to the same populations, the rivalries were sometimes very infelicitously expressed. In 391 Patriarch Theophilus of Alexandria led a mob into the Serapeion who burned the books of the famous library and hacked down the colossal wooden statue of Serapis. As it fell, hundreds of rodents, who had eaten away the inside of the effigy, poured out from its decayed innards. A church dedicated to St John the Baptist was built here, but of this, as of the Serapeion, nothing recognizable remains, and the site, now marked by 'Pompey's Pillar' is simply a huge mound of rubble. But the powerful Church of Alexandria, founded by St Mark, made better use of the Roman amphitheatre, rediscovered in 1963 and since excavated, at Kom el Dikka. This is, by any standards, an impressive site, with marble buildings and terraces. The first Christians converted it into a church – as witnessed in the carved and incised crosses and Coptic designs on many of the slabs of masonry which cover the area.

The cult of Serapis was one of many 'mystery' religions which offered its own form of personal salvation at about the time of Jesus, but which was destined to yield to Christianity. On this coin Serapis and Hadrian are shown jointly dedicating a shrine.

23

In Rome, similarly, the Pantheon was taken over entire as a Christian church, thus preserving the building intact to this day. At Pergamum, also, the magnificent red-brick Serapeion has survived to the present because of continued religious use. It is a large structure, in the form of a basilica, and may indeed have served some purpose associated with the nearby Asklepieion, since its function as a temple of Serapis has never been satisfactorily established. It is said that during construction the bricks were passed to the site by a human chain, hand to hand, so that they would touch neither earth nor sky. The result, at any rate, was an impressive Roman basilica, which the Early Christians converted into a church, and which, later again, has served as a mosque. The temple of Zeus on the acropolis of Pergamum also shows traces of having been turned into a Christian place of worship: doubtless in an attempt to redeem St John's reference to Pergamum, presumably to the famous altar of Zeus there, as 'Satan's seat'.

Occasionally a pagan temple was actually incorporated into the structure of a new Christian basilica. This occurred at Syracuse in Sicily, where the Doric temple of Athena, a building dating from the fifth century BC, had its walls recut to form the aisles of the early church. This example is also unusual in that the original appearance of the temple is known: Cicero describes its plunder by the Roman praetor Verres. Beneath the church of San Clemente in Rome, originally a basilica of the twelfth century, but still preserving, as do so many churches in Rome, the essentials of the early basilican design, are a series of descending vaults covering some very ancient ruins. Excavations here have revealed the walls of Roman houses and fragments of a temple. The depths are cold and damp, the stones in places almost luminously green with the discoloration of decay. But here, perhaps better than anywhere, the observer may sense the continuity of religious use, the visible evidence of enduring faith in the spiritual qualities of a site first chosen by pagan men as especially close to God.

The earliest Christian churches did not follow the design of the classical temples, however, because their use was different. The need for blood sacrifices had been superseded by the vicarious offering of Christ himself, and churches were intended primarily as meeting-places where the faithful could celebrate the Holy Eucharist. The very first followers of Jesus were accustomed to the worship of the synagogue, centralized in the rituals of the temple in Jerusalem; but, expelled from the company of the orthodox, the Christian converts plainly did not have resources to construct simulations. Nor would the encompassing official religion have tolerated it. The Hellenized members of the wider Church rejected the idolatrous rites of the pagan religions and the mystery cults although, as just noted, in some cases temples were converted.

But the normal pattern for the Christian churches which emerged with state toleration, at the start of the fourth century, was the Roman basilica. This was a civic building, for meetings, and was simply an extended rectangular hall with a wooden roof. It was symbolically satisfactory: a place of resort for the worshippers, not a house for the god as in classical pagan religion. At the end of the hall was a semi-circular apse, half enclosing the altar, and as these Christian basilicas became more ambitious in scale the whole apse area began to take on the appearance of an interior triumphal arch. Colonnades flanked the nave, with side aisles, and, since worshippers stood and did not need seating, pavements, usually of marble or mosaic, ran from one end of the church to the other. The effect was to draw the worshipper forward, as along the stoa of a 'sacred way' at an ancient sanctuary. These 'sacred ways' were colonnaded roads approaching – sometimes from quite a distance, but more commonly for the last hundred yards or so – the central mystery of a Greek or Roman shrine. In the Christian basilica this was the

No church evokes more vividly the triumph of Christianity over paganism than the cathedral of Syracuse, which is built inside a Greek Doric temple of the fifth century BC.

S. Paolo fuori le Mura in Rome gives an
excellent idea of an Early Christian
basilica in its pristine state, though it is
in fact almost completely a nineteenth-
century replica after a fire in 1823.
Architecturally it conforms to the
standard Constantinian pattern – two
rows of columns with aisles behind them;
clerestory lighting; flat roof; and apsed
east end. Right: the original façade of S.
Paolo, destroyed in the fire.

Veduta interna della Basilica di S. Maria Maggiore

altar: released from its function of actual sacrifice and regarded as the throne of Christ, the place for the symbolic re-enactment of his victory over the world.

As churches, again, became larger and more richly decorated within, later in the fourth century, it was the apse which received the greatest attention. Sometimes frescos, but more commonly mosaics, enfolded the altar with glowing depictions of Christ and the Virgin; decorative motifs in the main body of the basilica related episodes from the Scriptures. The whole development of the basilican style indicates a formalizing of the liturgy, and an increasing emphasis on the special significance attached to the position of the priest as the representative of Christ at the Holy Eucharist. It is scarcely accurate to refer, as scholars once did, to the 'emergence of the Church from the catacombs', because it is now clear that persecutions were not continuous, and that some measure of discreet public worship was in most places quite possible. But the impossibility of constructing or maintaining proper and distinct religious structures must have inhibited liturgical development, and with the Edict of 313 a whole new phase in the evolution of worship began, with the clergy representing themselves in the styles, and often in the adapted vestments, of imperial officials. There are enough surviving early churches in the basilican style to give a satisfactory impression of what the buildings were like.

Two Early Christian basilicas in Rome. Left: Sta Sabina, built in the fifth century and recently meticulously restored even to the transparent alabaster in the windows. Above: Sta Maria Maggiore, the grandest of surviving basilicas; its colonnade keeps a flat entablature instead of the arches seen in S. Paolo and Sta Sabina.

The art of mosaic perfectly suited the requirements of the early Church – rich and glowing but also hieratic and formal. Above: the apse of a chapel in Sta Costanza, Rome. Christ, seated on a globe against a background of palm trees, turns to a figure who approaches in an attitude of humility; the subject is uncertain but could be St Peter receiving the keys.

Two details from the tiny chapel of S. Zenone in the church of Sta Prassede, Rome. Left: one of four angels (c. 820) supporting a roundel in the ceiling which contains the head and shoulders of Christ. Right: the Virgin and Child between two angels, probably of the eleventh century. The Christ-child, his arms extended in welcome, holds a scroll reading EGO SUM LUX, 'I am the light'.

In 1854 the tombs of five early popes who had reigned between 230 and 283, when Christianity was not officially tolerated, were unexpectedly discovered in the vast catacombs of S. Callisto (above). Here too are rare wall-paintings portraying scenes from the New Testament, scenes of significance for the new Church whose liturgy was still evolving. Right: a communal meal, perhaps the Last Supper, perhaps the Wedding at Cana, perhaps a depiction of the Eucharist.

The best impression of the interior decoration, however, probably comes not from a church at all but from the catacombs of Rome. A catacomb was not a church but a Christian necropolis, and was used for religious worship only in times of extreme persecution: Pope Sixtus II was executed during the reign of Valerian, in 258, for celebrating mass in the catacombs. In the catacomb of St Callixtus are extraordinarily well-preserved frescos, some from the second century. The soft volcanic rock of the galleries had been covered with plaster and then painted with a huge range of subjects: Jonah and the fish, the Good Shepherd, Jesus at his baptism, loaves and wine representing the Eucharist, and – perhaps the most touching aspiration of faith – broken pots and birds, symbolizing the release of the soul from earthly cares into the spaciousness of eternity. The decorative splendours of the interiors of the early basilicas compensated for the austerity of the exteriors, rather like the country Baroque churches of the later European tradition. The outside walls of the basilicas were of unadorned and unplastered brick: the Christian life was perceived to be one of interior beauty.

The grandest surviving example of the basilican style must surely be Sta Maria Maggiore in Rome, founded by Pope Sixtus III in 431, and remodelled in the thirteenth century. The long nave here is flanked by Ionic columns, above which are fifth-century mosaic panels showing scenes from the Old Testament. The splendid apse mosaics, however, date from much later – the thirteenth century – as does the coffered roof – sixteenth century. The church of Sta Sabina in Rome is also of fifth-century origin, and again shows the basilican form with authentic clarity. The nave colonnade has Corinthian columns actually taken from destroyed pagan temples.

Very similar for its immediate visual impact, and for the impression of symmetry and simplicity, is the basilica built by Constantine over the grotto of the Nativity in Bethlehem. Christians had come to the cave of the manger to say their prayers from the very beginning, and the cult was so well established, in fact, that the Emperor Hadrian, in his attempts of 135 AD to eliminate the new religion in the Holy Land, had built a shrine to Adonis on the spot and planted a sacred grove in honour of the pagan divinities. In 326, when the commissioners of Constantine sought to restore the Christian shrine, local people led them to the place among the grove of trees beneath which the cave of the Nativity was known still to exist. The trees were felled and the rock beneath the soil was cut away to reveal the cave, which was then enclosed within an octagonal edicule, similar to the covering structures also placed over the Holy Sepulchre in Jerusalem and over the 'House of St Peter' in Capernaum. The grotto survives to this day, a silver star set into the floor at the traditional site of Christ's birth.

Above it is the church of the Nativity, in classic basilican form, but it is not the original church of 326. That had been so badly damaged during Samaritan rioting in the mid-sixth century that the Emperor Justinian had its remnants dismantled and a new basilica constructed. Work on this was completed in 530, and writers of the time described the splendour of its marbles and mosaics. Yet traces of the original church do remain: beneath the wooden covers of the nave floor are the mosaics laid down by Constantine. The church was unusual in being spared by the Persians during their sack of the holy places in 614; they found a mosaic panel depicting the Magi as Persians and took this for evidence of the inherent sanctity of the place. Later both Moslems and Christians used the church for their devotions. Extensive restoration occurred in 1165, when the Crusaders of the Latin Kingdom faced the grotto with marble. In 1480 further work took place. The roof, which still exists, was repaired using timber from

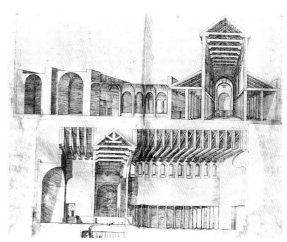

The church of the Nativity, Bethlehem, is still basically that built by the Emperor Justinian on the earlier Constantinian model. The diagram shows lateral and longitudinal sections from one of the earliest scholarly descriptions, published in 1609.

Naples Cathedral has been rebuilt several times, but miraculously the very first church of Sta Restituta was allowed to remain, with fragments of its early mosaic decoration. In the centre, the Lion of St Mark, with six wings; on either side the Apostles; and at the top a pastoral scene with sheep.

Venice and lead, a gift of King Edward IV, from England. In 1517 the Turks looted the church and some of the columns they took away can now be seen lying around the Temple Mount in Jerusalem. For all these variations of fortune, the church today still looks very much like the basilica of the Early Christian period. It is rectangular in shape, with double colonnades and five aisles. A few mosaic fragments survive on a south wall, but these date from the twelfth century; the whole of the interior walls of the Justinian building was once clad with mosaic panels. The columns are painted with twelfth-century representations of saints, in dark colours that once must have been bright.

The stone columns of basilicas, as was often the case, originated from pagan temples, and both they and the columns made exclusively for Christian churches sometimes received a further extension of use in still later buildings. In the Roman world columns were manufactured to order, and exported in bulk all over the Mediterranean. It was this, as much as anything, which gave the basilican style such uniformity. Beside the Duomo (the Cathedral) of Naples, for example, is the church of Sta Restituta – the original basilica of the city. Here may be seen classic columns of the fourth century still *in situ*, dividing the nave and two aisles. There are also remains of mosaics and sculpted marble slabs.

The site which perhaps most effectively conveys the main purpose of the basilica, however, is at Ephesus on the coast of modern Turkey. Visitors to the famous ruins often stop at the basilica of St John on the old acropolis, a church built by Justinian in 560 to cover the tomb of the Apostle. It is a splendid structure, even in decay. But the older basilica of Agia Maria, less visited, is an almost exaggerated example of the style. Here an extremely long and narrow double church ruin may be found in the ancient harbour area. The two churches lie end to end, nearly touching each other. There are Byzantine columns lying about all over the site, and the churches were clearly extensively remodelled in the Justinian period. Their origin is much earlier, however, and it was here that the Council of Ephesus was held in 431, at which the Virgin was formally identified as 'Theotokos', mother of God. It is perhaps no coincidence that Ephesus was also the centre of the cult of Artemis, the 'Diana of the Ephesians' whose votaries caused so much trouble for St Paul when he lived in the city. Artemis was a fertility goddess, whose own temple, some little distance from the centre of the city, on the road between Kusadasi and Selçuk, was the largest building in the Greek world. Now all that remains of it is a marshy depression filled with chunks of masonry, and a rather unhappily reassembled single standing column. The basilica of Agia Maria has fared a little better. In its long narrow construction may be seen a perfect representation of the function of the Christian basilica as the successor to the 'sacred way' of the sanctuaries of the ancient world. Here the faithful were led forward in spirit towards the scene of the great mystery of the Eucharist, to the apse with its altar of ultimate sacrifice.

The simplicity of the basilican form has not always commended itself, and most modern revivals of the style have tended to derive from the echoes found within Renaissance buildings, or from adaptations of Byzantine designs with longer naves added to meet the requirements of Western congregations accustomed to Romanesque or Gothic structures. But a splendidly authentic basilican revival may be seen at St Patrick's, the Irish national church in Rome. It was begun, on a plot of ground in the Villa Ludovisi, in 1888, and completed – after interludes of inactivity caused by lack of funds – in 1911. There is a long

Ephesus, in Asia Minor, was one of the holiest sites of early Christianity, the reputed home of the Virgin Mary and of St John, the beloved disciple, and the place of the latter's burial. Both had large basilicas dedicated to them, of which only fragments remain. The church of St John, reconstructed above, was built by Justinian in the sixth century.

The church of St Mary at Ephesus was constructed inside an ancient Roman public building, and eventually consisted of two churches lying end to end. The baptistry, to the north of the atrium through which the church was entered, contained the font, in which those wishing to be baptized were immersed.

nave, colonnades like those at S. Apollinare Nuovo in Ravenna (though here the columns alternate with square piers) and an enormous rounded apse of impressive nobility. The apse mosaic shows St Patrick explaining the mystery of the Trinity to the royal court of Tara.

It is to the Holy Land that it is necessary to return in order to sense, again, the importance to the first Christians of some kind of physical link with the life of Christ, and to discern, in the remains of those two hundred churches established in the Constantinian period, the original inspiration of a religious cult founded upon the knowledge of a man who was God. The remains are not always clear. The earliest basilicas, which were sometimes anyway very small, were usually later reconstructed in the mature Byzantine style. Indeed, the word 'Byzantine' is often rather loosely applied to virtually any church of a plainly early provenance in the Holy Land, regardless of its technical category. Mosaic floors are very durable, and several successive sets of walls in many cases went up, at various later dates, around the original pavements laid down in the aftermath of St Helena's mission to discover the scenes of the life of Christ. Tradition, in the end, has often surprisingly proved to be the best indicator of the authenticity of particular sites; places where complete desolation, caused by the pillaging of invaders, or where subsequent overbuilding has obliterated all signs of an early sanctuary, have in very many cases, upon excavation, yielded the remains of an early basilica.

The early years of Jesus have, for obvious reasons, left few material traces; the son of a carpenter of Nazareth was brought up in domestic circumstances which were necessarily unremarkable. Nazareth is not even mentioned in the Old Testament, and although the province of Galilee was not itself an obscure backwater – indeed, the ministry of Christ took place at a centre of considerable trading importance, for Galilee was an economic crossroads of the ancient world – the 'city' of Nazareth had a poor reputation: 'Can any good come out of Nazareth?' Local tradition later maintained that the Holy Family presided over the first Christian church of Nazareth, and did so for three centuries. In 570 a pilgrim from Piacenza found the town inhabited by both Christians and Jews, and remarks on the existence of both a church and a synagogue. The earliest church was thought to have been built over the scene of the Annunciation, the house and workshop of Joseph and Mary. The Crusaders, finding it in ruins in the twelfth century, rebuilt it, preserving the site of the first house as a grotto beneath the nave. Their church was destroyed by the Moslems in 1263, but the grotto survived as a place of pilgrimage, and is still there today, incorporated into the crypt of the new basilica which was opened in 1969.

It was during the centuries when the grotto alone existed that the tradition grew up of the 'Holy House of Loreto', that the original building of the carpenter's workshop had translated itself miraculously, eventually to Italy, leaving behind the cave beneath, in which the family partially dwelt. While the basilica was being rebuilt in 1955, excavation revealed the plan of the early basilica on the site: a nave, two aisles, and some mosaics. The most important discovery of all was made at the same time. Beneath the floor of the early basilica fragments of coloured plaster were found, evidence of a shrine from the end of the first or the start of the second century. The base of a nearby column, of the fourth century, bore an inscription to the Virgin, the words of the Annunciation, in Greek.

For an impression of the Nazareth of the time of Christ, however, it is best to visit the church of St Joseph which stands next to the basilica of the Annunciation. The church itself is modern, built in 1914; but it covers the remains of an ancient church, with a nave and two aisles, believed to mark the spot of St Joseph's original house. In the crypt are some remnants of the ancient village from the time of Christ: a cistern, some storage pits, and rooms – the latter, like the living quarters of the 'Holy House' in the lower church of the Annunciation basilica, doubtless the underground chambers frequently inhabited during the heat of summer by the inhabitants of ancient Galilee. The sense that the material associations of the life of Christ have been present here for centuries of believers is very strong.

The short earthly ministry of Jesus was centred around the town of Capernaum on the Sea of Galilee. Here he came after rejection in Nazareth, and the ruins of the 'town of Jesus' have been partially excavated, under the direction of the Franciscans, who are the Latin custodians of the Holy Places. The area was famous in the time of Christ for its wheatfields, a fact which gives additional resonance to the many sayings of Christ which use the images of corn and of trade to illustrate spiritual and moral truths. To the south is the city of Tiberias, a new venture begun by Herod Antipas in 18 AD: its famous hot-water springs perhaps suggested in Christ's words about living waters. The excavations at Capernaum started in the 1890s, and the most prominent feature of the site is the third-century synagogue, and the carved stones, lying around the place, which once adorned it. The synagogue gives a good impression, despite its later date, of the confidence and cultural assimilation of the official religion of Jesus' day. It is a Hellenistic structure, with Doric and Corinthian capitals and colonnades. Where it stood there was, in the time of Christ, an earlier synagogue.

Yet the real importance of this site, from the present perspective, is the nearby 'House of St Peter', revealed in the excavations of 1969. This is a first-century building, of simple and rather poor construction, which had plainly been subsequently converted into a shrine. In the fourth century additions were made, and the whole complex was turned into a church, the original simple house being encased in the octagonal walls which are the most obvious feature today, and which probably date from the fifth century. There is nothing else like it on the town site – as yet uncovered – and there can be little doubt that the small octagonal shrine sheltered what, to the early Christians, was regarded as the building most closely associated with the residence of Christ in the town. The 'House of St Peter' is clearly the home of Jesus.

Various episodes of the Galilean ministry of Christ received similar sanctification, and were, again, the sites of the earliest Christian churches. At Nain, on the edge of the plain of Esdraelon, an ancient church marked the place where Jesus, arriving near the gate of the town, had seen a widow grieving at the funeral procession of her son. The young man was raised from the dead, and local tradition never forgot the spot where the miracle had taken place. Today a chapel built by the Franciscans in 1880 covers the ancient foundations of the first sanctuary.

At Tabgha on the shore of the Sea of Galilee, there is no evidence of early settlement, because the area was known as a desert place, characteristic of those to which Jesus withdrew with his followers in order to teach and to pray. This particular spot was associated in early tradition with Christ, and in 313 three little churches were built in honour of Christ's miracles and the teaching which they illustrated. The modern basilica of the Multiplication covers the site of one of them. The first church had contained fine mosaics, some of which have survived, alongside some mosaic floor panels of the fifth and sixth centuries which are of such splendour, because of the brilliance of their colours and their designs, that they have become well known. Few places indicate the interiors of the first

Ruins of the synagogue at Capernaum, on the Sea of Galilee. It was in the earlier building on this site that Jesus preached. The present ruins belong to the third century and are entirely Hellenistic in style.

churches as well as Tabgha does; here may be seen, in excellent condition, a richly decorated surface where once the believers stood for their prayers and knelt before the miracle of the Eucharist. But its isolated location indicates that it was always a pilgrim church, probably originally served by the small band of monks whose predecessors had constructed it, and the humbler churches of less venerated sites doubtless displayed more rustic and austere characteristics.

The final sequences of Jesus' life, leading to the paradoxical apotheosis of the Crucifixion, took place in Jerusalem, and the churches built to mark particular events have always attracted special veneration. Constantine complemented his great basilicas at Bethlehem and the Holy Sepulchre by crowning the Mount of Olives with a monumental church on the site of so many of the discourses of Christ. There was a cave, quite near to the catacomb known as the 'Tombs of the Prophets', which in Jewish tradition once received the remains of Haggai, Zachariah and Malachi. Jesus had wept over the city from the nearby place now marked by the modern chapel of Dominus Flevit. Constantine's basilica over the cave of Christ's teaching was destroyed by the Persians in 614, rebuilt around 670, and destroyed again by the Caliph El Hakim in 1055. The Crusaders then built a church on the site which bore the title, as the present one does, of 'Pater Noster'; for it was here that by venerable tradition the Lord first spoke the words of his own prayer to the disciples (a tradition which corresponds to the account in St Luke's Gospel, but the Gospel of St Matthew places the event in Galilee). The modern church here was begun in 1868, and is in the care of the Carmelites. Beneath the church are two caves, believed to be the actual scene of Christ's ministry. Excavations in 1910 revealed the apse and crypt of the Constantinian church, with the base of columns and some mosaic fragments.

In the deep valley of the Kidron, where it meets the vale of Hinnom, by the village of Silwan, is the Pool of Siloam, where Jesus opened the eyes of the man born blind. The memory of the miracle never faded, and Christians of the early centuries came here in great numbers, many of them with afflictions seeking a miraculous cure in the waters. A church was built over the pool in the fifth century, with four porticos, a nave and two aisles. It, like most other churches, was completely destroyed by the Persians in 614, but the visitor today will still find some traces: the shafts of columns in the waters are all that is left of the healing sanctuary. The pool itself is once again exposed, and disappears into a rounded arch which is the start of Hezekiah's tunnel. Above it is a mosque, for the site is holy to Moslems as well.

The ministry of Christ in Jerusalem was also closely associated with the village of Bethany, on the far side of the Mount of Olives, for it was there that Jesus stayed in the house of Lazarus and his sisters Martha and Mary. The memories of Jesus drew pilgrims from the beginning: both Eusebius and Jerome refer to the tomb of Lazarus and the church built over it in the fourth century. The church existed until the end of the Latin Kingdom, when the Christian custodians of the Holy Places, who volunteered to stay behind and guard the shrines after the Moslem occupation, found their resources too stretched to include the outpost at Bethany, and the church there fell into decay. Eventually the site was turned into a mosque, but by then the whole superstructure of the ancient church had gone. What survived, apart from masonry fragments and an apse (now incorporated into the structure of the present church, by the door), was the tomb beneath the ground, in a gallery cut into the rock. A mosaic pavement, now in the courtyard, is also from the original building. The existing church was opened in 1953, and manages, still, to convey something of the holiness of the place. When Christ had raised the widow of Nain's son from the dead in Galilee it was said that he had had compassion because of her desolation; when he raised Lazarus it was because, in his words, the people might believe in his own relationship to the Father. The resurrection of Lazarus was thus an anticipation of the Saviour's triumph over the grave. There is a legend that Lazarus later crossed to Cyprus and became the first bishop of Larnaca. The cathedral of that city is to this day dedicated to his honour.

Gethsemane was another place which Jesus seems to have frequented while in the Jerusalem area. It was (and is still) an olive garden, and perhaps suggested to him some of the qualities of solitude which, in Galilee, drew him to deserted spots to pray and to teach. As the scene of his agony before the betrayal and Crucifixion, it was always venerated by Christians, and modern pilgrims, just as their predecessors have done throughout the centuries, take home olive leaves from ancient trees in the garden that must have witnessed the agony of Christ. In the fourth century Eusebius noted that the faithful came there to pray, and excavations in 1920 brought to light the foundations of that first church, built at the time of Theodosius. Mosaics of the church have been incorporated into the floor of the modern 'Church of All Nations', completed in 1924. The early structure was destroyed by fire in the seventh century – presumably by the Persians – and the medieval church of St Saviour later covered the area.

There also survives, though at some distance from the original location, another material link with the Passion of Christ. Twenty-eight marble steps from the residence of Pilate at Jerusalem, which Christ must have ascended at the time of his trial, were at some later date removed to Rome, where they were the centre of special devotions at St John Lateran. Tradition credits St Helena with moving the staircase. The steps were placed in their present position only in the sixteenth century, and now lead up to a venerable chapel, which is all that remains of the ancient Lateran Palace that Constantine gave to Pope Melchiades. But there must always be some doubt about the authenticity of the Scala Santa, because there is some difficulty about locating the exact site of Pilate's residence in Jerusalem, the Praetorium. It may have been either at the Antonia or at the Citadel, and the enlargement of the walls of the city in 44 AD by Herod Agrippa, a decade after the death of Christ, thereby extending the whole city to the north, makes identification still less precise.

The Mount of Olives still retains some of its original peace, though now clothed with commemorative shrines. In the foreground is the modern 'Church of All Nations'; in the middle distance the nineteenth-century Russian church; and beyond it on the right the chapel of Dominus Flevit, from which the view in pl. 8 was taken.

When Constantine's architects planned the first church of the Holy Sepulchre they took as their model the typical Roman 'martyrium', a circular structure with the right funerary and commemorative associations. An intriguingly close parallel is the round building built as a (presumably pagan) mausoleum for Constantine's own daughter, begun before his conversion and finished as a Christian church dedicated to Sta. Costanza. The etching is by Piranesi.

It was this alteration to the walls of Jerusalem which has caused some unnecessary confusion about the location of the Holy Sepulchre, the most venerable shrine of Christendom and the site of Constantine's first basilica. Golgotha, the place of Christ's execution and burial, was outside the city walls, but the site is within the area extended by Agrippa, and so, therefore, is the church of the Holy Sepulchre. The tomb of Christ was an ordinary Jewish chamber with an antechamber. Nearby were some deep-water cisterns, cut into the rock, and into which all kinds of debris was thrown: the one into which fragments of what was taken to be the True Cross were deposited now forms a chapel accessible from within the church of the Holy Sepulchre. A small gallery in the upper wall is where the mother of Constantine is said to have witnessed the discovery of the Cross.

The authentication of the Holy Sepulchre itself is rather more reliable. The first Christians had gone to the empty tomb from the beginning to say their devotions; so great had become the sanctity of the place, in fact, that in 135 Hadrian had the whole area buried beneath an enormous platform of stone and cement, on which was set a statue of Jupiter and an altar of Venus. The result, as it happened, was to mark the site permanently, so that when St Helena's workers sought the exact location of the tomb of Christ there was no problem at all in finding it. As the platform was removed, to the surprise and delight of everyone, it was found that the Roman construction teams had not bothered to destroy the rock tomb, but had merely buried it. The historian Eusebius was a witness. 'As layer after layer of the soil was removed,' he wrote, 'the venerable and most holy memorial of the Saviour's Resurrection, beyond all our hopes, came into view.'

In 335 began the construction of a huge church over the tomb, based on a Roman *martyrium*, a round, domed structure, in conception like the contemporaneous mausoleum of Constantine's daughter, the church of S. Constanza, in Rome, or the first church of St Peter in Rome, which was a rotunda built over the tomb of the Apostle in 333. The Holy Sepulchre was cut away from the rock and the ground around it levelled; the Anastasis (the tomb itself, the actual place of Resurrection) was covered with a small, internal, canopy-like structure, the edicule. The main church was, as it still is, an enormous rotunda supported by concentric pillars forming an ambulatory for pilgrims round the tomb. This rotunda construction, the *martyrium*, ultimately derived from the Pantheon, was to have great subsequent influence on certain types of church building, as seen in the round-plan 'Holy Sepulchre' churches of the Templars, for example, or in baptistries, for Christians are baptized into Christ's death and the font was sometimes, in grander churches, sited within a round building rather like a *martyrium*.

Constantine's basilica was destroyed by the Persians in 614, and was rebuilt in 629 by Modestos. But in 1009 that church was pulled down by Caliph El Hakim, who dismantled even the Holy Sepulchre itself, leaving just two of the rock sides. It is these that the modern pilgrim may still see; the side within the Greek chapel of the Anastasis covered with marble, but the side at the back, exposed beneath the altar of the tiny Coptic chapel which abuts the Greek edicule, still the original naked rock surface. The Byzantine Emperor Constantine Monomachos rebuilt the great church in 1048, and although it was quite different in many features from the original basilica of Constantine, it still preserved the essential rotunda form. The Crusaders, in turn, remoulded the church in 1149, and despite some damage, notably in the great fire of 1808, it is today more or less as they left it, although recent renovations have restored some of the colour and splendour of the earlier stonework.

The church of the Holy Sepulchre in Jerusalem has been many times altered, repaired and restored but retains the basic form given to it by Constantine. The main entrance (above), added at the time of the Crusaders' occupation, leads into a transept from which the sanctuary containing the tomb itself is reached (right). This engraving shows it in 1702. In 1808 a fire gutted the whole building, destroying the dome and the super-structure of the tomb itself.

For all the historical importance and sacred qualities of the church of the Holy Sepulchre, however, it is perhaps to the church at El Qubeibh that the Christian who seeks the atmosphere of the Resurrection should go. For this was perhaps the Biblical Emmaus, 'three-score furlongs' from Jerusalem, where Jesus appeared in his Resurrected form to the two disciples he had joined as they journeyed, and to whom he spoke of the events of his own death. Some of the Crusaders located Emmaus at Abu Ghosh, but none of the early remains there go back far enough to give the site any real significance. In 1335 the Franciscans identified the village of El Qubeibh (the 'Little Dome') as the place of the house of Cleophas, one of the two disciples. Their supposition was based on local tradition, seemingly without substantiation, and the passage through the village of an ancient road from Jerusalem. There was a Crusader township here, and a castle. The Crusaders had built a church whose foundations were uncovered in 1873. The structure was found to have incorporated the walls of an early house, of primitive construction, into the western nave. What seemed to have been discovered was a forgotten shrine. Further excavations of the village in the 1940s showed that it had been built over a Roman and Byzantine settlement. Piety has claimed the lost shrine as the house of Cleophas, and El Qubeibh as Emmaus, the village whose real location had never been established before. A modern sanctuary was raised over the ruined church in 1901. If this is indeed the place where Jesus took supper with the two disciples whose hearts had 'burned within them' as he spoke to them as they journeyed – and where he was made known to them in the breaking of bread – then it is, after the 'upper room' of Jerusalem, the first Christian church.

2 Divine mysteries on earth: churches of Byzantium

CONSTANTINE was not only the first Christian emperor: he was also the founder of a new capital. Constantinople, previously called Byzantium (and now Istanbul), stood for a new beginning. Remote from Rome and its pagan associations, it was to inaugurate a new era. The emphasis now was to be on the spiritual world; on the mysteries of the Incarnation and Sacrifice; on the glorification of Christ and his saints rather than of any earthly and physical powers. Byzantine art and architecture were able, for the first time, to express the full range of Christian belief in visual terms.

The Byzantine Empire endured for over a thousand years, from 330 to 1453. During that time it faced a continuing and increasing threat from the east, first from Persia and then from various waves of Islamic invaders culminating in the Ottomans; it suffered a bitter blow when the Fourth Crusade of 1204 was diverted by Venetian intrigues from its original purpose of conquering the Holy Land and was turned instead against Constantinople.

Compared with the West, the Byzantine Empire was politically more unified and the emperor more powerful than any European monarch. The Church, however, had less independence. The Patriarch of Constantinople was its head, but the emperor was God's vicegerent. No patriarch had the religious authority that the Pope had in the West. The Iconoclast controversy that shook the Eastern Church in the eighth and ninth centuries showed how closely religious and monarchical authority were interrelated.

The Eastern Church never acknowledged the primacy of the Pope, but it regarded itself as part of a united Christendom until 1054, when the two sides finally divided on the theological issue of whether the Holy Spirit proceeded from the Father only or from the Father and the Son. There were other points of contention, including the celibacy of the clergy. The liturgical differences between the Roman and the later Eastern (or Orthodox) Churches are reflected in the different architectural forms. There was no need for elaborate choirs and chancels. The most prominent feature in Orthodox churches came to be the iconostasis, a screen going from one wall to the other with a series of doors in it. Much of the ceremonial takes place behind these doors. Spatially the effect is one of confinement, dim light and rich decoration. Many of the most spectacular and atmospheric surviving churches are in regions on the fringe of the Empire, such as Russia, Greece and Serbia, now part of Yugoslavia.

For captions to colour plates 9–16, see p. 49

12,13

Colour plates 9–16

9 By the time of Justinian, two hundred years after Constantine, the Byzantine style was mature, and the Byzantine Empire had expanded to take in most of Italy. The imperial viceroys ('exarchs') ruled from Ravenna, and here a series of churches were built that were worthy of Constantinople itself. That of S. Vitale has all the qualities of Byzantine, as distinct from classical, aesthetic sensibility. The interior, instead of clearly and logically differentiating its structural members (columns, arches, walls), clothes them all in a coating of golden mosaic and marble veneer which transforms it into a grotto. Every surface bears its image and its meaning: scenes from the Old Testament (Abraham entertaining the angels in the lunette on the left); the New Covenant (Christ seated on a globe in the conch of the apse); and Justinian's own court (on the chancel wall, left) – all drawn together to form a theological programme that encompasses the whole of existence, human and divine.

10 Christ the Judge, a mosaic from Hagia Sophia, belongs to the thirteenth century, fairly late in Byzantine history. The technique is more delicate and the emotional tone (especially in the Virgin Mary who stands to the left of this figure and intercedes with him) more touchingly human. Christ's expression is severe; his left hand holds the jewelled Book that contains the Law; but the right is raised in blessing.

11 The great church of Hagia Sophia, in Constantinople, built under Justinian in the sixth century, was a turning-point in the history of architecture and is still one of the most exciting buildings in the world. Its technical achievement – the immensely high and wide interior space, the shallow dome without internal support, the flood of light from innumerable windows – was originally matched by equally spectacular decoration (mosaic, coloured marbles and rich carving) to create an organic whole dedicated to a single theological truth.

12 A small panel showing Christ in the familiar Byzantine pose of Ruler or Judge, with one hand holding the Book, and the other blessing. The material is coloured enamel set in a jewelled frame. The four roundels at the sides show the desks of the four Evangelists who surround him. The panel is part of the high altar ('Pala d'Oro') of St Mark's, Venice, a work made up partly of items looted from Constantinople during the Fourth Crusade (1204), partly by panels made in the same style by Venetian craftsmen. This is probably one of the latter.

13 St Mark's, Venice, is a Byzantine church on Italian soil, making its effect not through size and grandeur but through mystery and the glowing mosaic figures which cover every surface. It dates essentially from the eleventh century, though much of the decoration is later. Venice was culturally dependent on Byzantium until the sixteenth century.

14 The Presentation in the Temple, a Georgian enamel icon of the late twelfth century. Georgia and Armenia, which lay between Eastern Turkey and Russia, were flourishing parts of the Byzantine world before the Moslem invasions.

15 Church of the Transfiguration at Kozlyatevo, Russia (1756). After the fall of Constantinople in 1453 no large churches were built in the Byzantine style. But it continued to survive on a smaller scale in the churches of medieval Greece (e.g. on Mount Athos, see Chapter 3), and from there migrated to Russia, where in wood, the normal Russian building material, it assumed fantastic new forms.

16 The Holy Lamb, Agnus Dei, symbol of sacrifice and therefore of God the Son, who is one with the Father, the Creator, stands on the rock from which flow the four rivers of Paradise. Such an image, involving multiple layers of meaning which can never be completely separated, is typical of Byzantine Christianity. It is a small detail from the sixth-century apse mosaic of SS. Cosma e Damiano in Rome.

Divine mysteries on earth

ONSTANTINE'S SECOND ROME, the new Christian Empire of the East, was inaugurated in 330. Apart from an interlude of fifty-seven years following the seizure and sack of Constantinople by the Crusaders in 1204, the civilization and culture of Byzantium lasted until the Ottoman conquest of 1453. From the very beginning Constantine was determined that his new departure should be proclaimed in the most splendid of buildings, and from all over the Mediterranean world he gathered craftsmen and artists, as well as builders, to design and construct a city which would embody the Christian order of his new faith. Not only the human genius but the very materials themselves were often imported from the ancient centres of culture and religion: columns and marbles and monuments of stone and bronze. His successors, Theodosius and Justinian especially, continued this policy of cultural accumulation, and the result was a city of such splendour as to suggest, as it was intended to do, something of the divine magnificence, the earthly representation of a heavenly rule.

The first churches built by Constantine in Constantinople were in the basilican style, more or less exactly resembling the structures he inspired in Rome and in the Holy Land. The oldest church in the city, St John of Studion, built in 463, shows what they were like. The truly inventive form of Byzantine ecclesiastical architecture came with the reign of Justinian (527–563), and the development then made was decisive: from the basically rectangular hall structure which was the basilica, to the centralized building, with a dome resting on pendentives over a square base. Three of Justinian's churches still exist in the city: St Eirene, St Sergius and Bacchus, and – surely the greatest church in the world – Hagia Sophia, the church of the Holy Wisdom, named in honour of one of the attributes of Christ.

The 'Byzantine style' showed many subsequent variations, and the form itself allowed for several ranges of subtle treatment; but in essentials, and in its decorative traditions, it was to remain extraordinarily stable, just as Orthodoxy itself has been liturgically and theologically stable, for the best part of a millennium and a half. The basilica was a meeting-place for the faithful, in which they progressed towards the saving mystery of the Eucharist; the Byzantine church was itself a representation of the divine mysteries on earth. The great symbol of this was the wide central dome. Enormous architectural skill was deployed to leave the impression that the dome had virtually no support from the world beneath, that it hung downwards from heaven, enfolding the society or mortals within a space at once sacred and yet plainly earthly. But the very materials of the structure were intended to suggest a transfiguration of the world, as the light of the celestial order descended within the dome to touch the affairs of men. Within the dome, too, Christ was represented. On the flat, depthless background of gold mosaic or in painted colours, Christ as Pantocrator blesses the world, his face characteristically severe in judgment yet compassionate. The senses of the worshippers beneath, upon whom he gazes, are raised upwards to meet the descending levels of the celestial ranks. In fresco and mosaic the saints of

Justinian presents his church of Hagia Sophia (the Holy Wisdom) to the Virgin and Child, a detail from the mosaic above the main door (see p.54).

Opposite: the interior of Hagia Sophia as it was in the mid-nineteenth century, when it was still used as a mosque. This drawing by the Swiss architect Fossati, who restored the church, vividly conveys the feeling of lightness that was achieved by placing all the structural supports on the outside. It is essentially a square space covered by a shallow dome. On the east and west (we are looking east) the dome rests on semi-domes which themselves open into apses; on the north and south (left and right) there are relatively thin walls with arcades opening into aisles, the weight of the dome resting on massive external buttresses.

The church of SS. Sergius and Bacchus in Constantinople was also a foundation of Justinian. Though much smaller than Hagia Sophia it is equally refined in its details, including the exquisitely carved capitals whose filigree surfaces are a far remove from the conventional classical orders.

the lower walls of the church are transfigured men, pointing the way to other mortals. They are already detached from the world and serenely anticipate blessedness. Next, higher up, and around the base of semi-domes and the great central dome itself, are the Apostles and, perhaps also, archangels. And finally Christ himself, presiding over the universe, looks down with calm majesty.

Everything about the Byzantine church was intended to produce heaven upon earth. The decorative devices, the mosaics and the icons, were not in fact merely decorative: they were the actual and real embodiments of spiritual truths, their forms and colours mystically bringing the celestial order into the world of ordinary experience, their creators responsive to impulses which were, at least in part, thought to be derived from the divine essence. The entire unity of the church, expressed in its centralized form, was the canopy of heaven, a covering which preserved the harmony and balance of the celestial order and allowed men, not intimations only, but real experience of the union of this world and the unseen one. Matter is not dissolved; it is irradiated with the divinity that descends to the earth, as, through architectural genius, God is given material substance again and the Incarnation is re-enacted within the dome. Order and harmony, beneath the awesome majesty of Christ: the Byzantine conception of the universe, intended to be echoed within the structure of worldly government too, can be seen reflected in the still expressions of the patient rows of saints depicted in the mosaics and frescos.

The Byzantine church style did not develop slowly. It arose, instead, from the emulation of a single work of unique originality; it was fully mature right at the start. The preceding developments of the basilican form in the two centuries after Constantine were not without some significance, but nothing can have prepared men for the impact of Hagia Sophia, built between 532 and 537. The impact, indeed, was consciously planned by Justinian, who deliberately set out to fashion something new – both in terms of the ideological nature of his great cathedral and in terms of the effect it was intended to have on subsequent church building.

The first church of the Holy Wisdom, opened in 360, had been built by Constantius, son of the first Christian emperor, presumably on the basilican plan. It was destroyed by rioting in 404 and rebuilt by Theodosius II in 415. Something is known of this second church: it was designed by Ruffinos as a large basilica – excavations in 1935 showed that it had five naves. This structure, in turn, was destroyed by the mob in another of Byzantium's rather enthusiastic demonstrations of participation politics, the Nike riots, in 532. Hence Justinian's great opportunity to conceive and to construct the greatest church the world had seen. Columns and marbles were imported from Egypt and from all over Anatolia, and in the amazingly short period of seven years the enormous structure was completed.

For the eastern half of the Christian Church the form of Hagia Sophia has been the perfect embodiment of a church. So splendid and so breathtaking in its daring effects is it, in fact, that a thousand years after Justinian, when the Ottomans took over the city of Constantinople in 1453, the style of his church was used as the model for their mosques. From Istanbul to Cairo, the architects employed by the Turks put up buildings plainly based upon the centralized design and massive dome of Hagia Sophia. Some of these architects, like the greatest, Sinan, were actually converted Greek Christians, conscripted into the Sultan's service as young men. Sinan's Sulemaniye Mosque in Istanbul, for example, built in 1557, is a version of Hagia Sophia with subtle attempts to disguise the huge buttresses which had had to be added to the original over the centuries. The 'oriental' appearance of Hagia Sophia, which strikes the modern

Hagia Sophia is not impressive from outside. It was conceived from within, and the exterior shows simply the engineering necessary for the internal effect. When the Turks conquered the city, they added the minarets, which greatly changed its character.

observer, is purely the consequence of association: partly the effect of the minarets added by the Ottomans, partly the result of Eastern Mediterranean mosques being built as copies of it. In the Christian world itself the form of Hagia Sophia has, to some extent, been reproduced in every Orthodox church built subsequently. Older basilicas, as in the Holy Land, were often reconstructed in the centralized manner of Justinian's great building. There were, of course, numerous variations: octagonal as well as square bases to the dome, the lengthening of naves (for processional purposes), the clustering of subordinate domes in units around the central dome in the form of a Greek cross, and in Russia and Greece, from the end of the fourteenth century, the division of the interior by the addition of an iconostasis. The latter, a screen of icons, separated the altar from the church. In the older division of the interior, the laity observed worship from the side aisles, while the clergy occupied the nave for ceremonial preliminaries and the altar area for the performance of the central rites of the liturgy.

The only real discontinuity in the history of Byzantine churches came with the Iconoclast controversy of the eighth century, and even this was concerned not with structure, nor with the main ideological scheme of the structure, but with decoration. Opposition to depictions of figures in sacred art had Jewish antecedents and was also strictly maintained in Islam (as seen to this day in Hagia Sophia, where the winged cherubim in the pendentives beneath the great dome have had their faces blotted out with gold leaf, a legacy of the cathedral's long service as a mosque under the Ottomans). In Byzantium the destruction of the figural representations began in 726, under Leo III, and lasted until 843. Their restoration after that date seems to have been rapid; but the Iconoclast interlude does mean that none of the figural mosaics in Hagia Sophia come from the Justinian period, though some of the ordinary mosaics in the ceilings, of crosses and other motifs, do.

Mosaic was the Byzantine art *par excellence, an art intimately linked with Byzantine religious experience. The small tesserae, about the size of a thumb-nail, are made of glass, painted at the back with gold or enamel colours. Though it can approach naturalism, it is essentially a two-dimensional medium, reducing everything to jewel-like patterns and becoming one with the architecture. Left: above the entrance from the narthex at Hagia Sophia, the Emperor Leo VI (886–912) kneels at the feet of Christ; in the circles, the Virgin and Archangel Gabriel.*

Above: the Empress Irene, detail from a mosaic in the gallery of Hagia Sophia, c. 1120. Left: the main entrance, leading into the narthex; over the door Justinian and Constantine present their churches to the Virgin and Child, late tenth century. Right: Virgin and Child, ninth century, in the semi-dome of the eastern apse of Hagia Sophia.

Despite many subsequent modifications to the exterior, required because of periodic earthquake damage and the need to reinforce the weakened walls with huge buttresses to take the weight of the dome, Hagia Sophia is still recognizable as the church of Justinian and the interior, despite the decorative indications of its use as mosque, is structurally very much as it was when first built. Most of the Islamic decoration, in fact, dates not from the original conversion of the church, but from the restoration work of Caspare Fossati, a Swiss architect, in the mid-nineteenth century. In 1935 Hagia Sophia became a museum, following an edict of the Turkish government, and since then some of the mosaics of the post-Iconoclastic period have been uncovered. Others still remain hidden beneath painted plaster. In the inner narthex the mosaic above the imperial door shows Christ in blessing, with the Emperor Leo VI prostrate before him. The serene Virgin and Child in the apse is undamaged, but the best mosaics are in the galleries, where Christ and the Virgin are shown flanked by imperial rulers, and in the southern vestibule, where the Virgin and Child sit enthroned between Constantine, who offers her the city, and Justinian, who offers her the church. These mosaics, of great beauty, date from the ninth and tenth centuries.

Hagia Sophia, however, is dominated by the interior space of the dome; the church itself seeming to be but a mere enclosing curtain beneath. Even the 107 fine columns of rare marble, with their characteristic Byzantine capitals – whose surfaces are like lace, or perhaps filigree – which support the lateral walls and the galleries, do not distract from the dome. It is 180 feet high and 102 feet in diameter. Though constructed of light bricks, to lessen the weight, it has had to be repaired many times, and, in consequence, is no longer quite circular. Earthquakes in 559 destroyed the eastern side, and again, in 986, further damage was done; in 1348 the eastern half again collapsed. The interior ceiling is entirely covered with mosaics, arranged so that bands descending from the top suggest additional radiance; windows around the base light up the whole space and once gave upward illumination to the Pantocrator in the crown of the dome. Where Christ once looked down as the supreme ruler of the universe, there is now an

St Kyriaki Chrysopolitissa at Paphos, in Cyprus, severely plain and functional from the outside, belongs to the thirteenth century. The ruins in front of it are of a much earlier, fourth-century, structure.

inscription from the Koran. Beneath the dome are four winged cherubim of enormous size, two of them represented in mosaic and two in paint. The whole effect of the building, as it was intended that it should be (and despite the existing decorative chaos of competing Islamic and Christian motifs), is awesome and sanctifying. The very materials seem to radiate the majesty of God. Here, indeed, is the substance of the earth itself disclosing its divine purpose. Hagia Sophia, and the numerous churches which reflect its glory through copying its form, were not meant to inspire transcendence, as later Western European churches sought to do, but to bring heaven down to the world. Material structure is made to shine with divine purpose, and the earth itself is seen to be the throne of Christ.

When Justinian first entered his completed church he exultantly exclaimed that he had excelled Solomon. It was, perhaps, the truth. Straight away, so it seems, church builders throughout the Eastern Christian Empire abandoned the basilican style and tried to copy the perfection of Hagia Sophia. Quite often, too, existing churches were reconstructed in the 'Byzantine' manner following earthquakes or pillage, but sometimes, no doubt, in order to comply with ecclesiastical fashion. Thus at Perge, in what is now southern Turkey, there were two basilicas: St Paul had come to this malarial city, accompanied by Barnabas, and they had been identified by the inhabitants as gods descended from heaven. It became the seat of an archbishopric. The earlier of the two large fifth-century churches, on the colonnaded street of the ruins, has the remains of a large apse, and was plainly a basilican design which had been converted into a Byzantine form at some time of subsequent reconstruction. The second church is later in date – perhaps late sixth century (but not later, since the city fell to Islam in the seventh century and was largely deserted) – and was built entirely in the Byzantine style.

Paphos, in Cyprus, is another city associated with St Paul, and the pillar where he was scourged still exists in the ruins of the Roman forum. It is of dubious authenticity. It was at Paphos that St Paul converted the governor, Sergius Paulus, who became the first imperial official to accede to Christianity.

Here, by the thirteenth-century Byzantine church of St Kyriaki Chrysopolitissa (Ayia Kyriaki) lie the ruins of a fourth-century church. Formerly a large structure, basilican in style, it was subsequently remodelled in the Byzantine manner, and the surviving columns (though not the remnants of the floors) show the influence of the style spreading from Constantinople, existing alongside columns and masonry from the older basilica. Also in Cyprus, and not far away, are the remains of the Roman city of Curium. A fifth-century church of the basilican type had here, too, been adapted to the Byzantine style, while retaining most of the structure, including the classical columns of the original church. St Helena was said to have visited Cyprus on her return to Rome from the Holy Land, after the discovery of the True Cross, and to have ended a devastating drought on the island by the miraculous use of relics brought from Jerusalem. Her association with the island in the most expansive and buoyant age of Christianity gave its churches great importance. Curium itself was the seat of a bishopric.

If the structured and architectural perfection of Byzantium was achieved in Justinian's great church of Hagia Sophia, the artistic and decorative heights were probably reached rather later, in the eleventh and twelfth centuries, when mosaics and frescos attained their most developed form. At Daphni, only six miles from Athens on the old road to Corinth, stands one of the most important Byzantine churches in Greece. It was built on a site which, as its name ('Sacred Laurel') indicates, was once a sanctuary of Apollo. A church from the time of Justinian preceded the existing monastic church, which was constructed in 1080. The whole complex of monastic buildings was later converted, by the Frankish occupation of 1205, into a Cistercian house, and the result is the curious adaptation of the Byzantine structures to Gothic forms. Hence the pointed arches of the defensive walls, and the Gothicized exonarthex of the main building. But the church remains essentially Byzantine, and is, indeed, a gem of Byzantine artistic achievement.

In style it is entirely conventional: a large dome, and interior decoration intended to produce the visual sense of the descent of the celestial hierarchy to the

The monastic church at Daphni, near Athens, was built in the later twelfth century and decorated with mosaics of the highest quality. They have a freshness and lyricism which makes them particularly approachable. This is the Angel of the Annunciation greeting the Virgin on the opposite pendentive. Right: the church from the outside surrounded by monastic buildings mostly dating from the Frankish occupation of the thirteenth century.

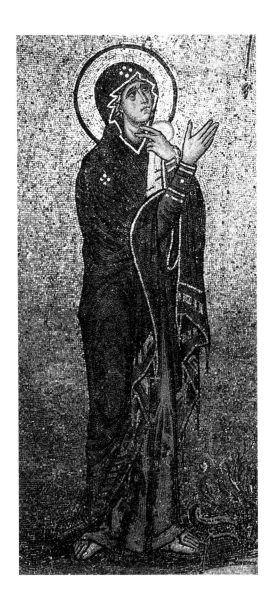

earth. In the dome is a splendid Pantocrator, the Christ accompanied by fully armed guardian angels. Beneath him are the Apostles and prophets who declare his sovereignty; and in the apse is the Virgin and Child, together with archangels. The lower walls are covered with the representations of the saints and scholars of the Church, their expressions calm and their forms still, as they bear witness to the truths of eternity. Above them, also in mosaics, are scenes from the life of Christ. Visitors come to Daphni for the splendours of the mosaic decoration, for it has a freshness of treatment and a technical quality which is quite remarkable. The Christ in the dome is shown as truly the supreme disposer of the universe; a dominant, even terrifying figure, whose countenance is magisterial and stern, whose distance from the affairs of men is proclaimed while he yet raises his hand in blessing.

Also particularly noticeable is the representation of the Virgin in the mosaic panels of the Crucifixion. Here it is, by contrast, humanity which predominates; as seen in the closure of the Virgin's features in sorrow and grief. The church is dedicated to the Dormition of the Virgin (the Assumption in Western tradition), and was restored to Orthodoxy after the Turkish occupation of southern Greece had resulted in the expulsion of the Cistercians. It fell into disuse in the nineteenth century, however, and was only restored in 1955; further restoration became necessary as a consequence of earthquake damage in 1981.

Two more mosaics at Daphni: the sorrowing Virgin from the scene of the Crucifixion and Christ Pantocrator (Ruler of the Universe) in the central dome.

Osios Loukas is a monastic complex near Delphi, founded in the eleventh century to commemorate a holy man whose grave had become the scene of miraculous cures. The scale and proportion of these Greek churches are markedly different from those of Constantinople, and became the norm throughout the Balkans for almost a thousand years.

Equal to Daphni in its artistic significance, and also monastic, is the church of Osios Loukas ('the Blessed Luke'), on the slopes of Mount Elikon, quite near to Delphi. Here are two interconnected churches, in fact; the older, dedicated to St Barbara, was built in 946 by the followers of Luke, a holy man who had come to the place and lived in a simple cell. In 953 he died, and was buried in the floor of his austere dwelling. Soon pilgrims were attracted to the site by miraculous cures, and in 1011 the second and larger church, the katholikon, was built by the Abbot Philotheos to receive the body of Luke. His remains were later removed to Rome, and have only recently been returned.

The fame of the shrine as a centre of pilgrimage led to the patronage of the imperial family, and the buildings were greatly enriched by Theophano, the daughter of a cabaret impresario, whose successive marriages to three emperors presumably left her well able to cope with the enormous cost. Her son, Basil II ('the Bulgar slayer'), added his decorative refinements early in the eleventh century when he was in the district, perhaps to slay stray Bulgars. The katholikon, in the usual manner, is a curtain to surround the spatial effects of the dome, 30 feet in diameter, and is lit from its base by sixteen windows. The wall-paintings of the dome were carried out later, in the sixteenth century. Here the Pantocrator has an expression of kindliness, as he holds an enormous book of the Gospels over 3 feet high. Below are the Virgin and the archangels. The walls of the church are banded with white marble, and the floors are of jasper and porphyry.

Everywhere there are splendid mosaics, covering the walls of the narthex and of the apse and transepts within. The Virgin and Child of the apse are seen seated upon a cushioned throne; the dome above has paintings by Michael Damaskinos, the sixteenth-century Cretan artist. The replacement of the earlier mosaics by frescos in some parts of the upper church was after earthquake damage in the sixteenth century. But the frescos of the crypt are the original covering. Here was the first shrine of the Blessed Luke, and the eleventh-century paintings, of primitive Cappadocian type, are among the most important in Greece. They are of astounding quality; their simple charm and numinous evocation make an immediate impression. Despite the passage of so many centuries, the colours are still fresh, and recent cleaning has revealed something of their original radiance. The figures are entirely serene; the events of the life of Christ portrayed against a natural background of landscapes and buildings of eleventh-century Greece.

Another important Greek church whose interior decoration represents the best of the golden age of Byzantine craftsmanship and artistic accomplishment can be found on the island of Chios. Nea Moni (the 'New Monastery') is contemporaneous with Osios Loukas; it was founded by the Emperor Constantine Monomachos and the main buildings were completed in 1056. They are of conventional Byzantine style, the main dome expressing the essential purpose of the church, and there is a large exonarthex and narthex. The church is best known for its eleventh-century mosaics, recently restored in all their brilliance after the neglect of the last two centuries and the damage caused by a great earthquake in 1881.

The mosaics are also the main attraction for visitors to the church of the Saviour in Chora (Kariye Camii) in Istanbul. This is a fairly small monastic building, outside the original Constantinian walls of the city ('in chora' means 'in

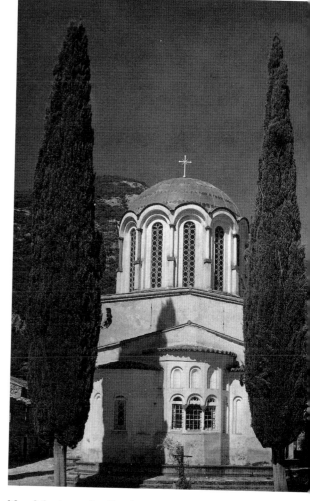

Nea Moni, on the Greek island of Chios, is also a foundation of the eleventh century. One of the mosaics (left) depicts the raising of Lazarus, who emerges from the tomb in the grip of Christ, to the amazement of those standing by.

61

The vivid scene of the Harrowing of Hell, with Christ literally dragging the dead from their graves, is a fresco from the church of the Saviour in Chora, Constantinople, built in the fourteenth century by Theodore Metochites – seen in a mosaic (below) offering the church to Christ.

the country') but within the enclosure of Theodosius's extension. The first church on the site has completely disappeared, however, and what the visitor sees today is an eleventh-century structure which was extensively repaired in the twelfth century. Two centuries later, following the Crusaders' occupation, the church was remodelled to its present appearance.

All the decorative accomplishments are from this period (1315–21) and are a memorial to the piety of one man. His portrait in mosaic may be seen above the door which leads into the nave from the inner narthex: Theodore Metochites, imperial Grand Logothete, the greatest man of his day. He was an important theologian – in the eastern Orthodox tradition of lay theology – a philosopher, historian, astronomer, poet, patron of the arts, as well as a high government official and a diplomat. He was, indeed, one of the leading figures of the Byzantine cultural revival, and his church in Chora, as he declared himself, was intended to secure 'a glorious memory to the end of the world'. It was also a momento of his sad later years. After the usurpation of the imperial throne by Andronicus III, Theodore Metochites, after a period of imprisonment, was exiled to the monastery and stayed there until his death in 1331.

His last years on earth were devoted to the decoration of the church. The mosaics are perhaps the finest in the world, and express the iconographic order of the universe – the church is dedicated to the Pantocrator. In the side-chapel on the south of the church (the parecclesion) are some important frescos of the same period, probably by the same unknown artist responsible for the mosaics. They indicate the function of the building as a mortuary chapel, and illustrate the Resurrection and Judgment. Thus the concluding preoccupations of Theodore Metochites's last unhappy years are preserved for all time in their hopeful and

The mosaics and frescos of the church of the Saviour in Chora have a humanity and drama that was new to Byzantine art. Left: Christ the Judge, a mosaic over the door of the inner narthex.

graceful depictions of the celestial world. The church became a mosque after the Turkish conquest of the city, and the decoration was plastered over. The plaster has now been removed again and the full harmony of the original design of the interior restored.

The legacy of Byzantium passed to the Greek Orthodox Church, whose buildings continued to be constructed up to and through the period of Turkish occupation. They are all on a small scale but richly decorated and full of treasures of every kind. Many of the most interesting are those on Mount Athos, to be described in the next chapter.

To Western eyes the interiors of Orthodox churches have a cluttered appearance. The patina of faith, the product of continued devotional use, can seem, to the observer from a more sanitized religious culture, like plain dirt. The smoke of incense, the wax of tapers, the sheer effects of applied holiness, do not always elicit immediate appreciation. In some churches, as in Moscow's Epiphany Cathedral, the decoration, though in the classic Byzantine-Russian style and heavily gilded, is relatively modern, and the whole building has a clean aspect which may commend itself. In most ancient churches of the Orthodox tradition, and especially in those continually in use – like shrines – the glowing icons, hanging lamps and blackened mosaics present an alien aspect to those accustomed to the devotional practices of Protestantism, who tend to evaluate the whole effect of an ecclesiastical building in the light of its decorative images and general state of preservation or cleanliness. It is unfortunate that this is the case.

The church of the Assumption in Gethsemane, for example, for centuries encased the traditional site of the tomb of the Virgin in Jerusalem, and what is left

The Armenian Cathedral in Jerusalem goes back to Crusader times, but its present furniture and decoration are typical of the Orthodox Church. This is the throne of St James, to whom the cathedral is dedicated.

of it perfectly illustrates the decayed decorative richness of Orthodox interiors. The original shrine here was first mentioned in the fifth century; the later church, built in the twelfth century by the Crusaders, has also gone, and all that remains is the Crusaders' Gothic doorway, with ancient steps leading down to the only surviving part of the church – the crypt and the tomb itself. The shrine is looked after by the Greek Orthodox, the Armenians, Syrians and Copts, and the combined physical traces of their faith, in the holy jumble of lamps and icons, is the most astonishing evocation of Eastern Christianity. The Armenian cathedral of St James, also in Jerusalem, the seat of the Armenian Patriarch, has the same ability to express the essence of Eastern worship. The tall building, another Crusader foundation, is fitted with the materials of worship and the marks of liturgical splendour. To the unsympathetic it is a tinselled contrivance; to the faithful it is an anticipation of eternity.

The political and cultural influence of Byzantium extended westwards as far as the Adriatic coasts of Italy, and it was there, in fact, that some of the most interesting variations of the church style occurred. At Ravenna the centrality of the dome in the Byzantine church of S. Vitale accords exactly with the theological basis established in Constantinople, and the famous mosaics of the city, especially of S. Apollinare Nuovo, are all very close to their Byzantine originals. But it was in the churches of the Venetian lagoon that the Byzantine style showed its most inventive variations. Venice was technically a 'dukedom' of the Eastern Empire; in reality the rise to power of the 'Serene Republic' was an essay in playing the Byzantine emperors off against the Germanic Holy Roman Empire in the West.

The Venetian policy of balancing East and West is represented in its architectural history, too, with the gradual introduction of Romanesque and Gothic additions to the original Byzantine structures. Venice took a major part in the sack of Constantinople in 1204, and thereafter began to turn increasingly to the West – a change which became decisive in the fifteenth century, when its artistic achievements, too, point to a decisive break with the Eastern world. The island of Torcello, once equal to Venice itself, some six miles across the lagoon, has a cathedral church (Sta Maria Assunta) built in 639 in the Byzantine style, and rebuilt, with a bell-tower, in the eleventh century. There are mosaics here from the original church, and columns of marble from classical sites in Greece. The outstanding apse mosaic of the Virgin and Child with the Apostles beneath, is twelfth century. The nearby church of Santa Fosca, an eleventh-century foundation, preserves much more of the external appearance of a Byzantine church. It is a large central dome resting upon a Greek cross design, with a kind of open exonarthex forming an arcade around the outside of the building – all in brick and tile, with marble columns.

But it is the basilica of St Mark, in Venice itself, that represents the most extraordinary Western development of the Byzantine church. The first building here, a canopy for the remains of St Mark himself – rescued, as the Venetians put it, from the Islamic occupation of Alexandria – was pulled down in the year 1000 when the doge, Domenico Contarini, decided to house the relics in a more splendid structure. Completed in 1073, this was a unified Byzantine church, on a Greek cross basis, with a series of five domes. There were Romanesque influences, too, and with the successive need to accommodate monuments, columns, statues and relics brought back from their overseas trade (or conquest or pillage) by Venetian entrepreneurs, the artistic and architectural styles which have been added to the basilica have made for a rich but chaotic confusion both inside and outside. Many of the columns and decorative panels have come from

Venice was the heir of Constantinople – in some ways all too literally when the infamous Fourth Crusade (1204) led to the sack of the city and the transfer of many of its treasures to Venice. This jewelled book cover is made up of Byzantine work of the eleventh century: the Archangel Michael in the centre is surrounded by small enamel panels of saints.

Opposite: the old cathedral of Torcello, the mother church of Venice, was founded as early as the seventh century. All its features are strongly Byzantine – the mosaic of the Virgin in the apse, the screen of paintings with portraits of the Apostles, the stone panels beneath carved with pairs of peacocks, symbols of eternity because their flesh, according to legend, was immune to decay.

St Mark's, Venice, is a treasure-house of mosaics of all periods, from Byzantine to Renaissance. This figure of St Athanasius dates from the fourteenth century.

older Byzantine churches: the famous Greek horses, of the fourth century BC, which for centuries adorned the façade above the main door, were looted from Constantinople during the sack of 1204. The narthex/atrium has ancient marble columns and splendid mosaics, in the Byzantine-Romanesque style of the twelfth and thirteenth centuries.

The whole of the interior of the basilica suggests what the great Byzantine churches of the Eastern Empire must have been like before the Islamic occupation. It is luminous with mosaics, most with flat gold backgrounds, and all in excellent condition. Worship here has never been discontinued. The name of the architect is unknown, but tradition insists that Contarini instructed him to build the most beautiful church in the world. Whether he was successful in his commission is a matter of judgment: he at least produced, despite its variations and cultural accretions, a classic Byzantine church. Here, in the rather heightened central dome of the Ascension, with its slightly Westernized thirteenth-century mosaic interior, is Christ in Majesty, with the Apostles beneath, and, lower again, on the pendentives, the four evangelists. Here, too, are apse mosaics of pure Byzantine design, survivors of the great fire of 1106. The aisles are flanked by Byzantine marble columns. St Mark himself now rests within the main altar, beneath the Pala d'Oro, designed by artists in Constantinople in 978 and encrusted with sacred enamels looted from the city during the Fourth Crusade. The patterned marble floors are strikingly undulating: a reminder of the subsidence to which Venice is subject, as the piles on which the whole place rests sink unevenly through the unstable mud to the clay substrata. The exterior of St Mark's is untypically ornate, and crowded with later additions in the Venetian-Gothic style. The extravagance and richness of the whole structure, indeed, suggest a kind of 'Baroque' variant of the Byzantine style, a later flowering on the fringe of the Eastern Empire.

In the Greek heartlands of Byzantium the church pattern established by Justinian has continued: to visit modern churches in the suburbs of Athens is to see buildings in the same centralized form, and with the same iconographic intentions and details, as the great original in Constantinople. Just as there were developments of the Byzantine style to the far west, however, so there were to the north. The background to these developments, and the main reason why the West turned to Romanesque and then Gothic styles of ecclesiastical architecture, while the East and the North retained the Byzantine forms, lay in the separation of Greek Christianity from the Germanized inheritance of Rome. Developments were gradual and uneven. By the sixth century the Nestorian and Monophysite churches of the eastern provinces of the Empire had more or less ceased to have any connexion with the Byzantine Church, and with the Islamic conquests of the seventh century they disappeared behind an alien religious curtain. Of the four ancient Patriarchates, three (Alexandria, Antioch and Jerusalem) were lost to Christendom. Thus the fourth, Constantinople, became the leader of Greek Christianity in the eastern and central Mediterranean world. But the absence of centralized authority in the Eastern understanding of the nature of the Church meant that nothing like the dominant position Rome was achieving in the West was visited upon the Patriarchate of Constantinople. In 800 the Pope gave the imperial crown of the Holy Roman Empire to Charlemagne in what amounted to an actual, as well as a symbolic, recognition of the separation of the Latin and Greek worlds.

Differences of language and learning were also, by then, becoming enormous. Greek Christianity was speculative in its theology, yet its worship was committed to a liturgy whose unchanging form itself disclosed the fullness of religious truth;

Latin Christianity was more practical and its patterns of worship began to show, beneath a deceptive appearance of uniformity, a wide range of localized rites. In 1054 came the Great Schism, when the Patriarch was excommunicated by the Pope, but by then the reality of two separate Christian worlds had for some time been in existence. When the Latin Christians ransacked Constantinople in 1204, stripped Hagia Sophia of its riches and removed its relics to the West, the two halves of Christianity seemed separated for ever. The Greeks never forgot the dreadful desecration. With the fall of Constantinople to Islam the remnants of Byzantium passed out of Christendom altogether: on 29 May 1453, the last Christian service was held in Hagia Sophia. Yet there was a final remnant, a 'Third Rome', a northern extension of Byzantine Christianity, which was, until 1917, to preserve something of the ancient splendour of the Eastern Church.

One of the by-products of the revival that followed the Iconoclastic controversy was the ninth-century mission to the Slavs: the Patriarch Photius commissioned two Greek brothers, St Methodius and St Cyril, to travel to territory to the north of the Empire. Orthodoxy has normally worshipped in the local tongue: the two Greeks had recognized the need, from the start, to translate the Scriptures and the liturgy into the Slavic languages, and so to integrate Christianity into Slavic culture. National churches were also formed in the Christianized lands, thereby, as it turned out, associating the faith with national self-consciousness, and issuing in that close relationship of Church and State – a direct legacy of Byzantium – which has characterized the Orthodoxy of Eastern Europe. Missionary enterprise moved north to Kiev, and in 988 King Vladimir adopted Christianity. Monasticism, always a vital part of Byzantine religious tradition, became hugely important in the conversion of Russia that followed.

The Mongol occupation of the whole area in the thirteenth century actually assisted the advance of Christianity, for the Church became the repository of national sentiment, the spiritual basis of resistance to the alien invaders. The Russian state which emerged in the fourteenth century was triumphalist in its acclamation of Orthodoxy, and the great apostle of the new nation was St Sergius. It was an Orthodoxy redolent of the monastic ideal, and from the great foundation at Zagorsk, Sergius and his followers set up some fifty monasteries as the guardians of the Christianity of Russia. The new kingdom was identified as the successor to Constantinople; in 1448 the independence of the Russian Church was demonstrated by the election of a separate Metropolitan without securing the authority of the Patriarch – and this was a few years before the fall of Constantinople. Russian Grand Dukes began to adopt the old Roman-Byzantine imperial titles; the double-headed eagle of Byzantine became the symbol of the Russian state, as the standard-bearer of Christian civilization. A patriarchate was set up in Moscow, the new holy city of the Christian world.

The Byzantine Church style was adopted in the north as well. At first it was retained in a pure form, a straight extension of the churches of the old Romanian territories of the Byzantine Empire – many of which still exist. But in the frontier conditions of the Russian mission the walls of the churches began to grow taller in emulation of the defensive secular buildings. Domes became more rounded and exotic, decorative additions for external appreciation rather than the utilitarian coverings of sacred space. Above them rose the distinctive cross of three bars – the topmost suggesting the superscription proclaiming the kingship of Christ, and the lowest, the foot-rest (*suppedaneum*), recalling the divinity resting upon the earth, the essence of the Incarnation.

The extraordinary elaboration of the exteriors of Russian church towers and domes can be seen at its most dramatic in Moscow: St Basil's Cathedral, which

In Romania a type of church decoration evolved which seems to have existed nowhere else: painting on the exterior, partially protected from the weather by a wide overhanging roof. At Suceviţa, in the province of Bucovina, the walls of the monastic church are covered with figures of saints, angels and prophets. It dates from 1582 to 1584.

St Basil's Cathedral, Moscow, seems to combine every element of the late Byzantine style. Built in the mid-sixteenth century, it is a fantastic assemblage of spires, domes, and all-over patterns; the interior space hardly exists.

Two churches in the huge monastic complex of Zagorsk: Nikon's Church (1548), and the Trinity Cathedral (1423).

comprises no less than nine tall-domed chapels, is surely comparable to St Mark's in Venice, in the sense that both are extravagant and dramatic versions of the Byzantine style. St Basil's, the cathedral of the Intercession, was built in the 1550s by Ivan IV to commemorate the annexation of Kazan to the Russian Empire; the architect was Posnik Yakovlev. The polychrome walls scarcely seem real. The building is like something from a book of fables, at once vulgar yet breathtaking in its architectural skills, proto-Gaudí, an ecclesiastical anticipation of Disneyland. In fact, though constructed of brick, St Basil's actually continues to suggest the wooden churches of the first Russian expansion; it is the perpetuation in an urban context of the dark forest churches of the Russian landscape. It is now a historical museum.

The general principles of Byzantine church design were retained in Russia: the centralized form, still basically a Greek cross, with apse, shortened nave, plain exteriors, and interior decoration of mosaic and fresco. The increased height of the buildings, however, has tended to alter the spiritual effect. In place of the sense of Christ's descent to the world, where he meets the assembled witnesses to his truth – which was the main characteristic of the huge and wide central domes of Byzantium – there is an experience of ascent, the eye is drawn upwards and the aspirant to spiritual truth is called away from the world.

This is certainly the effect in the Trinity Cathedral at Zagorsk, the great centre of Russian spirituality, where St Sergius founded his monastery in the middle of the fifteenth century, and where successive churches have produced the finest examples of Russian ecclesiastical architecture. The Trinity Cathedral was completed in 1423, in huge slabs of white masonry. Its high walls, with small narrow windows, suggest defensive features. Doorways and the gables of the vaults form pointed arches, drawing attention upwards from the massive walls to the slender and elevated central dome, with its gold cover. Inside, light from the narrow windows adds to the impression of height. Here, too, is the iconostasis, the screen of icons separating the nave from the sanctuary, which was so magnificently developed in the Russian Church. The example at the Trinity Cathedral is especially celebrated: it is the work of Andrei Rublyov and Daniil Cherny.

The exuberance of the Russian style is seen in the Assumption Cathedral, also in the monastic complex at Zagorsk. Completed in 1585, this is a tall building from whose roof, like exotic mushrooms, sprout five bulbous domes, all except the central one, which is gold, brightly painted in green and blue, with golden stars. Yet the structure beneath them, the church itself, is massive and austere. Inside, the walls are covered with frescos of the later seventeenth century, by Yaroslav and Troitsk artists.

The same basic form of these two masterpieces of Russian church design are echoed in the famous cathedrals of the Kremlin in Moscow and in numerous smaller churches. As in the case of classic Byzantine churches, the earlier the date, the simpler and less ornate are the exteriors. Thus the splendid church of the Theotokos, on the banks of the Nerl not far from Vladimir, is a tall twelfth-century structure, surmounted by a single slender dome, with virtually no exterior decorative effects. Here the upper gables are rounded, in the Byzantine manner, and have not yet attained the pointed shape of the later building. These are churches designed for the performance of the liturgy, houses for the sacred mysteries of Orthodoxy, refuges of spirituality in a warring society. They are less ideological than the more linear descendants of Hagia Sophia; they attempt rather less to evoke the celestial order in the form of earthly materials, and rather more to provide mysterious and exalted chambers for the Eucharistic presence.

Despite the development of the iconostasis, which divides the people in the nave from the priests in the sanctuary, there has also been a shift of emphasis towards the worshippers themselves, who have, at least, managed to occupy the nave, once reserved only for processions.

Humbler versions of the Russian church style, often of wooden construction, spread across the Russian Empire with the great expansion of the eighteenth and nineteenth centuries. Some are to be found in seemingly unlikely places. Thus at Kenai and Kodiak in Alaska there are splendid small, weather-boarded Orthodox churches, rising to slender ornate domes: rustic copies of the great churches of the Russian heartlands. Sometimes there is a touch of Western influence, as at Ninilchik, where a wooden cruciform church rises to two domes, one square and the other octagonal, both rather squat, and both suggesting the domestic architecture of the Victorian era. These churches are here because Bering claimed Alaska for Russia in 1741, and the spread of Orthodoxy followed. When ten Russian monks arrived in 1794, intent upon a missionary push to the south, Spanish Catholicism spread further northwards from southern California, in order to counter what was perceived as the Orthodox and imperial threat. The little wooden churches of Alaska are the reminder of an almost forgotten past expansion of the Russian Church.

Russian church styles at home were greatly influenced by Western European taste in the eighteenth century: as seen in the bell-towers at the Lavra of the Caves in Kiev and at Zagorsk, both superb examples of Western Neo-classicism. Peter the Great's reforms of the Church, in 1721, were accompanied by serious and persistent attempts to adapt Orthodoxy to Western ideas and patterns of organisation. There were monastic reforms as well, with many of the lesser foundations disappearing altogether. Reaction to the changes came in the next century, just as in England nineteenth-century religious enthusiasts acted in self-conscious rejection of what they supposed the dry rationalism of the eighteenth-century Church had been like. The popular spiritual revival of nineteenth-century Russia looked to Mount Athos, not the West, for inspiration, and the monastic and missionary enterprises which were evidence of its vitality and extent restored a distinctly Russian note which was very emphatic in the ecclesiastical architecture of the century.

The Moscow Kremlin contains many churches and four cathedrals. Here the onion dome left of centre belongs to the cathedral of the Archangel Michael (early sixteenth century); the tall tower is the Bell Tower of Ivan Veliky (also sixteenth century), and to the right of that, the cathedral of the Twelve Apostles (1656). On the extreme left, actually outside the Kremlin, is the cathedral of Christ the Redeemer, built between 1838 and 1880, and demolished in 1934.

The Russian monastery on Mount Athos is the largest of the whole peninsula.

In England the most outstanding example of the Byzantine Revival is the Catholic cathedral of Westminster by J. F. Bentley, begun in 1895.

The Russian monastery of St Panteleimon on Mount Athos itself is perhaps the greatest monument of the revival. It was an ancient foundation, but the existing buildings date from the first half of the nineteenth century. In 1875, with the election of a Russian abbot, the monastery came entirely under Russian (rather than Greek) control; and by the end of the century there were over a thousand Russian monks in residence. The enormous extent of the buildings is as impressive as their characteristic Russian appearance. The katholikon, with its cluster of green domes, was built between 1812 and 1821. Since 1875 the services have been held in both Greek and Russian.

There have been successful, twentieth-century, adaptations of the original Byzantine style in Western countries. The Catholic cathedrals of the capitals of both the United Kingdom and the United States are outstanding examples. In both cases the forms of the Byzantine model have been radically altered: they are basically extended cruciform churches with long naves, like the Gothic structures more familiar to the worshippers of those countries, but with classic Byzantine arcades and vaults, and with central domes. In both cases, too, the Byzantine style recommended itself for utilitarian reasons. It was foreseen that construction would be over an extended period, because of uncertainty about financing, and the Byzantine style had the great advantage that decorative effects, like interior mosaic cladding, could be left to the future, and were not – as with Gothic buildings – an integral part of the structure itself. Byzantine architecture, additionally, was very unfamiliar in the West at the start of the twentieth century, and Catholic churches in the style would not be regarded as being in competition with the Gothic Protestant cathedrals.

Westminster Cathedral in London was the supreme achievement of J. F. Bentley. It was also his only building in the Byzantine style. Begun in 1895, the structure is an enormous mass of brick, with layered stone on the exterior more suggestive of Siena than of Constantinople. There are Renaissance hints, too, in the slender campanile, surmounted by a cross which contains a fragment of the

True Cross discovered by St Helena in Jerusalem. It is Byzantine only in the tapered domed cover. But within, the cathedral is a masterpiece of Byzantine adaptation. The huge vaults of the nave, the highest in England, and the arches of the arcade, are mysterious and splendid in their undressed brick: shortage of money has meant that they have never been covered with mosaics, as originally intended – covered like the side-chapels, once described as reminiscent of 'bathrooms by Harrods'. The stains and patina on the naked brick surfaces are like the bowels of some Victorian railway terminus; the dark interiors of the three domes of the nave have mysterious cavernous qualities, emphasizing the light and splendour of the ceremonies in the space beneath. The highest, central dome, above the sanctuary, is lit from its base by twelve windows, in the classic Byzantine manner. But its function is not Byzantine. It is to illuminate the great baldacchino which rises over the high altar, an enhancement to the offering of the Mass, not a special experience of the presence of the Pantocrator. The yellow Veronese marble of the baldacchino contrasts with the green Byzantine columns of the nave, which came from the same marble quarry used by Justinian for the construction of Hagia Sophia. The capitals are of white Carrara marble from Italy.

The mosaic adornments of the interior of the National Shrine of the Immaculate Conception in Washington D.C. are rather nearer to completion than those in Westminster. Indeed, the depiction of the Descent of the Holy Spirit, in the chancel dome, is the largest mosaic in the world. Designed by Max Ingrand, it was finished in 1968. The first stone of the cathedral was laid in 1920: an enormous block of New Hampshire granite containing a slice of marble from Mount Carmel in the Holy Land. The architect of the building was Charles D. Maginnis, Senior, who had previously designed over a hundred American churches, many in Neo-classical styles. For the Shrine of the Immaculate Conception he elected to use a mixture of Romanesque and Byzantine, with more of the classic sense of the ideological importance of the central dome than the extended cruciform shape of the cathedral might at first suggest. Building techniques were traditional; only brick, stone and tile (not steel) were employed. The sixty-two interior columns, supporting arcading in the Byzantine style, are of imported marble; the massive walls, three feet thick, support Byzantine vaults and five domes. The slender Romanesque campanile, beside a Romanesque west front, precede a thoroughly Byzantine church, dominated by a wide central dome. The exterior, brightly coloured tile decoration of the dome is a feature of the Washington skyline. The crypt of the cathedral was completed in 1931, and the superstructure in 1959. Although the ingredients have been assembled in an original way, this great church retains the leading attributes of a classical Byzantine building. The apse mosaic, it is true, is not of the Virgin, as was always the case in early Byzantine churches, but of Christ in Majesty. It is by John De Rosen, and is the largest mosaic representation of Christ in existence. This is all some distance, it must seem, from Justinian's great original church in Constantine's ancient city, but the thread of continuity is still easily discernible, and something of the awe evoked by Hagia Sophia will affect the visitor to this, as surely to most, of the subsequent structures that have aspired to reproduce shadows of its perfection.

The National Shrine of the Immaculate Conception, Washington, contains this vast mosaic figure of Christ by John De Rosen.

3 Monastic seclusion: the active and contemplative life

AT THE SAME TIME as the Church was growing great and powerful, exercising an authority that is reflected in the scale of its buildings both in Byzantium and Western Europe, another way of religious life was turning its back upon all these values and finding holiness in poverty and solitude. The monastic movement goes back to those hermits, later known as the Desert Fathers who, in the early years of Christianity, decided to dedicate their lives to prayer and meditation in the area of the Nile Delta. In the course of time they gathered together in loosely organized communities, but the tradition of the desert – that of monks living secluded lives in places remote from the great urban centres – was still fundamental to Eastern and Celtic monasticism. Some of the most evocative sites now remaining are in Ireland, where primitive stone huts and churches no bigger than wayside chapels were the setting for a spiritual culture that, for a time, outshone everything else in northern Europe. Contemplating the sparse remains of Kells or Clonmacnoise, it is difficult to believe that such monasteries could have produced masterpieces of manuscript illumination and sculpture. Yet the Irish Church was flourishing enough to send missionary expeditions all over Europe and to found a tradition that was independent of Rome and in some ways closer to Christian origins.

In the Latin world, monasticism was radically transformed by the establishment of the Benedictine system in the sixth century. St Benedict's Rule formed the basis of all subsequent monasticism in the West. In Britain the two systems could not coexist, and at the Synod of Whitby (664) it was decided that the authority of Rome, which entailed the Benedictine Rule, should prevail.

For captions to colour plates 17–24,
see p. 81

18,19

22,23

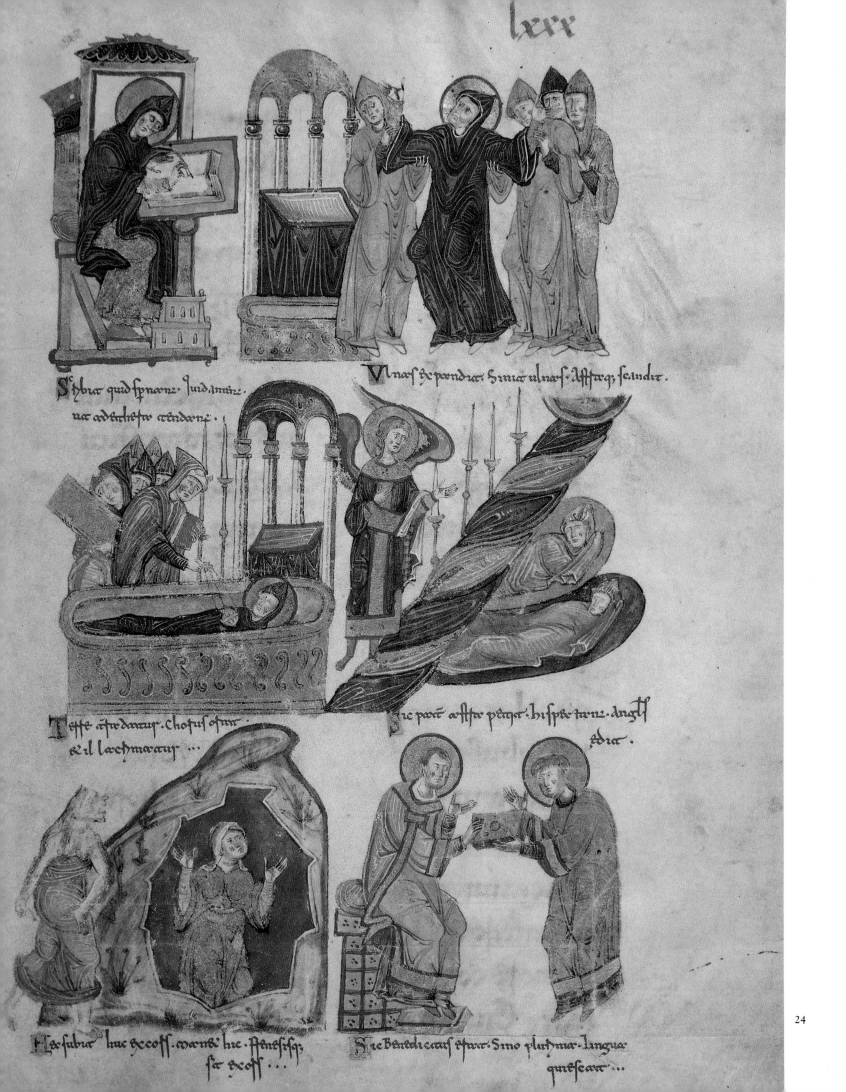

Sibris quid spiritiv. quid amicic
uix ad sicuhesio cendoris.

Vluas dependirc. hinc ulnas. Asstarq; scindir.

Teste ccredarur. chorus osum
&il lacrimarur ...

hic part astare pergit. hispe tuvie. angli
edia.

hec subir huc de coss. coarnc hic ffenessq;
far deoss ...

hic Benedicearur esswer. Sino pluchmor. lingue
quiescarur ...

24

Colour plates 17–24

17 *The lives of the Desert Fathers attracted a whole series of picturesque legends involving temptations by devils, harrowing privations and miraculous rescues. An Italian Renaissance painting by Starnina represents them in a charmingly schematic form sitting in their cells, calling upon one another and experiencing various supernatural interventions.*

18 *To come closest to the early monastic ideal we have to go to Mount Athos in Greece, where a series of independent monasteries have continued uninterrupted from Early Byzantine times until today. This photograph shows the installation of a new head of the whole community in the church of the Protaton at Kariai. This is the oldest church on Mount Athos, dating from the tenth century. The rich iconostasis in the background was added in 1607.*

19 *Edward Lear's painting of the monastery of St Paul (Ayiou Pavlou) on Mount Athos is one of the most vivid evocations of its remoteness and seclusion. Since Lear's visit in 1856 it has been substantially rebuilt and now houses about fifty monks.*

20 *The peaks of the Meteora, in northern Greece, are even more striking in appearance than those of Mount Athos. The monasteries here were similarly founded as a refuge from the world and made deliberately hard of access. Some could only be reached by baskets wound up by windlasses. Unlike Mount Athos, however, its communities have in modern times failed to attract sufficient new members and they are now supported by tourism.*

21 *The monastery at the foot of Mount Sinai goes back to at least the fifth century, probably earlier. One of its first abbots was Climacus, which means 'ladder', so called after his work* The Ladder to Paradise. *A ninth-century illustration shows the monastery. A monk, bottom left, looks out of the upper window which was the only way of entering. In the background is Mount Sinai and Climacus himself in a cave where he lived for nearly forty years, drawing up his food in a basket.*

22 *Mountain tops were sacred to the Archangel Michael. Mont St Michel, off the coast of Normandy, was sufficiently isolated to attract an early monastic community, which grew to be one of the most celebrated in France. In this sixteenth-century manuscript the monastic buildings are shown in realistic detail (the two west towers later collapsed into the sea). In the sky above, St Michael defeats the satanic dragon.*

23 *Montserrat, in Spain, became celebrated for its miraculous image of the Black Virgin. It was a flourishing pilgrimage place throughout the Middle Ages but was badly damaged in the Napoleonic wars and the church was rebuilt in a Neo-Romanesque style. The setting, with its strangely shaped rocks, makes it one of the most extraordinary of all monastic sites.*

24 *Benedict of Nursia was born in 480. He lived first as a hermit, then as a member of a community on the Egyptian model. But in 529 he founded a monastery at Montecassino, in southern Italy, and drew up a Rule for its members that has been the basis of Western monasticism ever since. Abandoning the extremes and austerities of the Desert Fathers, he devised a way of life equally divided between practical work and spiritual devotion, economically viable and sufficiently disciplined to allow it to survive in a violent and unstable world. These miniatures, from a manuscript of St Gregory's Life of Benedict, show (top left to bottom right): St Benedict writing the Rule; his death, supported by monks; his burial; two sleeping monks seeing a vision of the angel path leading to heaven; a mad woman cured by spending the night in the cave where he had once lived; and St Gregory as he completes writing Benedict's life.*

Monastic seclusion

THERE IS AN IMPORTANT STRAND in Christianity – some have supposed it the ideal – which directs believers away from the world and into the seclusion of prayer, austere self-denial, and spiritual contemplation. Monasticism began in Egypt around the start of the fourth century. Its earliest hero was St Antony, who died in 356, and its style was extremely ascetic. The aspirants to religious perfection went off into the desert, or dwelt among the caves and catacombs of cemeteries, or sometimes, even, in the tradition of St Simon Stylites, they passed their lives on pillars. The monasticism of Egypt attracted many pilgrims from other parts of the Christian world in the early centuries; so that by the end of the fourth century Egypt was regarded as a second Holy Land, to be visited at the same time as a journey to the Holy Sepulchre in Jerusalem, its monastic sanctuaries providing additional occasions of solace and instruction in spiritual discipline. As it spread to the Byzantine world, monasticism was often coenobitic: the monks lived in communities (as distinct from idiorrhythmic practice, the life of the solitary lived either as a hermit or in groups). The communities associated themselves with the general monastic ideals of St Basil, though he had founded no rule, as such, and the patterns of their lives therefore showed some variations, but were united in the priority given to the contemplative over the active life. The monasticism that inspired the Church in the West was ultimately indebted to St Pachomius, and shared a common origin therefore with the basilican ideal, but was more systematic. Its great founder was St Benedict, who died in 543, and it was centred on a unified and specified rule of life. Nearly all of the monasticism of the Latin Church is derived from the Benedictine vision, and most variations have been prompted either by a desire to return to its first simplicity or by adaptations of the monastic ideal to changes in society.

Both the collective, communal life of monasticism, and the individual and perhaps more sacrificial life of the hermit, have continued to coexist within the Eastern and the Western Churches. Some of the most successful penetrations of culture have proceeded from monastic work, and some of the most effective expansions of Christianity have been enormously assisted by a monastic spearhead. Examples include the Irish mission to Europe in the seventh century, the work of the friars in the assimilation of South America to Iberian Catholicism, the Christianization of the Slavs by Orthodox monks, and the conversion of the Russian Empire by the religious forces associated with St Sergius. Because the monastic life and the life of the Church in general have been so closely associated, there has never been a distinct 'church style' for monastic building. The churches of the orders have echoed prevailing modes, and have invented variations or assisted transitions to new styles in ways which do not set them apart. A great Cistercian church of the medieval West looked very much like the secular churches, just as the Byzantine styles of Eastern monasticism followed the tradition general within Orthodoxy. But there were some monastic communities who, by their peculiar choice of sites, stood apart from the rest of the evolution of mainstream Christendom, and these are now considered

The abbot was the father of his monks and his decision was law. This tombstone of an abbot is from a Coptic monastery of the sixth or seventh century.

Opposite: St Anthony, the most famous of the desert hermits, was subjected to unceasing temptation by the devil. Beautiful women were sent to overcome his chastity; food appeared when he was supposed to be fasting; horrible demons tried to frighten him into submission. All in vain. 'The illusions of the devil soon vanish,' he said, 'if a man arms himself with the sign of the cross.' St Anthony's legend lived on and was a favourite subject in art. This fresco, showing defeated devils cringing away from him, is by the Lorenzetti brothers at Pisa.

Coptic monasteries survived in Egypt through the centuries of Moslem occupation, pursuing their way of life unaffected by the Benedictine Rule of the West. This chapel is at Wâdi el Natrûn.

separately because of their importance as expressions, both to contemporaries and to subsequent observers, of a kind of monastic purity.

Monastic clusters – concentrations of several houses in remote places – usually followed the pioneering work of a single hermit who had taken himself into isolation to achieve spiritual insights through extraordinary severities of living. His sanctity attracted others, and small communities were the result. Egypt, again, showed the earliest examples, and of these the best impression may still be received by visiting the little monastic 'city' at Wâdi el Natrûn, just off the old road from Alexandria to Cairo, in the western desert. The area has been notable since the earliest times for its nitrates and other minerals, and the Coptic monks who first came here to seek a life of separation from the world were not, therefore, quite as remote from some of its industrial activity as the modern desolation of the area suggests. The founding hermit seems to have been St Fronto, who arrived in the middle of the second century from Alexandria; a century later there were said to be five thousand monks. It was from Wâdi el Natrûn that the army of monks came who invaded Alexandria in 399, after the Patriarch, Theophilus, had accused them of Monophysite heresies. They were Egyptians, Copts, and represented a rather different version of the faith from the Greek Christianity of the coast.

Set among the ruins of many others, four of the Coptic monasteries survive. They have surrounding defensive walls, and inside are the two or three churches and the monastic quarters. All four are sixth-century foundations: St Pschoi, St Macarius, St Baramus, and the convent of the Syrians. This last, as its name suggests, was staffed by Syrian monks, and is dedicated to the Virgin. Here, in 1833, the English traveller Robert Curzon discovered a rich collection of early manuscripts, which are now in the British Museum. The church, of the sixth century, has a nave and vaults with pointed arches, and splendid frescos and ivory panels, depicting scenes from the life of Christ. These date from the seventh and eighth centuries. There hangs around the whole of the Natrûn complex a surprisingly strong sense of the sanctity of the place. Set amidst the scarred evidence of ancient and modern industrial activity – the soda works – the numinous associations somehow persist, as if the maintenance of the divine worship for so many centuries has laid a second landscape on top of the original one. The harsh brightness of the desert gives a surreal dimension to the buildings.

The Europe to which Christianity spread was rather short of deserts, and the early ascetics here sought out the heights in their attempts to find godly isolation. Monastic communities were perched on rocks, hidden in the clouds, or surrounded by the sea, in the search for places which reproduced the primitive privations of the Egyptian deserts. Many of these sites were named in honour of St Michael the Archangel, lover of heights, the guardian of Christian armies, protector against the devil, the one who conveys Christian souls after death to the merciful judgment of God. But the original deserts, too, had offered the chance for rock-dwelling monasticism, and among the earliest – and in direct emulation of the privations of Christ himself – were the monastic cells that clung to the Mount of the Temptation above the Jordan valley, near to Jericho. In the 300 years between the conversion of Constantine and the Islamic occupation of the Holy Land this line of high cliffs provided bleak shelter for numerous hermits and small communities of monks. They sought to live again with their Lord the fastings of the forty days.

The first settlement was made in 304, by St Chariton, whose monastery was on the top of the cliff. It was destroyed by the Persians in 614 and rebuilt by the Crusaders. This house, in turn, was destroyed, and the site thereafter occupied by

Georgian monks, who built a small hermitage. Soon afterwards Greek Orthodox monks began to build here – and have been here ever since. But the present monastery, pressed into the rock face and preserving, still, the shrine of Christ's fast, the first Lent, is fairly modern. It was begun in 1845 and finished in 1874, with the main church, dedicated to the Annunciation, completed in 1904. The cliff all round is pitted with caves and crevices which once gave uncomfortable refuge to hermits.

To the west of the Christian world the rock pinnacles, which the monks made their homes, were sometimes given additional isolation by the sea. The most famous of these is surely Mont St Michel in Normandy, opposite the coastal town of Avranches. No traces survive, however, of the earliest monastic cells that once clung to the top of this enormous rock, rising 240 feet above the sea, for in 966 Duke Richard-Sans-Peur handed it over to the Benedictines, and more formal monastic life, based upon the Rule and under centralized discipline took over. The abbey church, the work of Abbot Hildebest, was built on to the living rock itself, instead of excavating the top of the mount to form a platform. The work was begun in 1024 and finished in 1084. The apex of the rock now lies immediately beneath the intersection of the nave and transept. Huge infills of masonry supported the building from the sides, to prevent slippage down the face of the rock; but with the addition of more structures the weight became progressively too great to bear and one of the towers fell in 1300. In 1618 the outer walls began to slide away, and in 1776 the whole façade and seven bays of the nave had to be demolished. Nevertheless, the remaining portion of the original

'This monastery consisted of a high stone wall, surrounding a square enclosure of about an acre in extent. A large square tower commanded the narrow entrance, which was closed by a low and narrow iron door. Within there was a good-sized church in tolerable preservation, standing nearly in the centre of the enclosure.' – Robert Curzon at Wâdi el Natrûn in 1833. He would still have recognized it today.

The buildings on Mont St Michel grew throughout the Middle Ages. The church was rebuilt in the twelfth century and most of the nave survives. In the mid-fifteenth century a new choir was built in the Gothic style with light flooding through the glazed clerestory and triforium.

eleventh-century church is still impressive, and not just because of its dramatic site, for it retains its original and rare wooden roof. The first choir has also collapsed through insufficient support, and the present one, in late fifteenth-century Gothic, contrasts, many think pleasingly, with the Romanesque of the truncated nave. Mont St Michel became one of the most celebrated pilgrimage centres of northern Europe, and there are surviving architectural traces of each successive phase of its history.

This richness of building was completely absent from another site which was, in origin, very similar. Skellig Michael (Sceilg Mhichil), is also a conical rock rising out of the sea – off the coast of Kerry in south-west Ireland. It, too, is named in honour of the archangel. St Finan has traditionally been credited with making the first settlement of monks on the rock, seeking isolation and harshness from the distractions of the world. If there was also a secondary intention of achieving a measure of security the monks' expectations were not fulfilled: the rock was successfully stormed by the Vikings in the ninth century. It evidently survived the sacking, however, though it passed out of use some time in the eleventh century – or, at least, to be more accurate, it is not heard of again after that time and so it may be presumed that the monastery was abandoned around the time that Celtic monasticism in general was being assimilated into the general Latin pattern of the West. Its inaccessible site has made it the most perfectly preserved of early Irish monastic settlements. The monks had banked up such earth and gravel as they could find within small enclosing walls near the top of the rock, 600 feet above the sea, and there they had built six dry-stone cells (clochan), with inclining corbelled roofs, two small oratories, and a later church known as St Michael's. A further small enclosure may have been the cemetery. Nearby, and slightly lower down, are enclosed ledges forming small artificial terraces for growing vegetables. It was doubtless from settlements like this, and the numerous comparable houses throughout Ireland, that the first monks came who occupied the rock at Mont St Michel in Normandy, as part of the great seventh-century expansion of Celtic monasticism.

Not only isolation, and a measure of protection, but also a sense of awe and mystery must have dictated the location of some of the early monastic clusters. As the mists descend upon the curious fingers of rock which surround the great Catalonian monastery of Montserrat, not far from Barcelona, it is still possible to appreciate something of the unearthly quality of the place, which the founders took for holiness. The limestone bluffs have been carved by the winds of countless centuries into weird shapes, and the light catches them oddly to heighten the atmosphere of strange grandeur. There is a local legend that a Roman temple of Venus built up here was destroyed by the miraculous intervention of St Michael. The first hermits, at any rate, were living among the rocks by the eighth century, and seem to have managed to hold out here during the Moorish occupation. At the end of the ninth century, after the expulsion of the Moors from this part of Spain, four small monastic houses were in existence, and one of those, dedicated to the Virgin, later grew into the present famous monastery.

In the eleventh and twelfth centuries Montserrat became a pilgrimage centre for the cult of the Black Virgin, whose image is to this day the central feature of the more modern basilica. It is the work of some long-forgotten Romanesque wood-carver, but the effect of his skill and faith has been universal; wherever the Spanish extended Catholic Christianity, churches and images of Our Lady of Montserrat are to be found. Parts of the first Romanesque chapel also survive, but most of the monastic buildings here date from the sixteenth century, including the existing main church. There was, however, very extensive and

Eastern monasticism, with its communities of monks each living in separate cells or stone huts, was adopted in Early Christian Ireland. On a rocky island, Skellig Michael, off the coast of Kerry, are the remains of beehive cells, terracing, two rectangular oratories and several gravestones. The site was occupied from the ninth to the twelfth century. The smaller island is Little Skellig.

The monastery of St Varlaam in the Meteora, as it was in the nineteenth century. Founded in 1517, its church still contains Byzantine frescos and a notable sixteenth-century iconostasis.

severe damage to the fabric during the French occupation in the Napoleonic period, and most of the visible reconstruction of the monastery was undertaken in the nineteenth century. The monastery has been under the Benedictine Rule since the eleventh century, but thirteen hermitages also existed among the high rocks of the mountain until the Napoleonic era, and the deserted remains of these may still be visited.

One, that of St Onofrius, perched on a rock, recalls another early monastic group which owed its special characteristics to Baroque geological formations. The Orthodox monasteries of the Meteora, in a remote segment of the Thessalian plain near the deep canyon of the Pindus in Greece, occupy the summits of tall rock outcrops so steep that the monks used to lower ropes to haul visitors to their sacred platforms in the sky. The landscape here is extremely dramatic, but the choice of site by the first hermits was not due to any sense of the inherent beauty of the place, but the need for security. The ancients had no love of natural scenery and this area of the plain was shunned for centuries. The hermits chose it as a refuge from the increasing violence which was visited upon the fringes of the Byzantine Empire. In the fourteenth century came the first formal settlement in the convent of Panaghia Doupani: originally simply a series of eyries and caves at the top of a rock pinnacle where the hermits lived and prayed and periodically climbed down to the plain beneath in order to join in communal worship. Some, like the later Parsees of Bombay, left explicit instructions that their poor mortal remains, on death, should be exposed on the rocks in order to be consumed by birds of prey.

There were eventually twenty-four proper monastic houses, each one set upon a separate needle of rock, though only four remain inhabited. First in importance is the Great Meteoron, founded by a monk from Mount Athos some time before 1372 and dedicated to the Transfiguration. The convent of St Varlaam, founded in 1517, used to maintain the Athos tradition of forbidding access to the rock by any woman. The monastery of Ayia Triada (Agia Trias), the Holy Trinity, sits on a rock which is said to move further away from the contiguous hillside in earthquakes. The churches of the monasteries are filled with primitive frescos showing the mortifications of the ascetic life and the glories of the divine presence. The Meteora was a last outpost of Byzantine art, a preservation of Greek culture through successive Ottoman occupations of the plains below. The buildings, with churches and wooden galleries along the skyline, seem almost unearthly in their extraordinary suspension, yet very material with their crude styles and poor condition. Decline set in during the seventeenth century and continued until very recent times. The monasteries have been saved by tourism.

The same cannot be said of Mount Athos itself, the great centre of Orthodox spirituality, where the slow decline of recent decades has been reversed, not by visitors (who are restricted, to preserve the sanctity of the life of the monasteries), but by a renewal of Orthodox monasticism itself. An increasing number of younger monks are now arriving to supplement the older men, who were mostly rural in origin and not markedly informed with modern learning. The newer recruits are from urban areas; many are university graduates and professional men, attracted to the spiritual life and finding at Athos, as centuries of their predecessors have done, some intimation of the serenity and order in the religious explanation of the world. The whole peninsula itself preserves something of the past. The isolation of the place, the primitive methods of tillage used for so many centuries by the monks, and the determination to keep the holy mountain as a religious reserve, have made it a unique surviving remnant of

Europe as it probably was a couple of thousand years ago. Extending down between the Singitic Gulf and the Aegean, Athos rises at its southernmost extremity to a huge cone: the Holy Mountain itself, its exposed higher region faintly glistening with the whiteness of its marble. The Virgin is believed to have landed here, in the Bay of Iveron, when her ship was blown off course on a visit to St Lazarus in Cyprus – so beautifully interlocking are the rustic legends of the earlier centuries of Greek Christianity.

When the Islamic Arabs overran the ancient centres of Christianity, monks fleeing to the West found in this distant and lush stretch of land a measure of welcome security. In the eighth century holy men sought refuge from the Iconoclastic controversy here, and Athos has ever since been a centre for the veneration and production of icons. Many of the icons still treasured in the monasteries of Mount Athos were believed to have been thrown into the sea at Constantinople and to have floated here with unseen and miraculous guidance. The first of the solitaries of whom there is record was Peter the Anchorite, in the ninth century, who lived in a cave for half a century. By 872, the year in which the Emperor Basil I granted a charter of protection to the monks, there must have been quite a number of them, and already the evolution from the solitary hermit life to coenobitic monasticism was occurring. The clusters of monastic houses attracted pilgrims, too, so that in 1046 a chrysobull of Constantine IX formally recognized the special and holy status of the peninsula. It was, thereafter, an

The Great Lavra is the largest and best preserved of the monasteries of Mount Athos. Its church, the katholikon (above), goes back to the eleventh century. The whole precinct is surrounded by a wall like a fortified village. It is entered through a long vaulted passage protected by several iron gates.

independent religious state, a kind of sanctified republic, and even the Patriarch of Constantinople has a jurisdiction limited to the spiritualities of the monks and not over their monasteries.

The first hermits had settled at the landward end of the peninsula, where the soil is richer and flatter. But the accessibility of the place attracted Saracen raiders and sea-pirates, and so a retreat was made down the length of the peninsula towards the barren rocky heights in the south. There, on the slopes of the Holy Mountain itself, the first lavras were built, and here, also, coenobitic monasticism began, at the Great Lavra, Vatopedi, and Iveron. Expansion was rapid. By the eleventh century there were 180 monasteries, most, presumably, extremely small. In the next century monks began to arrive from non-Greek lands, called by the sanctity of Athos: the presence of these Georgians, Slavs, Serbs and Russians has ever since made the place the centre of Orthodox spirituality, a training ground for great Christian teachers and administrators, the exemplar of holy living. The austere determination of the monks to preserve a pure form of Orthodoxy was tested after the Fourth Crusade when the Franks, in occupying the peninsula for some sixty years from 1204, attempted to convert the houses to Latin Christianity. They did not succeed, and a crop of martyrs testified to the Greeks' religious tenacity.

With the rule of the Ottoman Turks after the fall of Constantinople in 1453, however, the conditions were less testing, and the monks managed to achieve tolerably good relations with the Sultans – Murat II recognized the right of the monks to the monasteries and guaranteed their possession. Heavy taxation, not persecution, was the problem, and this resulted in some of the monks reverting to idiorrhythmic patterns of monasticism. Houses were occasionally abandoned altogether; in some cases the monks developed *sketae*, small dependencies of the main monasteries, as a means of reducing costs. Yet the Turkish period, despite a decline in the overall numbers of monks, saw an important elevation of their utility to Greek religious life in general. For, in the seventeenth and eighteenth centuries, Athos became an intellectual centre, virtually the only place in the Greek world where Christian education could flourish. Bishops and ecclesiastical administrators, teachers and monks, were furnished by Athos to the Orthodox world in general. So important became the association between Greek culture and Orthodox spirituality at this time that it left an enduring imprint on modern Greek concepts of nationality. Many monks left the Holy Mountain in 1821 to take part in the War of Independence against the Ottoman Empire.

Much of the building on the sacred peninsula is fairly recent, undertaken in the last three or four centuries. But some of the earlier church structures survive, and they give a very clear impression of what Byzantine churches were like in their most developed form. The Great Lavra was the first of the monastic foundations, built directly under Mount Athos itself at the end of the peninsula, and dedicated to the founder, St Athanasios the Athorite. That was in 963, and the founder himself built the katholikon. It was extensively reconstructed in the fifteenth and sixteenth centuries, but retained the style and structural form of the first building. This shows the usual large, wide, central dome over a Greek cross, with narthex and exonarthex. It became the model for most other churches in Mount Athos, and, like them, is surrounded by monastic buildings and chapels, mostly of much later date, and protective walls, which give the monastery the appearance of a small fortified town. The frescos in the katholikon of the Great Lavra were painted in 1535 by the Cretan master Theophanes.

The monastery of Vatopedi, on a small inlet on the north-east side of the peninsula, is of uncertain origin. Tradition claims Emperor Theodosius I as its

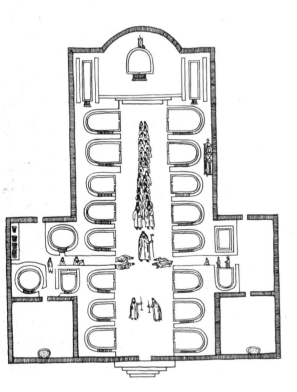

The refectory of the Great Lavra: an old plan showing the seating arrangements, which have not changed up to today (compare Vatopedi, opposite).

founder. This would make it a fourth-century establishment, but its origin may perhaps more accurately be located in the later decades of the tenth century. The name is no real clue: it suggests the bramble bushes which grow abundantly in this part of the peninsula. The monastery is dedicated to the Virgin, and so, therefore, is its katholikon, built in the tenth century. It is in the conventional Byzantine style, with an exonarthex and bell-tower as later additions of the fifteenth century. The interior frescos, painted early in the fourteenth century, were rather too enthusiastically restored on two occasions, in the eighteenth and nineteenth centuries, and so the vigorous Macedonian characteristics of the original work

The refectory of Vatopedi is one of the most atmospheric rooms in Athos. In the foreground are the monks' benches and tables. The frescos at the end are: top left, the three angels entertained by Abraham and Sarah (in Orthodox iconography an image of the Trinity), and on the right the Last Supper; below, at the sides, the Annunciation; in the apse, saints of the Eastern Church.

are patchily overlaid. Some of the mosaics, however, are the only early Byzantine examples left on Mount Athos, and there is a particularly fine representation of the Annunciation above the eastern columns of the nave.

There were once 40,000 monks on the peninsula; today there are a little over 1,000, though the numbers are rising. The majority are now Greeks, and have been since the Russian Revolution of 1917 and the advent of socialism to the Eastern European countries after 1945 cut off, as the Islamic and Ottoman Empires had once done, sections of Orthodoxy from the Greek world. In this, too, though, there are recent changes, as monks from Western Europe and North America have begun to find at Athos something of the spiritual splendour which seems exuded by every stone of the place. Women are still excluded, as required by pious tradition and by the order of Athanasios, founder of the Great Lavra.

The peninsula today presents a picture, not of decline – despite the large empty buildings and the deserted fields – but of gradual recovery, and renewed international interest in its ancient spirituality has given new vitality to Athos. The atmosphere of the past survives everywhere, however. The old Julian calendar is still kept, and so is Byzantine time (in which the hours are determined by sunset). Many of the monasteries have fortified appearances, the cells and churches and other conventual buildings retained within walls and towers. The enclosures are ancient, but the buildings within are often fairly modern, dating from the eighteenth and nineteenth centuries: a result of the many fires, caused by the large number of candles in daily use, which destroyed the earlier structures. Twenty of the monasteries are still inhabited, and the peninsula has been divided into twenty districts, giving each a territorial exclusivity. Thirteen of the houses are coenobitic, and seven idiorrhythmic; in addition are twelve *sketae* and some remaining hermits' cells in the southern extremity of the cape. In style the churches of Mount Athos show no variations on the general Byzantine type and its developments. Russian and Serbian monks have left traces of their presence in the decorative and architectural effects of the monasteries in which they have been numerous. The most dramatic buildings, which recall the styles of the Meteora, are found on the western cliffs. The monastery of Dionysiou is perched on an outcrop of rock 260 feet above the sea. It was founded in the fourteenth century by St Dionysios of Korseos with help from Alexios III Comnenos, Emperor of Trebizond. The present buildings are those put up after a great fire in 1535, and the tiers of balconies outside the cells of the monks, for all their quaint appearance, were only built in the eighteenth century. Their construction and purpose was very like the balconied rustic houses of contemporaneous Greece.

The same feature can also be seen at the monastery of Simonopetra, further up the coast. This, too, is a fourteenth-century foundation – by St Simon of Mount Athos. Tradition insists that he was led to this spot by a mystical light. Another story relates how Simon and his servant were climbing the precipitous rock face to give refreshing drinks to the monks, during the period of construction, and that the servant fell and was rescued by miraculous intervention. The first building work here must have involved great heroism and a collective head for heights. During a fire of 1580 the trapped monks threw themselves over the balconies to terrible deaths on the rocks beneath. It was this fire, in fact, and another in 1626, that destroyed the first buildings. The seven tiers of balconies that may be seen today actually date only from 1891, after yet another fire.

In buildings like this we are clearly a long way from the first hermit life of Athos. Yet remains of some of the first *kellia*, or hermits' dwellings, can still be seen at the southern tip of the cape. Here the sea and the strong currents drench

Within the tenth-century katholikon of the Vatopedi monastery of Mount Athos is a rich profusion of images and works of art. Here an icon of the Virgin stands in front of the mosaic showing the Angel of the Annunciation.

Opposite: Simonopetra clings to a precipitous cliff over 1000 feet high. Like many of the Athos monasteries it has suffered disastrous fires, and was reconstructed after 1891.

At Tintagel, in Cornwall, are sparse vestiges of cells built by Irish monks in the early centuries of Christianity in Britain. Irish monasteries consisted of primitive stone huts built round a small oratory – the farthest possible remove from the great basilicas being erected in Italy and the East.

the rock face for many parts of the year, and serenity does not seem so obviously attainable where nature is powerful and violent. Excommunicated monks also lived in caves here, their bodies, on death, it is said – in a local reversal of what is usually taken as an indication of sanctity – remaining undecomposed as an additional punishment of their unworthiness. Many early hermits had lived in tombs in Egypt; hence the association of the site. The *kellia* were joined to one another by ropes and pulleys, enabling periodic communication, of a sort, on the cliffs. As at Skellig Michael in Ireland, narrow shelves retain enough soil for terraced cultivation: just enough for the survival of each solitary. Today there are tracks etched into the rock face, allowing less hazardous movement among the settlements, for towards the west of the tip of the cape there are still inhabited *kellia*. The peninsula thus retains evidence of all stages of its development, from these barren dwellings to the splendid churches of the major monastic houses. Mount Athos is a whole religious world in itself.

The same combination of coenobitic and idiorrhythmic monasticism existing within a single expression of Christianity was to be found in a country whose early church was virtually entirely monastic. Celtic monasticism in Ireland was important not only because of its great missionary influence in Europe, and because of its intellectual and cultural vitality, but because it offered in itself a unique development of church styles. Society was Christianized in Ireland sometime in the first half of the fifth century; by the sixth century Irish Christianity was expansive and already richly endowed with learning. Ireland itself, and the coasts of Scotland, Wales, Cornwall, and Brittany, formed a single religious unit, and Celtic monks were founding houses in the heartlands of Europe too – at St Gall in Switzerland, for example, and at Bobbio in Italy, Luxueil in France, and Würzburg in Germany. Wherever they went, the Irish built small oratories and cells, whose successors, constructed in stone and often with Romanesque additions, in many places still exist. St Guirec sailed to the Breton coast in the sixth century, and on the beach at Ploumanac'h, where he landed and built his oratory, there is still the ruin of a small church, containing a shrine with a statue of the saint.

Cornwall was even more accessible from Ireland. Visitors to the romantic ruins of the twelfth-century castle at Tintagel, on a dramatic headland of the north coast, are often unaware that before the castle was built this remote spot was inhabited by a colony of Irish monks. Their small cells and an oratory were found during the excavations of 1933–36. These seem to date from the fifth to the ninth centuries, and it is clear that the monastery had been abandoned sometime before the headland was fortified. St Piran's Church, near Perranporth, further along the coast, shows what a Celtic monastic building looked like. The saint himself is said to have floated over from Ireland on a millstone; the early lives of the Celtic holy men are filled with such folk miracles. In all probability, St Piran had brought an altar-stone with him, and pious memories have enlarged upon its miraculous capacities. He arrived, at any rate, sometime very early in the sixth century and built a church where he landed. It is possible that the remains of the church which still exist are actually those of St Piran's first structure, but even if not, they are still of very early date, perhaps no later than the seventh century.

After a few centuries the church was buried by drifting sands, and worship was transferred to a new building, to the east. What was doubtless a disaster to the good Christians of Cornwall, however, is a blessing to us: the ruins of St Piran's little oratory were preserved by the sand and when it was removed, in the nineteenth century, the church and the shrine which contained the saint's remains came to light. It is a small, rectangular building, 30 foot long, with only one narrow window, and, originally, a pitched roof. The stonework is crude, and there is no ornament. Services must have been held by the light of tapers, but the darkness within was surely worth the protection from the winds of this desolate spot. Such churches existed all over Ireland in the early centuries of Christianity, and, as in Ireland also, at St Piran's the faithful buried their dead as near as possible to the sanctifying remains of the founder. The oratory was surrounded by hundreds of burials, many of which were discovered in the first excavations of 1835. St Piran died in 530, and was later venerated as the patron of the tin miners of Cornwall.

Another of these early heroes of the Irish diaspora was St Petroc. He was said to have been born in Wales and educated at one of the great monastic schools in Ireland. He arrived in Cornwall, seeking the solitary life, in 518, and settled at Padstow. Of his cell and oratory there is now no trace, and the existing church of St Petroc is of thirteenth-century origin, though it was greatly reconstructed in the fifteenth. Above the chancel piscina, however, there is an early stone-carved effigy of the saint. It was from this church that for centuries pilgrims, having landed from the southern Irish ports, crossed the Cornish peninsula to re-embark for Rome, so avoiding the perilous sea journey round the tip of Land's End.

At the other extremity of Britain the early Irish monks also left evidence of their labours. Ireland and the western seaboard of Scotland, in fact, were scarcely distinct areas – they formed a single cultural and religious territory – and the material relics of the monks show no features which are peculiarly Scottish. At Iona, the best-known monastic site in Scotland, the early Celtic monastery has left a few traces, though these are much overlaid by subsequent religious occupation. St Columba arrived here from Ireland in 563; from his monastery others were founded throughout southern Scotland and northern England. The first Viking raids upon the island were in 803, and the early buildings doubtless suffered in this period; though their disappearance is mainly due to the transfer of the monastery to the Benedictines, around 1200, and its reconstruction on the general plan of Western monasticism. Iona, therefore, paralleled the demise of the old Celtic monastic uses that occurred in Ireland itself. Late in the ninth century the main body of monks evacuated the island, because of the Viking danger, taking the remains of St Columba with them, and settled at Kells in Ireland.

It is difficult to determine in what sense the site was occupied between then and the Benedictine foundation. A small group of monks may have remained behind, rather like the custodians who volunteered to protect the holy places of Jerusalem after the fall of the Latin Kingdom. It was in this period, between 800 and the closing decades of the twelfth century, that Iona became the burial place of the kings of Scotland; a processional way, the 'Street of the Dead', was built from the landing-place up to the monastery. The small church at the burial ground itself provides a link to the earliest monastic life here. Known as St Oran's Chapel, it is a small rectangular stone building of the ninth or tenth centuries, perhaps on the site of an earlier oratory: St Oran was one of Columba's first monks, who came over with him from Ireland, and the association of his name with this later chapel, and with the burial ground itself ('Relig Oran'), can hardly be without some significance. The Romanesque door of the church, later in date than the main structure, was made in the second half of the twelfth century.

Iona is one of the sacred places of Christianity in Britain, since it was here that St Columba landed from Ireland in 563, bringing the new faith with him. His monastery lasted until the Viking raids of the ninth century; it was subsequently refounded as a Benedictine house. The present church is basically early sixteenth century, though most of the conventual buildings belong to the twentieth.

From St Columba's first monastery there remains, on Tor Abb, a cell – a circular, walled bed cut into the rock – the foundations and post-holes of some wooden huts, discovered by excavation of the site, and the remains of a large enclosing wall, very much like the walls of the Celtic monasteries in Ireland. At Iona, unlike most Irish monasteries, however, the enclosure is roughly square-shaped, with one side open to the sea, as if the model was that of an Iron Age 'promontory fort', rather than the rath or cashel origin – a circular bank of earth and stone containing dwellings – of most Irish monastic settlements.

Further north still, in the Orkney Islands, stands another good example of an early Celtic church. St Magnus Church, on the small island of Egilsay, is built of mortared stone, and has remained, apart from its roof, structurally intact. The building is in the usual rectangular form, a large version of its type, and with a round tower attached to the west end. This is one of the few towers like this in Scotland, though they are common in Ireland, where, however, they were usually free standing. The roof is thought to have been of stone slabs; the windows are characteristically small, and there are two doors. The church probably dates from the twelfth century, and was perhaps built on the site of an earlier oratory. But of that, and the Celtic monastic life which its style indicates, there is now no surviving trace.

What, then, of the original Irish Church to whose religious vitality these scattered remains bear witness, whose expansion was so impressive for centuries? The first Christians in Ireland lived in the south of the country, but the first of whom there is any clear evidence were followers of St Patrick in the middle years of the fifth century. Patrick was a Roman Britain who was captured as a boy during a raid, and became a slave in County Antrim. After escaping from Ireland he was trained for the priesthood, perhaps in Gaul, and then experienced a call to return to the land of his captivity as a missionary. By the time he arrived he had been made a bishop, and the Church he founded was Episcopal. But it was not quite Episcopal in the usual sense. There had been no Roman occupation of Ireland, and there were, as a consequence, no Roman (or other) cities around which a regular network of Episcopal sees could be established. Ireland was governed from the raths and cashels which were the seats of the hundreds of petty kings. In many places raths were handed over by converted chiefs to become the centre of local churches, but where this happened the chief himself moved out, and so the blend of civil and ecclesiastical administration, which occurred in the Roman Empire and in Byzantium, did not take place in Ireland. There, the religious centres were rural raths, and there must have been a very large number of them by the end of the Patrician mission.

From almost the beginning, these raths organized themselves on monastic lines, as the local followers of St Patrick attached themselves to particular holy men. Monasticism was particularly suited to Celtic society, with its rules of overlordship and its respect for kindred. Boys who had previously entered the learned class of Celtic society by going to centres where traditional knowledge was passed on now resorted, instead, to the great schools set up in the monasteries. By the end of the sixth century the process was more or less complete: the Irish Church which emerged being run by local bishops who were also the heads of monastic communities. The process was not universal, and in some places a non-monastic clergy seems to have continued, but of their purpose and numbers there is no real clue. During the sixth century the first patrician houses were succeeded by groups of larger foundations inspired by bishops of administrative genius. Thus Darrow and Derry were established by St Colum-cille; Bangor by St Colman; Clonmacnoise by St Ciaran; Clonfert by St Brendan;

The twelfth-century Doorty Cross at Kilfenora, County Clare, bears figures of three bishops. The different types of crosier are of interest. The large figure has a continental one; the other two have Tau and Irish types.

Kells, County Meath, Ireland, was a typical Celtic monastery with beehive cells, an oratory and a round tower. The early ninth-century oratory, now known as St Columcille's House, is a square stone building with a steep roof. It was originally entered by a door six or seven feet above the ground.

and Clonard – which together with Lismore was the greatest of the educational centres – by St Finnian. These larger houses had numerous smaller churches attached, and were grouped together into *paruchia* or *familia*. They were united, that is to say, by common adhesion to the founding tradition of a particular holy man. Derry, Durrow, and Iona, for example, were part of a group inspired by the ideals of St Columcille. There is a good stone-carved representation of one of these bishop-abbots of the early Irish Church in the little cathedral at Kilfenora in County Clare. It is late – twelfth century – but wholly Celtic in style.

The monasteries began to receive wealth and to acquire influence, as gifts of land came to them, and by the seventh and eighth centuries, the great age of expansion, there were also signs of worldliness. This prompted an ascetic revival at the end of the eighth century, and a new wave of hermits betook themselves to isolated places, and new foundations were made. At the same time the Viking raids plundered the wealth of the older houses and doubtless, also, helped some in their return to Christian simplicity of living. The annals list over 900 sackings of churches and monasteries, but it has to be noted that the Vikings were sometimes not the exclusive perpetrators of outrage: native Irish lords enlisted their help to settle old scores. Often the monasteries were obliged to make treaties of protection with local chiefs, and this had a progressively secularizing effect, and, together with the gradual recession of the ascetic revival, led to a long decline of the monastic ideals within the Church generally.

The Church still had some vitality, however, and when the Vikings settled and were converted, it was the old Celtic form of Christianity which they adopted in very many cases. In some other cases they began to look to the Latin patterns of Episcopal government in Britain and Gaul, and this, together with the reform movement led by St Malachy (a friend of St Bernard of Clairvaux, who died in 1148) precipitated the final reformation of the Irish Church – one which destroyed its Celtic monastic bases and arranged it, instead, in regular dioceses like the Church of the West in general. That occurred at the Synod of Cashel in 1110. With the arrival, in the twelfth century, of the European monastic orders, the Cistercians, the Augustinians, the Benedictines, and the Cluniac monks, the ancient monasticism of the converted raths was abandoned altogether.

There is no way of knowing if the liturgical practices of the Celtic Church in the early centuries were peculiar to Ireland – probably not. The Christianity of St Patrick was orthodox in everything except its ecclesiastical administrative system, and some controversial matters like the practice of the tonsure for the regular clergy. The first churches, and the monasteries in which they were built, did not express any liturgical or theological ideas but were rude huts within earthen compounds: they were not even copied from the pagan structures around, for they were actually those very structures, simply turned to religious use. The conversion of Ireland was carried out without bloodshed and in a single generation; the continuity of use and of culture is very striking. The earliest wooden churches have passed away, their sites occupied by the small, rectangular stone buildings that succeeded them. These first churches were described in later writings, and their simplicity is evident. Within the circular enclosing walls of the rath the cells and oratories of the monks were put up next to the founding oratory of the first holy men.

The Viking raids stimulated the conversion to stone structures, and the first essays in stone construction, like the Saxon churches of England, retained something of the formalized design of the wooden buildings they replaced. In stony districts, as in the remote western seaboard of Ireland, construction in dry-stone, with inclining corbelled roofs, both for oratories and for little round monastic cells, was usual. The Gallarus Oratory at Kilmalkeader in County Kerry is a perfectly preserved, boat-shaped example. It is windowless and narrow, with a single small doorway. Such buildings are not easy to date precisely, for their methods of construction and style were retained in the remoter areas for centuries after changes had occurred elsewhere. The Gallarus Oratory was probably built in the eighth or ninth century. A similar structure can be seen at Carrownaff, near Moville in County Donegal. In most of the monastic centres throughout Ireland, where the first churches had been of wood, their stone replacements were plain, single-chamber churches, whose roofless ruins, often set in what are now rural churchyards, are a common feature of the Irish countryside. Some have later Romanesque additions: doorways, niches, windows, with ornamental rounded arches. The great Columban monastery of Kells, in County Meath, is a good example. The early Celtic monastery here was turned into an Augustinian house in the twelfth century, and most of the surviving buildings belong to that refoundation. The building known as 'St Columcille's House', however, is a splendidly preserved oratory, perhaps of the ninth century, with mortared stone walls and high-pitched roof. It, too, is without windows.

The best impression of an early monastic cashel can be gained by visiting the remote Ilauntannig Island, in County Kerry. Cashels were simply raths built in rocky areas, where trees and earth were scarce. Ilauntannig has cashel walls of limestone which are 18 feet thick, and within the enclosure are the remains of an oratory and three clochan of dry-stone construction, three graves and a cross. The site is not quite complete, and the present appearance, of a headland or promontory fort, is deceptive: the cashel was originally circular, but coastal erosion has swept a part of the containing wall away. When members of the Royal Society of Antiquaries visited the site in 1897, the remains of a second small oratory were in existence. They have since fallen over the cliff. Stone construction also led to the famous Irish round towers. These belfries and watch-towers began to be built during the Viking raids, and most date from the tenth century. They are found only at monastic sites, and eighty survive, though some only as circular stumps amidst the grisly rubble of rural graveyards.

The Gallarus Oratory, County Kerry, is another well-preserved monastic church, of a type that has been likened to an upturned boat. This shape presumably derives from the dry-stone methods of construction, and may also be seen in the navetas of the island of Minorca in the Mediterranean.

On Ilauntannig Island, County Kerry, the monastic enclosure survives, though perilously close to the cliff edge, with originally two oratories, three beehive cells and several burials.

The great age of Irish monasticism would have little to show today were it not for two things: the illuminated manuscripts and the great stone crosses. Both reveal a degree of artistic sophistication that is hard to imagine in the setting of the crude stone buildings that we have just seen.

Above: the Temptation of Christ, from the Book of Kells, perhaps the greatest of the Irish illuminated books, made in the early ninth century. Christ is shown on the pinnacle of the Temple, the black figure of the devil is to the right. The crowds of tiny people to the left and at the bottom seem to be an allusion to the events following the Temptation, when Christ preached at Nazareth and Capernaum. Left: the Cross of Muirdach at Monasterboice. The panel at the top shows the meeting of St Paul and St Anthony; in the centre is Christ in Judgment with St Michael weighing souls underneath; then the Adoration of the Magi; and three Old Testament scenes not conclusively identified. Opposite: Glendalough, another early monastic site with a church known as St Kevin's Kitchen incorporating a round tower. The picturesque gravestones are all relatively recent.

The raths, or farmsteads, which local chiefs handed over to the monks at the time of the conversion of Ireland had walls of earth which were never intended to be defensive. They were to keep out cattle, and perhaps, also, to secure some measure of privacy. They were sometimes an indication of status: a more substantial local king in his *tuath* would have a rath constructed with more than one concentric circular bank. Double earthworks were quite common, and triple banks and ditches showed real status. The monks who succeeded to these more elaborate structures retained them, and with the symbols of status must have themselves achieved greater prestige and influence. But whether the raths of the monastic church were single- or multi-vallate, the internal arrangement was always the same. A series of subdividing internal walls marked out the living quarter, where the monks built their huts of wood and clay (later replaced by simple stone structures), and the sanctuary itself, with the main church and the cemetery.

As the communities developed and enlarged, additional huts were put up, both inside and outside the enclosing walls, for the scribes, metal-craftsmen, and clients of the monastery who came to live within its sanctifying protection. As the population grew, so one or two more little oratories were built to accommodate the additional worshippers. Later writings describe these expansions as sometimes running to thousands of people, and the resulting monastic 'cities' as great centres of economic as well as religious and scholarly activity. In a country which had not before had towns, the Celtic monks provided the first experience of a kind of urban living.

It was for long imagined that the accounts of the size of some of the monasteries amounted to little more than pious exaggeration, but modern techniques of aerial photography, which are able to show surviving traces of early occupation of a site in terms of crop-marks, soil stains, and unevenness of elevation invisible from the ground, can now substantiate the claims. St Finnian's great house at Clonard, County Meath, for example, was described in the annals as having a population of three thousand. Aerial photography of the site has indeed shown indications of huts or cells and other buildings over an enormous area, certainly enough to give substance to the early estimates. Aerial photography has also revealed that many isolated country churches in Ireland are actually situated within the characteristic circular enclosures that indicate an early Celtic monastery.

At Kiltiernan the monastic site is best seen from the air; it is one of a large cluster of similar monastic establishments in southern Galway. Nothing is known of the founder of this place, but as there was no later building here, in the Middle Ages, and no subsequent use as a churchyard, the site has remained undisturbed. In the centre of the circular enclosure lies a single-chamber stone church ruin, of the eighth or ninth century, and around it the monastery is divided by internal walls into fifteen or so segments. There are also the foundations of three cells and half a dozen fragments of other buildings. Excavations in 1950 uncovered a monastic cemetery in the central church area, and a few pieces of slag showed that there was once an iron works maintained by the monks; but no other finds were made which might help to date the site. Across Ireland, however, there are hundreds of comparable monastic remains – another testimony to the expansive nature of the Celtic Church.

The scholarship and artistic achievements of the Irish monasteries were also set upon a generous scale, but early remains at the major sites are scant, since the very success of the houses led to much subsequent rebuilding, and the first monastic buildings have long since been buried or their materials reused. The

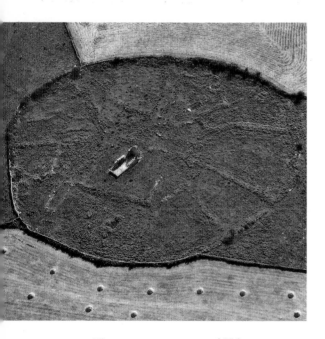

The monastic precinct of Kiltiernan, County Galway, is a stone-walled enclosure with a church in the middle. It was divided into segments by smaller walls.

splendours of the late La Tène decorative styles – best known in the Book of Kells – may still be seen in the memorials and crosses at some of the great monastic houses. At Clonmacnoise in County Offaly, an important monastic school founded by St Ciaran in 544, are five hundred gravestones, ranging from the eighth to the twelfth century. At Monasterboice, in County Louth, founded by St Buithe (who died in 521), are some splendid early figured crosses, whose decoration, of scriptural scenes, declares the spirit of Irish monastic piety in a manner which transcends the division of centuries. The crosses are topped with stone-carved representations of high-gabled single-chamber churches, showing in decorated stone what may still be seen intact at Kells.

Such a church may also be seen at one of the most famous of all the Celtic monasteries: the oratory of St Kevin at Glendalough in County Wicklow. Known popularly as 'St Kevin's Kitchen', presumably because the attached round-tower belfry (rather like the one at Egilsay in Orkney) may look to the rustic eye like a great chimney, this church, dating from the eighth or ninth century, is vaulted and corbelled in mortared stone. The walls slope slightly inwards, and within the steep roof there was once a small chamber, supported on a wooden floor – perhaps the dwelling of the monk who served the church. There were three small windows, one of them in the upper chamber, but their size is such that they can only have been intended for ventilation since the light they afford is minimal. St Kevin was born in 498, and was educated by Petroc, before that saint retired to Padstow. Desiring the life of solitude and prayer, Kevin was said to have been led by an angel into the mountains of Wicklow, and in a deep valley, beside the upper of two lakes, he built a small round stone cell, which still exists – a tribute to Kevin's choice of an extremely inaccessible spot on a stone ledge above the waters. Pilgrims and aspirants to the sanctified life were soon attracted to Glendalough, and Kevin reluctantly consented to the foundation of a monastery lower down the valley. The buildings on this site, including 'St Kevin's Kitchen', form the nucleus of the great monastic 'city'. In fact the expansion must have taken place sometime after Kevin's death, doubtless in the general enlargements of the sixth century. The monastery was plundered and burnt frequently, yet, amazingly, many of the earliest stone buildings survive; and excavations near the first cell of Kevin have even revealed the carbonized traces of the first wooden huts. The simple, rectangular remains of the seventh-century stone church at the site (known as Temple Na Skellig) also survive, and are approached by rough stone steps leading from the lakeside.

It is hard to realize that these simple memorials of Celtic Christianity were built at the same time as the Byzantine splendours in the eastern half of Christendom; that the little monastic cashel at Ilauntannig Island, off the western coast of Ireland, was being constructed at about the same time that Justinian's architects were creating Hagia Sophia in Constantinople. But the spiritual life which emanated from the dark little oratories, set amidst the formidable and dripping landscape of the western seaboard of Europe, had a quite extraordinary vitality; and the smoking tapers which must have lit the interiors of those humble buildings succeeded in lighting a much wider Christian life. The Irish monks spread over Europe, and Celtic Christianity became a major missionary influence, as well as a protector of Christian learning, in the dark years of pagan incursion from the north and from the east.

White Island, in Lough Erne, County Fermanagh, contains a series of early carvings associated with the monastery there. This figure is a bishop carrying a crosier and a bell.

4 The feudal order in stone: Romanesque Christendom

During the confused period known as the 'Dark Ages', the monasteries were virtually the only institutions to preserve literacy, learning and technical and artistic skills. More tightly organized and more expansionist than their contemporaries in the East, Western monasteries provided society with teachers, scholars, administrators and clerks.

They also provided churches. Not until the eleventh century could the secular clergy (the bishops and archbishops) afford to build cathedrals that matched their claims to authority. When they did, they took the great abbeys as their models. Here the style that has come to be known as Romanesque was forged.

These great abbey churches and cathedrals were larger than anything found in the East except for half a dozen imperial foundations. Already by Carolingian times great churches had assumed the form that they were to retain: cruciform in plan, with a three-storey elevation (arcade, gallery, clerestory), massive piers supporting round arches and – if funds allowed – a stone vault, at first groined, later ribbed. Their interiors were far more colourful than they appear now: walls and ceilings were frescoed and the numerous altars adorned with images and rich furnishings. On the great festivals of the Christian year and increasingly, with the growth of the cult of relics, as the settings for pilgrims worshipping at the shrine of saints, they came fully into their own.

As the centuries passed the monasteries too became great and powerful, so that there was a constant tension between organized institutional life and the urge to restore the austere values of St Benedict's Rule. Most of the great monastic movements of the Middle Ages, such as the Cistercian and the Carthusian, were attempts to renounce worldly wealth and return to the simplicity of the early principles. The Franciscan order can be seen as an ultimate expression of this desire, the renunciation of all possessions. Although their ideals were inevitably compromised with time, the early churches of these orders are often severely functional and with a stark beauty of their own.

For captions to colour plates 25–32, see p. 113

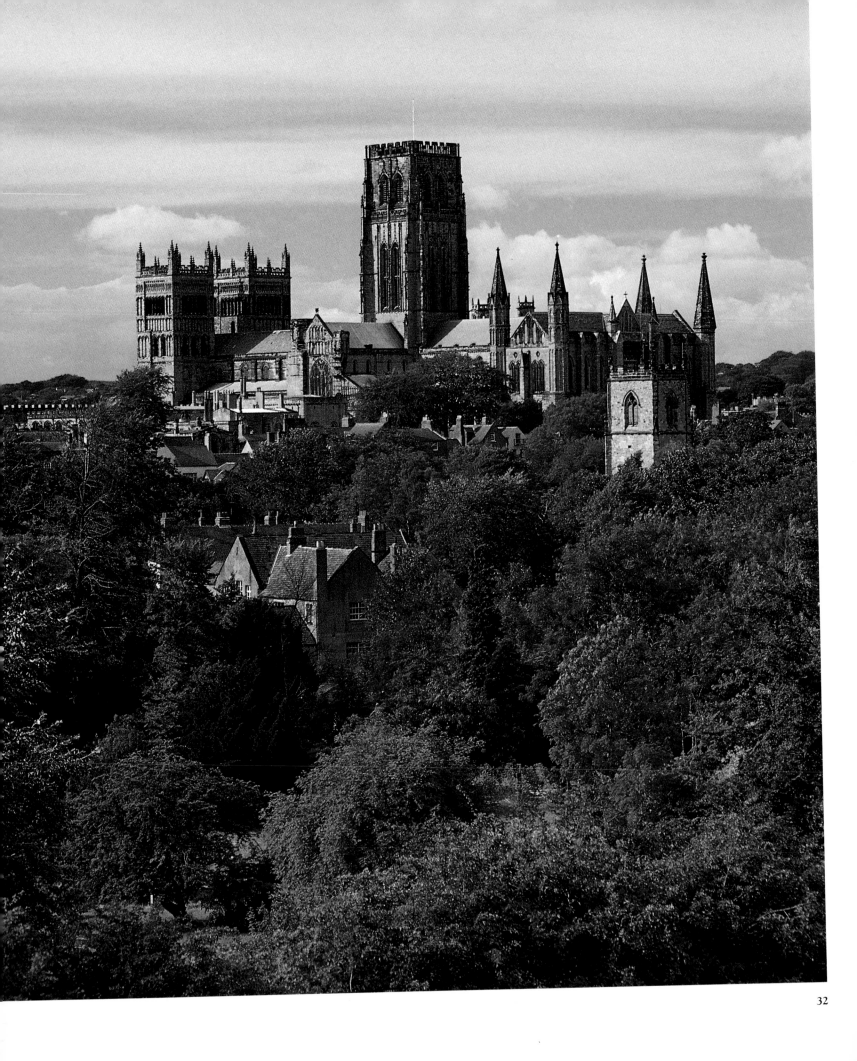

Colour plates 25–32

25 Portal of the abbey church of Vézelay, in Burgundy (1120–32). In the centre of the tympanum the risen Christ sends the Apostles out into the world to preach the Gospel. The crowd of figures on the lintel represent the peoples to whom the Word of God is to be carried; the eight panels beneath the arch show miracles worked by the Apostles in the course of their evangelism. The small circles of the arch itself contain the Labours of the Months and the Signs of the Zodiac. On the trumeau stands John the Baptist. Through the open door we see the Romanesque nave and beyond it the lighter Gothic choir.

26 Charlemagne presents his Palatine Chapel at Aachen to the Virgin and Child. This gold relief was made as part of a shrine in the late twelfth or early thirteenth century, long after the time of Charlemagne, but it shows the building before the later Gothic additions.

27 The throne of Charlemagne in the western gallery of the Palatine Chapel of Aachen. This gallery communicated with the emperor's rooms in the palace. Here Charlemagne took his place facing the high altar, and here, throughout the Middle Ages, the Holy Roman Emperors were enthroned.

28 The image of Ste Foy, kept at Conques, was the object of a popular cult. Pilgrims on the way to the shrine of Santiago de Compostela stopped here to pay their devotion to the little saint. Ste Foy was a girl of twelve who was martyred by the Romans in the fourth century. Her body was brought to Conques in the ninth century and began to work miraculous cures. This crude image is made up of elements from various sources. The head is probably a late Roman parade helmet. For hundreds of years pilgrims added precious gems to it. The triptych on her breast dates from the thirteenth century.

29 The church dedicated to Ste Foy at Conques is one of several great churches built along the pilgrimage routes in the twelfth century. The little town still has something of the atmosphere of the Middle Ages. Here we are looking from the east, with the apse of the choir in the foreground.

30 The Deposition from the Cross, a panel from the early twelfth-century bronze doors of S. Zeno, Verona. During the Dark Ages, the iconography that had served the Early Christians largely disappeared and had to be re-invented. Here Christ is shown as a regal figure even on the Cross, wearing not a crown of thorns but a kingly crown. The pointed caps of the executioners denote Jews. Above the Cross are personifications of the Sun and Moon, and at the sides stand the Virgin and St John. The scene has its own expressive power, though there is as yet no idea of creating a unified space in which the figures can exist.

31 S. Miniato al Monte, just outside Florence, is a well-preserved church in the Tuscan Romanesque style of the eleventh century. Here classical Rome still seems close, especially in the marble columns and the capitals, which are a variant of the Corinthian order. The coloured marble inlay of the walls is characteristic of Italy, as is the raised choir at the east end with, beneath it, steps leading down to a crypt containing the tomb of the saint.

32 Durham Cathedral is one of the supreme monuments of Romanesque architecture. It represents a particularly English institution – a Benedictine abbey that also functions as a cathedral, the bishop being at the same time nominally the abbot. Begun soon after the Norman Conquest and standing fortress-like on a defensive hill-top position, it was technically one of the most advanced buildings in Europe. Its most prominent external features, however, are late medieval additions, the upper stages of the west towers dating from the thirteenth century, the central tower from the fifteenth, and the wide transverse structure at the east end, the Chapel of the Nine Altars, from the thirteenth.

The feudal order in stone

WHILE BYZANTIUM was developing its rich and theologically sophisticated style of Christianity, the West of Europe was transformed by the Germanic and Norse peoples who – after the fall of the Western Empire in 476 – increasingly asserted an independent sovereignty. The new arrivals soon adopted the Christianity of the people among whom they settled in the Romanized provinces of the West, and one of the great expansions of the faith began. It has left few physical traces; their wooden churches have not survived. Building in stone came virtually to an end with the collapse of Roman order, and when it was revived, in the Carolingian churches of the late eighth and ninth centuries, and in the stone Saxon churches, the ruins of the remaining Roman structures were plundered to provide most of the materials. The styles were either crude adaptations of Roman and Byzantine models, or simulations in rubble and stone of the wooden buildings that were being replaced.

Then, in the middle of the eleventh century, a quite distinctive and monumental style began to be adopted in the West – and in Germany and France in particular – later known as the 'Romanesque' because scholars came to imagine that the authors of the new style were seeking a revival of the building techniques of the Roman Empire. The new style lasted for 200 years. Many of the structures put up in these centuries continued to be of wood (some massive fortresses, almost alone, forming an important exception). Some scholars have associated the sudden acceleration of church building in the eleventh century with the survival of Christendom itself – presuming that the widespread anticipation of the end of the world in the year 1000, or at least of some portentous apocalyptic event, inhibited the construction of permanent building in the immediate century preceding. The increase, however, may be attributed in fact to the successful development of two stable institutions, in Church and State. The evolution of Benedictine monasticism into a uniform religious style, and the consolidation of feudalism, were both indications that the Germanic penetration of the Western Empire was complete, and that what had emerged had an unexpected coherence and solidity.

Romanesque was a monumental representation in stone of the mature feudal order. It was an order represented, again, in both Church and State. In Byzantium and in the Celtic Christianity of the extreme West, the relationship of civil and religious authorities was expressed within an almost mystical harmony: the rule of Christ over the world was regarded as uniformly resident within a single order of authority among men, where emperor and patriarch (or, in Celtic Christianity, local petty-king and bishop) exercised different functions within an agreed society whose purposes and structures were directly ordained by Christ himself.

In the Germanic West, on the other hand, the governance of Christ was seen as given jointly to the two powers, civil and ecclesiastical, who were each to possess their own separate authority and exercise it within defined spheres. The definitions could never be agreed, and the history of the Church in the West was punctuated by disputes between the papacy and the Holy Roman Empire (inaugurated in 800 by Charlemagne), and, at the local level, between the clergy

King Louis VI of France presents his church at Avenas to St Vincent. The model is almost a diagram of a Romanesque church: the high nave on the left, the tower at the crossing and the apsed choir.

Opposite: the nave of Durham Cathedral, early twelfth century. Here are all the qualities that make Romanesque architecture so powerfully expressive – its solidity, simplicity of structure and sense of permanence. In its own way the cathedral is the equivalent of the castle only a few hundred yards away. The castle stood for the political dominance of the Normans, the cathedral for ecclesiastical. Henceforth the Church would function like the State – hierarchic, organized, efficient, exacting obedience but sure of its mission to teach and to save.

Stone relief of Christ in Blessing, from the church of St-Sernin at Toulouse, late eleventh century. The sculptor's model was probably a Byzantine ivory, but the scale has increased enormously and the whole effect is transformed. Christ, seated in a nimbus and flanked by the symbols of the evangelists, raises his right hand in blessing and in the other holds a book inscribed 'Pax Vobis'.

and the feudal magnates over jurisdiction and authority. Feudalism was a rival world hierarchy to the harmonious order of the Byzantine universal scheme; it was earthly and broken down into numerous detailed obligations which had an abiding tendency to absorb the Church. In some large measure the Church, especially in Germany, did indeed become feudalized, often with the active support of local senior clergy, anxious to find in a sympathetic civil power some effective counter to the distant authority of Rome. The rights of the laity over the Church were pressed at all levels, and especially in the matter of ecclesiastical appointments.

Proprietary churches emerged, in which the lay founder or protector achieved the rights of patronage; at a higher level the larger feudal magnates and kings expected, and often succeeded in acquiring, the right to scrutinize the appointment of bishops. Sometimes the Church revolted against the growing strength of civil control, as in the pontificate of Hildebrand, or the monastic revivals associated with Cluny and later with the Cistercians. But more usually, in the early Middle Ages, lay domination of the Western Church absorbed it into the texture of Germanic society, the local clergy generally willing accomplices in the subordination of religion to the prevailing social customs. Christianity became itself an ingredient of the feudal hierarchy.

This is nowhere better demonstrated than in the *tympana* of Romanesque churches. Here, in the semi-circular space above external doorways, were sculptural reliefs representing Christ in Majesty or in Judgment. The style is astonishingly uniform throughout Western Europe, and everywhere Christ is shown as a feudal overlord surrounded by heavenly beings, while beneath him are his senior vassals – the Apostles – and the other members of the subinfeudated society. The most accomplished of these *tympanum* depictions is at the great pilgrimage church of La Madeleine at Vézelay, where Christ is shown instructing the Apostles. At Moissac, also in France, Christ sits enthroned above a row of seated disciples, the whole tableau arranged in the manner of a feudal court. At Barfreston, in Kent (England), the twelfth-century south doorway has a seated Christ surrounded by angels and beasts entwined in riotous foliage, but there are warriors at the base of the carvings at each side, and the world being blessed by the raised hand of Christ is clearly intended to be the host-in-arms which the feudal order represented. How greatly all this contrasts with the serene Pantocrator of the Byzantine churches, removed from the affairs of men, mysterious in awesome and distant governance. It is as if the source of authority has removed himself from the descending dome to the entrance doorway, and in the process become the great reminder to men of their obligations of loyalty in the existing world of graded service.

The triumphalist intentions of lay patrons, expressed in the massive grandeur of the Romanesque style, can be seen in many of the great cathedrals and churches of Western Europe built between 1000 and 1200 or so. At Speyer, the huge cathedral was begun in 1030 by Conrad III as a monument to the power and authority of the German emperors. Everything about the building – and especially its long nave and four towers – is on an enormous scale, the sense of weight reinforced by the addition, early in the twelfth century, of masonry to the piers to carry the groin-vaulted roof which replaced the original wooden one. Speyer can be taken as a typical great church: a vast structure which offers up the power of the world to the sovereign in heaven, the payment in stone of the obligations of a vassal to a greater lord. The numerous carvings of royal and noble figures seem far to outnumber religious representations.

Romanesque churches showed some diversities of style throughout Western

Europe. Yet whether put up by secular lords or by monastic authorities, the buildings were just the same: feudalism may have used the Romanesque to express its ideals but it did not invent the style. The multiplication of the Benedictine houses, and the increasing tendency to a measure of centralization within the order, must have helped to foster uniformity of building techniques. So did the existence of itinerant craftsmen. Particularly successful churches were copied in other places. St Michael's at Hildesheim, built in the first third of the eleventh century, elicited many imitations, of which one of the most splendid, almost a century later, was the great abbey church of Maria Laach. German Romanesque was especially given to the construction of towers, and both these churches had six each.

Influence was spread over huge areas. Cormac's Chapel, on the Rock of Cashel in Ireland, was constructed under the direct inspiration of German Romanesque, and is, by any standards, a superb example of the style. It is unusual in Ireland for having two square towers – a German feature – with storeys of blind arcading and a barrel-vaulted roof. Most Irish Romanesque was blended with existing Celtic methods of building and decoration, with corbelled roofs and a single round tower. The Rock of Cashel was associated with St Patrick; in 1101 it was given to the Church by the kings of Munster. As a good defensive site in the Golden Vale of Tipperary, it was eventually crowded with buildings: a Romanesque church, a thirteenth-century Gothic cathedral, a castle, and a round tower.

The Romanesque Cormac's Chapel, consecrated in 1134, showed the continuing proximity of Irish and European monasticism, even after the great days of the early Celtic missions had passed. The seventh abbot of Ratisbon (Regensburg), Dionysius, was an Irishman, and he dispatched a small delegation from the monastery to his native land to collect funds for the rebuilding of his own Benedictine foundation. Among those sent were two craftsmen, William and Conrad – we know that the second of these was a carpenter – and their influence is plainly evident in the church constructed on the Rock of Cashel after their visit. Cormac's Chapel is a simple nave and chancel building, but decorated in a mature Romanesque fashion. The two doorways have *tympana*, which are very rare in Ireland, and both are unusually filled with sculpted beasts, rather than with depictions of Christ: the feudal order was unknown in Ireland before the arrival of the Anglo-Norman knights. There are arches decorated with chevrons, blind arcading both inside and outside the building, with pilasters in the conventional German or French Romanesque manner. It is, altogether, a remarkable demonstration of the international nature of the style. Even the 'Mozarabic' versions, developed in Spain during the tenth century, which show strong traces of Islamic art, are still very obviously Romanesque.

Detail of the head of Christ from the tympanum of the abbey of Moissac, southern France. A little earlier than Vézelay (pl. 25), the Moissac Christ is even more commanding in his pose and expression.

Opposite: Speyer Cathedral, on the Rhine, was begun in 1030 on an unprecedentedly huge scale, to demonstrate the authority of the German emperor. Here we are looking at the east end, with its apse meeting the gabled choir. Flanking the choir are two tall towers topped by a type of spire called a 'Rhenish helm'.

Right: the abbey church of Maria Laach, also on the Rhine, showing the more developed form of the great church that began at Speyer. Here the eastern towers (which are round) are at the ends of the transepts rather than in the angles. There are two pairs of transepts and two crossing towers.

Cormac's Chapel, on the Rock of Cashel, Ireland, could be called an example of German Romanesque away from its native soil. The exterior (above) has the dwarf arcading to be seen on the apse at Speyer and the interior (right), uniquely for Ireland at this time, is stone vaulted.

119

Saxon churches in England must often have been made of wood, but only one survives today, that at Greensted, in Essex. The nave walls are of split logs. Roof and dormer windows are later.

The 'Fordwich Stone', a tomb or shrine from St Augustine's Abbey, Canterbury, is made like a miniature church with a row of columns down the sides and a tiled roof.

The origins of Romanesque are very difficult to determine. The period between the collapse of the old Empire in the West and the emergence of Carolingian and Ottonian stone churches, and the Saxon churches of England, was a time of great Christian expansion. There must have been an enormous number of small wooden churches. What were they like? There is really no way of knowing, but it is surely possible to assume that they copied, in simple rectangular wooden form, the shape of the Roman basilican style. In Rome itself, indeed, Christian basilicas in a virtually unchanged style continued to be built until the end of the twelfth century – like the church of S. Clemente. Elsewhere the basilican style as such must have passed into the crude wooden churches. How faithfully and to what extent did they preserve aspects of the traditional basilica? Did they manage to keep, in wood, the rounded apses at the east end, or did they begin what was to emerge later as a feature particularly noticeable in England – the square-ended chancel? It is impossible to tell. The making of bricks ceased with the end of the Empire, and a couple of centuries were to pass before the Christianized peoples of the West began to dig among the rubble of the surviving Roman buildings to recover building materials for secondary use. The techniques of the wooden churches can still be seen in Russian and Scandinavian church buildings; an interesting English example has survived at Greensted in Essex. A nave of massive split oak logs, of some indeterminable Saxon date, supports a Gothicized medieval superstructure.

Stone churches were initially so rare that they caused remark: the oratory built by St Ninian at Whithorn in Galloway was, because of the colour of its stone, known as 'Candida Casa', the 'White House'. Why was the move to stone structures made at all? The reasons were probably similar to those which prompted the conversion in the Celtic Church: defensive requirements in the age of Viking raids, the vulnerability of wooden construction to total destruction by fire, and perhaps, even, the first beginnings of a relative scarcity of large timbers once the deforestation of the countryside had proceeded.

The first stone churches showed two structural features which linked them strongly to the past. They preserved the rectangular design. There was no attempt to copy the common Byzantine pattern of a Greek cross. They also used recovered Roman materials, especially bricks and columns. Roofs were originally of wood; they gave a high-pitched effect, as in the Celtic oratories of Ireland. None has survived, but an indication of what these little churches must have been like is suggested by 'Hedda's Stone' at Peterborough Cathedral. It is an eighth-century carved block, with figures of Christ and the Apostles, and perhaps once served as part of a shrine or a tomb. Like so many reliquaries, it represents the shape of a church, and in this case particular interest is attached to the high-pitched roof. Similarly in the later 'Fordwich Stone', now in the parish church at Fordwich near Canterbury, but originally from St Augustine's Abbey in the city, the church shape has a high-pitched roof. It is eleventh or twelfth century, with Romanesque blind arcading on the side. But the roof is the most intriguing detail with fish-scale tiles. This feature of Romanesque roof decoration was comparatively common in France, as in the twin towers of Notre-Dame-La-Grande at Poitiers, for example. The 'Fordwich Stone' therefore indicates some considerable advances on the first roofs of churches: it is a testimony to the arrival of mature European methods of construction.

Stone Saxon churches before that had revealed great variations. In some examples the decorative effects rather crudely preserved a suggestion of the wooden structures that preceded them. The most famous is the tower of the Saxon church at Earls Barton, which was probably built in the late tenth century.

It is decorated with pilaster strips like wooden slats, arranged in rude patterns. In contrast is the basilica at Brixworth, also in Northamptonshire, which dates from the eighth century. Here Roman bricks have been used for the arches of the nave arcading and clerestory, and a certain elegance and classical sense pervades the building.

Roman materials were also used in the Saxon church of St Peter-on-the-Wall at Bradwell-juxta-Mare in Essex. This tall, rectangular building, constructed in 654, represents what the basilican style must have looked like when first translated back to stone from wood. It is rather a large example, for the site was also a shrine to St Cedd, who was the bishop and apostle of the Christians in the territory of the East Saxons. The church was not only built out of Roman rubble, it was also constructed into the inner wall of the Roman fortress of Othona. As in the Early Christian basilican churches, there were originally two small chambers, or *porticus*, projecting from the nave, which served as sacristies. At Bradwell the foundations of one of these buildings have been discovered in excavation. The surviving church is simple and austere, but has great dignity and is well proportioned.

The ruins of St Augustine's Abbey at Canterbury cover an extensive site where once there were three churches of the Saxon period. Of these St Pancras' Chapel is the most useful for illustrating the design of a stone Saxon church since excavations have carefully marked out the original plan. Most of the early work here survives to just above floor level, although the apse wall and the *porticus* on the north side have disappeared. The wall of the west porch still stands to almost its original height, and is of such fine workmanship that it can only have been constructed by craftsmen from the Continent. The bricks throughout the whole building are Roman, and so are the columns of the chancel arch. The two side arches of this triple arch had been filled in not long after their original installation, leaving a central, rather narrow entry into the chancel. This may have indicated some sort of liturgical change: an acceleration of the tendency to divide the

The late tenth-century tower of Earls Barton Church, Northamptonshire (above left), is the grandest and most spectacularly decorated of the remaining Saxon buildings. The decoration is simple – flat bands of stone forming patterns, possibly derived from timber prototypes.

Brixworth church, Northamptonshire (above), is the most impressive surviving Saxon church. The arches originally led into 'porticus', separate chapels opening off the nave on both sides. The bricks are Roman but the technique by which they are laid is still unsure.

Gaunt and lonely by the Essex sea-shore, the church of Bradwell-juxta-Mare has a claim to be the oldest church building in England. It was probably erected by St Cedd in 654. What remains now is just the nave. There was originally a west porch and an apsed chancel.

mysteries of the sanctuary from the place of assembly for the laity. This triple-arch feature is clearly of southern European origin, and also existed at Brixworth, Bradwell, and at Reculver.

The abbey church of St Mary at Reculver, on the bleak north coast of Kent, was built within the massive walls of the Roman fort of Regulbium, the first to be established in defence of the 'Saxon Shore'. The earliest church here was the work of a priest called Bassa, to whom the site was given by Egbert, King of Kent, in 669. There was a rectangular nave, and a semi-circular apse, very much in the southern European manner. The entire church was constructed with flint and stone rubble taken from the ruins of the Roman fort, bonded together with spaced layers of Roman brickwork. Shortly after construction the *porticus* on each side of the nave were slightly enlarged, perhaps to accommodate burials. Between nave and chancel was the triple arch.

By chance, we know exactly what it looked like, because the Saxon church at Reculver was demolished in 1809 in circumstances of some controversy. Coastal erosion had eaten into the low clay cliff on which the original fort, and the church, were built, and by a majority of just one vote in the parish vestry meeting the vicar secured authority to dismantle the building and construct a new church about a mile inland. Feelings ran exceedingly high, and this meant that the demolition, as it proceeded, was recorded. An engraving by R. Adlard, made in 1826 (and published in 1830) shows the chancel arches as they were being taken down. The rounded sides were of Roman brick, resting on two large Roman pillars. The

Reculver, in Kent, possessed one of the most perfect Saxon churches in England until 1809 when most of it was demolished, leaving only the western towers which had anyway been added in the twelfth century.

towers appear to be of Early English Gothic design, for the whole Saxon church was incorporated within a Gothic structure in the thirteenth century. There is a fine Early English entrance door, and good lancet windows.

The return to stone building by the Saxons was on a modest scale. For larger stone structures, and for a further step towards what was to become the Romanesque style, it is necessary to turn next to the churches of the Carolingian monarchy in France and Germany. Charlemagne's Palatine Chapel at Aachen was built in the last decade of the eighth century and was plainly intended as a monumental testimony to his claim to stand as the successor to the rulers of imperial Rome. The impressive Roman buildings of Trier were an obvious source of inspiration for the great church, and Roman ruins were indeed ransacked to provide the materials; yet Charlemagne's structure, designed by Odo of Metz, was an emulation on a large scale – as the Saxon churches were on a small scale – not of the Roman basilica, but of the Byzantine style. The main chapel at Aachen, a central octagon, was based upon the Italian-Byzantine church of S. Vitale in Ravenna. The belfry was by the Armenian architect, Oton Matsaetsi. It is clear that as the use of stone construction revived, the ideal of a church to which the Germanic patrons looked came from the East. Adaptation, however, was extremely radical. The Greek cross and the domed roof were not copied in the north of Europe; instead the basilica shape was encased within massive stone walls whose rounded arches suggested Byzantine originals. Inspiration may also have come from the more eastern territories of the empire; some have noticed the similarity between the massive solidity of Romanesque forms and the Roman-Syrian churches which existed in large numbers to the north of the Holy Land in the fourth and fifth centuries.

The roofs of Romanesque churches were of wood, and then, as techniques developed in the eleventh century, of stone vaults. Vaulting required more substantial walls to carry the additional weight of stone, and this in turn added to the ponderous grandeur of the style. The *porticus* of the basilican church – the small projecting side chambers – developed into transepts, and this produced the elongated cruciform shape so familiar in the Western tradition of church building. The old rectangular basilica space became the nave; a choir, often raised above a crypt, appeared beyond a chancel arch; the sanctuary moved beyond that to an apse-end which was still characteristically rounded, and in the larger churches the sanctuary was itself encased within an ambulatory. The old basilica was a unified building with the single purpose of leading the worshipper forward; the Byzantine church was a centralized space beneath a descending dome which was intended to bring heaven down to the society of men; the Romanesque structures, as they developed, were a collection of units which, like the feudal assembly itself, was an architectural representation of the duties and obligations of the Christian life.

The Byzantine influence was more noticeable in interior decoration than in structure, yet there were some churches in central France which retained domes. It is possible that the Crusaders were so impressed by the Byzantine churches they saw in Cyprus and in the Greek islands that they copied some of their features when they returned to France. The last surviving example of a Romanesque domed church – out of the seventy or so which once existed in France – is the cathedral of St-Front at Périgueux. This eleventh-century building has five domes set on pendentives, and the Byzantine influence is heightened by the fact that the church was designed in the shape of a Greek cross. The lofty interior, which owes its austerity to nineteenth-century restoration, evokes a strong sense of Byzantine spirituality. This group of domed churches is quite exceptional.

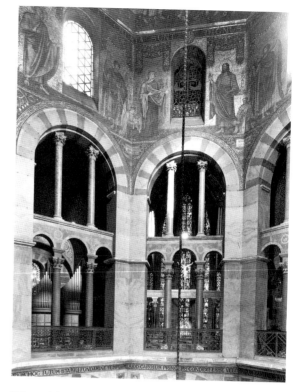

When Charlemagne built his Palatine Chapel at Aachen in the early ninth century, he consciously took as his model Justinian's imperial church of S. Vitale at Ravenna (pl. 9).

St-Front, Périgueux, eleventh century: one of the few clearly Byzantine buildings in the West. Its series of domed spaces resembles St Mark's in Venice.

Crypts developed as the burial places of saints whose remains were often removed here from previous places of pilgrimage. In Italian churches they were commonly only half underground, the choir being raised up over them on steps (e.g. S. Miniato al Monte, pl. 31). Left: S. Zeno, Verona, whose bronze doors we have already seen. Here stood the tomb of S. Zeno himself.

Crypt of Speyer Cathedral, the oldest part of the building. The simple 'cushion' capitals speak of a time when sculpture was still a rarity.

Right: crypt of Canterbury Cathedral, early twelfth century. Most great churches were provided with a crypt, whether they had a saint to put in it or not. Canterbury had to wait until 1170 before the murder of Thomas Becket made it a popular shrine. The capitals here (see p.131) are among the most sophisticated in Romanesque art.

Byzantine decorative techniques were more common in Romanesque churches: mosaics were often the work of artists from Constantinople itself. In the Norman kingdom of Sicily the combination of styles was most advanced, but the resulting churches were still clearly Romanesque rather than Byzantine. The movement of travellers between Western Europe and the Byzantine Empire was frequent, and contact with the further East, with the territories occupied by Islam after the seventh century, was steady. Monasticism helped to maintain links with the East. The Byzantine influence upon the development of the Romanesque style had many channels, therefore, and it was evidently quite usual for Western patrons to buy entire church kits from workshops in Constantinople and have them shipped back home. A ship raised from the seabed by marine archaeologists working in Sicily a few years ago was found to contain the complete furnishings of a church, including a chancel screen (like the one at Reculver). It had sunk to the bottom of the sea sometime in the sixth century.

Romanesque churches became progressively larger. Of course not all did: the larger examples have tended to survive (while smaller ones have been rebuilt in other styles) simply because they were created for specialized functions which attracted sacral qualities – abbey churches, cathedrals, monuments to the dynastic splendour of great rulers. There is no doubt, however, that the large churches influenced the general development of the style, and this was especially true of the 'pilgrim churches' which were put up along the European pilgrimage routes. Apart from the longer journey to the Holy Land, pilgrims also made their way to Rome and to the great shrine of St James at Compostela in the extreme north-west of the Iberian peninsula. From four main starting points, the routes crossed France to join up beyond the Pyrenees. Some of the churches along the way developed subsidiary cults, like the relics of St-Martin at Tours or of Ste-Foy at Conques, and these added to the splendour of the churches. The pilgrim trade had its own requirements, and catering for these made important contributions to the general evolution of the Romanesque style. The cathedral at St-Martin of Tours, for example, (now replaced by a Gothic building) was widely copied in many of its features. Larger churches, more extensive crypts, and ambulatories to enable the pilgrims to circulate around the east-end altars of the raised sanctuaries, and upper galleries, were all creations of the pilgrimage churches which became part of the ordinary Romanesque church style.

The allure of shrines was not the only reason for enlarged churches. The old basilican style was adapted for a world in which the civil and the ecclesiastical authorities existed side by side in the same cities and towns of the Roman Empire. In the Germanic kingdoms of the West the Roman civic organization disappeared, and their buildings fell into ruin. Churches succeeded as the only structures of any size in the new centres of settlement, and were therefore used for a number of civic functions. Their size, accordingly, was further enlarged to accommodate multiple use. An increase in the numbers of clergy may also have been a contributory factor, since more altars, and more side-chapels, were required for the daily Mass of each. This is a difficult point to establish, however, since there is virtually no way of knowing, even in the monastic churches, exactly how liturgical use and daily custom may have affected alterations to church buildings.

The cult of relics did certainly provide the incentive for one important feature of Romanesque churches: the bodies of saints were buried in crypts, and the size and importance of crypts accordingly developed enormously. Sometimes entirely subterranean, and sometimes half above ground level, so that the choir was raised, Romanesque crypts were also the first part of the churches to have

Sta Marta de Terra, in Spain, is on the pilgrim road to Compostela. St James (Santiago), whose body was miraculously discovered in Galicia, and served as an inspiration in the war of reconquest against the Moors, is often shown in the guise of a pilgrim wearing the badge of the scallop-shell.

125

Pilgrims converged on the shrine of St James at Compostela from all over Europe, and the towns through which they passed are marked by a specific type of church which has been labelled the 'pilgrimage church'. One of the grandest is that of St-Sernin at Toulouse. At the east end, shown here, the ambulatory (an aisle encircling the choir) enables pilgrims to make a circuit of the whole church.

stone-vaulted roofs. It was a development shown at its most splendid in the cathedral of Canterbury. In 1070, following the Conquest, Lanfranc began to rebuild the old cathedral of Augustine in the Romanesque style. His successor Anselm radically altered the plan, by raising an enlarged choir upon a huge crypt. It was so far above ground that the many windows make it the most well-lit as well as the largest Norman crypt in existence. Another good English example of the raised crypt is at Worcester; fine continental parallels are at Speyer and Cologne.

At Canterbury the crypt is perfectly preserved, having remained unaffected by the great fire of 1174 that did so much damage to the rest of the cathedral. The crypt nave contains twenty-two columns, supporting a groin-vaulted roof. The capitals have some of the best Romanesque carving anywhere, mostly dating from the 1120s. They show fantastic animals, often in combat with others representing the forces of evil; the inspiration seems to be the illuminated manuscripts of the period, the lively imagination of the *scriptorium* applied with a chisel. Some of the columns have characteristic Romanesque chevron decorative bands. In the thirteenth century there was a tendency for the relics of saints to be translated to the churches above, and the golden age of the crypt came to an end.

Another legacy of the pilgrimage churches was the ambulatory. To enable the pilgrims to circulate around the building, a walkway was created around the apse, behind the sanctuary altar, and to the outside wall of this passage was attached a series of radiating side-chapels. This rearrangement of the east end is known as the *chevet*, and was widely copied from the original Romanesque cathedral of St-Martin of Tours. There are splendid surviving examples in most Romanesque cathedrals, and perhaps the best among the French pilgrimage churches is to be seen at St-Sernin at Toulouse, which was begun in 1080. Galleries above the main arcades of the nave and choir, allowing a complete circuit of the building, formed a kind of upper church. The mystery and potency of the cult of the saints in Christianity has no more obvious memorial than these features of the Romanesque style.

The development of stone-vaulted roofs had a dramatic effect on the nature of the church beneath. The slender columns of basilicas had supported wooden roofs, and the early Romanesque churches, which also had wooden covers, were characterized by relatively light columns. The barrel vault was introduced in the eleventh century – built, not in concrete as Roman vaulting had been, but in brick and stone. The barrel-vaulted roof had been developed in the Syrian and Anatolian provinces of the Byzantine Empire, and its addition to the Romanesque style testifies to the Eastern influences which helped the evolution of the style generally. Later groin vaulting was employed, which was even heavier. There were two results. One was that churches became a series of bays. A vault is defined by four arches, and the nave became a series of such units, end to end, capable of being extended if the prestige or use of the building required it. To look down the length of a Romanesque nave is to see a sequence of spatial units; the effect is utterly unlike a basilica.

The second result of stone roofs was the thickening of the supporting walls and columns. The most typical of Romanesque churches have massive supporting structures. What most strikes the visitor to Durham Cathedral, which is one of the most impressive Romanesque churches, and very characteristic of the Norman achievement in the style, is the sheer size of the nave columns. The huge circular and composite piers alternate, and some have bold incised chevron or spiral designs. Many Romanesque buildings had to be strengthened when wooden roofs were replaced by vaults, but Durham, begun in 1093, was stone-vaulted throughout from the beginning. So great is the weight of

Right: it is a tribute to the effects of the cult of relics that a major church, Kirkwall Cathedral, should have been built in the twelfth century in the remote Orkney Islands to house the body of St Magnus.

The White Tower of the Tower of London was among the first permanent buildings erected by the Normans after the Conquest. Inside it is the chapel of St John, the prototype Norman church.

the roof, indeed, that the church has concealed flying buttresses, in anticipation of the Gothic style which was to succeed it.

A similar impression of the solidity of Romanesque architecture can be received at the chapel of St John in the White Tower of the Tower of London – the huge castle built by the Normans to guard the river approach to the capital. The chapel is a small Romanesque church, built into the structure of the keep, in the 1080s. It is entirely without decoration except for the sober cross-motifs on the capitals of the massive columns.

At the other end of the British Isles, the small cathedral at Kirkwall in the Orkney Islands, begun in 1137 to house the relics of the martyred St Magnus, shows the same massive qualities. Stone-masons from Durham were almost certainly employed in the construction. A softer effect than is usual in

Left: Mainz Cathedral, another of the great Rhineland churches. Like Speyer (p. 118), it had towers flanking the choir. In this case we are looking at the west end of the church, for German churches favoured the strange arrangement of an apse at both ends. The tops of the two smaller towers, and the upper part of the central octagon (beginning with the large traceried windows) are later additions.

Romanesque churches sprouted towers, a legacy which was to pass on to their Gothic successors. Old Canterbury Cathedral, before the rebuilding of the late twelfth century, had towers in the position favoured in Germany, flanking the choir, and they still remain, though the choir has been transformed (above: St Anselm's Tower).

Romanesque buildings was achieved by the use of the local red sandstone, blended with yellow sandstone from the nearby island of Eday to give a polychrome effect. The cathedral was completed in Gothic style in the fifteenth century. It is rare in Scotland for having remained undamaged during the Reformation – a happy consequence of its remote location: until 1472 it had been under the jurisdiction of the Archbishop of Trondheim in Norway.

Towers are a feature of the Romanesque style. Originally, in Italy, they were free-standing belfries – the famous 'Leaning Tower' at Pisa is a late example – but in northern Europe towers came to be built for purely decorative reasons, to add to the grand and majestic qualities of the buildings which they enhanced. Sometimes they were square-shaped, but in the more elaborate cathedrals, such as at Mainz, they were octagonal, and in some other cases, as at Worms, they were round. Twin towers, usually square, were a feature of the west end of churches in Normandy and England, giving them, too, a monumental appearance, especially when the west wall between them contained a 'wheel window', another Romanesque favourite. At Jumièges in France, a Benedictine church begun in 1037, the fine square twin towers of the west end became octagonal for their uppermost two stages. This magnificent ruin, its walls pockmarked by the ivy (now removed) which for centuries covered them, is one of the best examples of Norman Romanesque. As at Durham, enormous round columns in the nave alternate with compound piers; at Jumièges, however, these massive structures supported a wooden, not a stone, roof. Square-shaped towers in northern Europe could sometimes achieve the slender appearance of southern European belfries, even when integrated with the main buildings. This was certainly the case with Cormac's Chapel in Ireland, and with St Anselm's Tower at Canterbury Cathedral. The latter is covered with decoration, and it is clear that the top three of the four rows of arcading were added after the original work of Anselm had been completed. The effect is somewhat chaotic from a decorative point of view, but the tower itself is splendidly proportioned.

Before turning to Romanesque decoration itself it is worth noticing that, as in all other Christian styles, Romanesque designers sometimes built churches in honour of the Holy Sepulchre: round or octagonal. At St-Bénigne, Dijon, Abbot William of Volpiano created a church of striking originality, completed in 1018, which included a large rotunda, with three circles of columned arcades. These arcades extended upwards in three storeys to an aperture which was unroofed. This large church has now virtually disappeared, but St Augustine's Abbey in Canterbury still preserves the remains of a church unquestionably built in imitation of it. Abbot Wulfric's rotunda, like the rest of the original abbey site, was cleared in the post-Conquest rebuilding of the abbey. It had never, in fact, been completed, and Wulfric himself had died, in 1059, while the work was still in progress. The area has now been excavated, and the lower walls of the rotunda, which was anyway designed to be partly below ground level, revealed. It was an octagonal building externally, but round inside, with eight massive circular columns supporting a groin-vault. In the course of building the outer walls had evidently been strengthened – perhaps indicating a late decision to switch from a wood to a stone roof. As at St-Bénigne, a church was to extend to the west of the rotunda, but at Canterbury only a small start had begun on this before the whole work was demolished. Wulfric's rotunda, one of the few examples of a circular church in the Romanesque style in England, stands in a long tradition of sacred buildings based on the Holy Sepulchre, and like so many preceding examples, there is evidence to suggest that it was intended as a *martyrium* or a grand cover for an illustrious tomb: that of St Augustine himself.

Paired western towers were favoured in Normandy, and probably from here passed into the repertoire of French early Gothic, where they became standard. Jumièges (above), near Rouen, was a great Benedictine abbey, cathedral-like in its scale, and now an impressive ruin.

The decorative genius of Romanesque lay in sculpture and in arcading. Originally, in the eleventh century, only the capitals of columns were carved; in the succeeding century sculpted decoration covered many surfaces, both inside and outside the churches. Portals and the edges of arcade arches were especially rich in symmetrically carved devices – chevrons, dog-tooth, pyramid, twisted-cord, and so forth. To these were sometimes added the forms of beasts and human heads. Some are barbaric, reminders of the surviving, if veiled, presence of the Germanic gods whose formal abandonment the Romanesque churches were intended to declare. At the small cathedral of Clonfert in County Galway in Ireland (now the Protestant parish church), the west doorway is a magnificent testimony to the vigour of primitive Romanesque carving. Rows of human heads look outwards above a rounded arch of six concentric types of carved decoration. The cathedral was built by the king of Ui Maine between 1140 and 1180. A sophisticated example of decorated portals can be found at Bamberg Cathedral in Germany. Here, as very commonly, for it is a Romanesque hallmark, the shafts of the decorative side-columns are sculpted with human forms, the decoration and the structure thus achieving complete integration. Some of the apparent crudity of the rustic examples of carving is the consequence of the Romanesque habit of representing humans and beasts, not in realistic dimensions, but in sizes appropriate to the space to be filled. All these carvings, both inside and outside churches, were once painted.

The other great Romanesque decorative achievement was blind arcading, sometimes stacked in rows above one another, separated by string-courses. Pilasters extend along the walls, and arches sometimes intersect. Originally an interior device, it was soon being used all over the façades and other external spaces. The Lady Chapel at Glastonbury Abbey in Somerset has lower walls with intersecting blind arcading, inside and outside, almost all the way round the building. The great abbey here was destroyed by fire in 1184, and the Lady Chapel was the first part to be rebuilt. It is in a mature Romanesque style, with excellent portals which were once, as at Bamberg, flanked with columns carved into human forms.

Doorways were often the occasion for lavish displays of sculpture. Clonfert Cathedral, Ireland, is unique: the gable over the door is filled with a pattern of alternating triangles and human heads.

Far left: Bamberg Cathedral, Germany. Although still Romanesque in style, these figures are inspired by the great Gothic portals of Chartres, Amiens and Reims with their 'figures-colonne'. At Bamberg they represent St Stephen, the Empress Kunigunde, the Emperor Henry II and (on the other side) St Peter, and Adam and Eve.

Left: the Lady Chapel of Glastonbury Abbey, Somerset. Here tiny figures are intermingled with foliage and abstract patterns. On each side of the door is the leitmotiv of English Romanesque, intersecting arcading.

A bizarre monster from the crypt of Canterbury Cathedral (see p. 124). The Romanesque carvers were fascinated by fierce animals devouring each other or attacking humans: an indication, perhaps, of the persistence of pagan folk symbolism within Christianized Europe.

A capital at Hildesheim, Germany, clearly descends from classical Roman art, yet even here strange faces emerge from the foliage.

The sculpture of Moissac, in southern France, is perhaps the most fantastic of all Romanesque art. On the central trumeau of the porch (right) the outer face is carved with hybrid beasts like lions and lionesses, climbing over each other. The sides have Old Testament prophets bearing scrolls foretelling the birth of Christ – impossibly elongated and incorporeal, yet with faces of poignant humanity.

Tuscan Romanesque is a subcategory of
its own, a lively and inventive style but
mostly relying upon one single motif,
miniature arcading spread across every
surface. Right: the façade of S. Michele
at Lucca, St Michael himself on the
gable.

White, high-quality marble gives these
Tuscan churches a texture of jewel-like
richness, which is enhanced when
coloured marbles are used as decorative
inlays. Above: Lucca Cathedral, the west
front. Right: the west front of Pisa
Cathedral. Opposite: the east end of
Pisa, with dwarf arcading surrounding
the apse and, on the extreme left, the
campanile, or Leaning Tower, whose
decorative vocabulary consists only of the
same arcading.

In Florence the effect of arcading is suggested by the use of coloured marbles on a flat surface. Above: the façade of S. Miniato al Monte (see pl. 31).

The Baptistry of Florence Cathedral, which functioned as the cathedral itself until the present one was erected. Renaissance Florentines believed this to be an ancient Roman building.

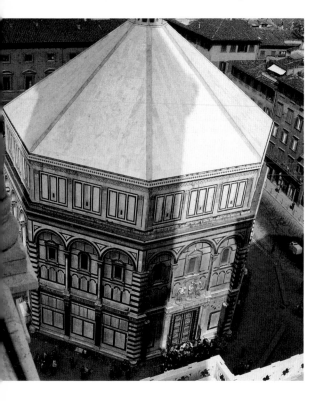

A further development of blind arcading came when the pilasters were actually separated from the walls again, and open arcaded galleries, purely decorative in purpose, resulted. The effect of both devices, and especially of blind arcading, can be experienced at their most exuberant in the west front of Ely Cathedral in Cambridgeshire (England) – a late Romanesque example. For the most sophisticated versions it is best to go to Italy, and to Tuscany, where the 'Lombard frieze' underwent inspired changes.

Architectural and decorative styles seem to reach their most extravagant forms in the final stages of development – like the termination of Gothic in the extraordinary elaboration of the Portuguese Manueline style of the fifteenth and sixteenth centuries. The Romanesque of Tuscany had always had distinctive features, particularly in the use of banded marble, but its final stages produced some truly remarkable articulations of arcading. Lombardy saw the first Italian renditions of Romanesque, in the ninth century. It was heavily indebted to north European architecture. In Tuscany the style produced unusual variations from the start; and the reopening of the great marble quarries of Carrara – very little worked since the end of the Roman Empire – provided the marble which inspired many of the earliest Florentine buildings of note. The Baptistry was the original cathedral of Florence: a structure believed by the citizens to have been of great classical antiquity, once a temple of Mars. In fact it is a fourth- or fifth-century building, which in the eleventh century was covered with green and white marble panels. Inside, the existing Roman marble columns and capitals were enriched with more marble cladding. The result was a Romanesque building quite unlike the massive versions of the north of Europe. In Florence it is classical symmetry which is most evident, and a geometric use of the stone panels to produce an effect at once delicate and clearly defined. The layered marbles combine with the rounded Romanesque arches in a way which seems to side-step the Gothic interlude and almost to anticipate Renaissance architectural styles. At the little Florentine Benedictine church of S. Miniato al Monte, similarly, the use of green and white marble in a façade that combines Romanesque arches and panels with classical gable-pediments produces a highly distinctive building, quite unlike the monumentalism of the north. The façade dates from 1090.

Pisa produced an almost florid development of arcading. The famous buildings of the Campo dei Miracoli, set upon their vast green field, and thus seen without any kind of relationship to other structures, are dominated by the Duomo – the most important Romanesque church in Italy. Here, again, is the distinctive marble cladding, and the rounded arches. The cathedral, by a master called Buscheto, was constructed between 1064 and 1118. There are large transepts, and the nave was extended in the middle of the thirteenth century. Interior mosaics remind the visitor of the Italian liking for Byzantine enrichment, even in Romanesque buildings, and the classical inheritance is once again represented by the use of ancient-Roman granite columns to support the interior arcades. But the great glory of the cathedral is the west façade, added in the twelfth century by Rainaldo. Five tiers of open arcaded galleries rise above three ceremonial doorways, set in blind arcading of huge proportions. The lower parts of the nearby Baptistry show the same kind of extravagant arcading. This was begun in 1152 by Diotisalvi and completed a century later by Pisano. In the lowest band are four portals, set in blind arcades which echo those of the Duomo; above are galleried arcades of extraordinary elaboration. Yet the whole rotunda has a simple and dignified aspect, capped by a later Gothic dome.

At Lucca the Pisan Romanesque version of arcading reached its greatest extravagance. The church of S. Michele in Foro, begun in 1143, has a façade added in the thirteenth century which is crammed with galleried arcades of white marble. The Duomo at Lucca, an eleventh-century building greatly altered by Guidetto da Como in the first years of the thirteenth century, also shows the florid progression of the Tuscan Romanesque style. The earlier work is seen in massive arches and piers; the later in the profusion of open galleried arcading.

Modern revivals of the Romanesque style have borrowed all its features. The church of St Anne in Dawson Street, Dublin, is a highly unusual case. A Neo-classical building (designed by Isaac Wills in 1720) was given a Romanesque façade in 1868 by Sir Thomas Deane. All the Romanesque elements are present: square twin towers, elaborate portal with *tympanum*, open galleried arcades, and a wheel-window.

Sometimes the Romanesque style has been adopted because of its association with particular parts of Europe: thus the German immigrant settlers who came to Victoria, in the American state of Kansas, in the later decades of the nineteenth century, built themselves a thoroughly German church. St Fidelis Church, known as the 'Cathedral of the Plains', is a noble limestone structure with square twin-towers, wheel-window, and rounded arches. It was completed in 1911. A triple-arched front portal perfectly echoes the monumental qualities of Rhenish Romanesque.

Because the Romanesque church is an addition of units, rather than an organically conceived whole, it is extremely suitable for projects whose completion may have to be envisaged over decades, yet where a certain massive and impressive quality is easily achieved. Thus it has sometimes found favour in new countries where resources are uncertain. The Anglican cathedral of Harare in Zimbabwe was started in 1913, in a style which is basically Romanesque. Though austere in conception, there are even some upper decorative blind-arcaded friezes, rather chunky in the undressed stone. Inside an impression of solemnity pervades, the rounded, rather narrow windows – a very authentic Romanesque feature – excluding just enough light to suggest awesome mystery. There is still a trace of the earlier mission church which stood on the site: its altar cross, made of cigar boxes, is now preserved in the St George's Chapel of the existing building.

A last example shows the complex nature of Romanesque origins. The basilica of the Transfiguration, at the summit of Mount Tabor in Israel, was built in 1924, where once there had been an early Christian church, of the fourth century, and a Crusader monastery. It is in the Roman-Syrian style of the fourth and fifth centuries, and therefore happily illustrates the Eastern influences upon Romanesque design. The rather stunted twin towers are joined at the lower level by a sculptured triumphal arch supported by slender columns; above is a gallery of three rounded arches, and both the towers and the west front are completed with classical gable-pediments. Inside, there is a large apse mosaic, in a Neo-Byzantine style, of the transfigured Christ, and a crypt which preserves the sanctuary of the earliest basilica on the site. Huge rounded arches predominate. So do strength and massive form, the robust qualities which Eastern churches bequeathed to north European Romanesque.

The basilica of the Transfiguration on Mount Tabor, Israel. Though built in the 1920s, it represents a style prevalent in the Near East in the fourth century and one which was a source of Romanesque in Western Europe.

5 The majesty of God: the achievement of Gothic

By 1150 the Romanesque masons were able to respond to all the demands made upon them by their ecclesiastical patrons. They could build churches of any size; they understood structural principles adequately, in practice if not entirely in theory; and they could provide all the required opportunities for figural art on capitals, portals and interior walls. Until the Reformation the liturgy remained essentially the same, at least as far as its architectural setting was concerned. There was no pressing reason, therefore, why the design of churches should have changed.

How, then, should we account for the dramatic emergence of the Gothic style at this time? The answer seems to lie not so much in mechanics or engineering as in the realm of symbolism, of mysticism, of religious experience and spiritual values. Gothic could express aspiration, exaltation, a feeling of upward movement towards God in ways that were impossible in Romanesque.

The verticality of Gothic was achieved by a new mastery of the pointed arch. The height of a round arch depended upon its span; that of a pointed arch could be varied to almost any degree. This not only gave the masons much greater flexibility in the management of vaults but significantly altered the system of statics which enabled them to stand up. The weight supported by pointed arches or ribs can be concentrated at particular points and transferred to the ground via carefully placed flying buttresses on the outside of the building. The result is a structure like a skeleton depending on a balance of forces rather than one depending on load-bearing walls. It allowed architecture to soar with a new freedom, leaving the spaces in between the supports to be opened out as windows; a new art – tracery – was invented to fill these windows which now glowed with coloured glass on a scale never seen before. On the exterior, the upward movement of all these flowing lines was continued into pinnacles, towers and spires pointing towards heaven. Gothic architecture was the perfect fusion of form and function, means and ends.

For captions to colour plates 33–40, see p. 145

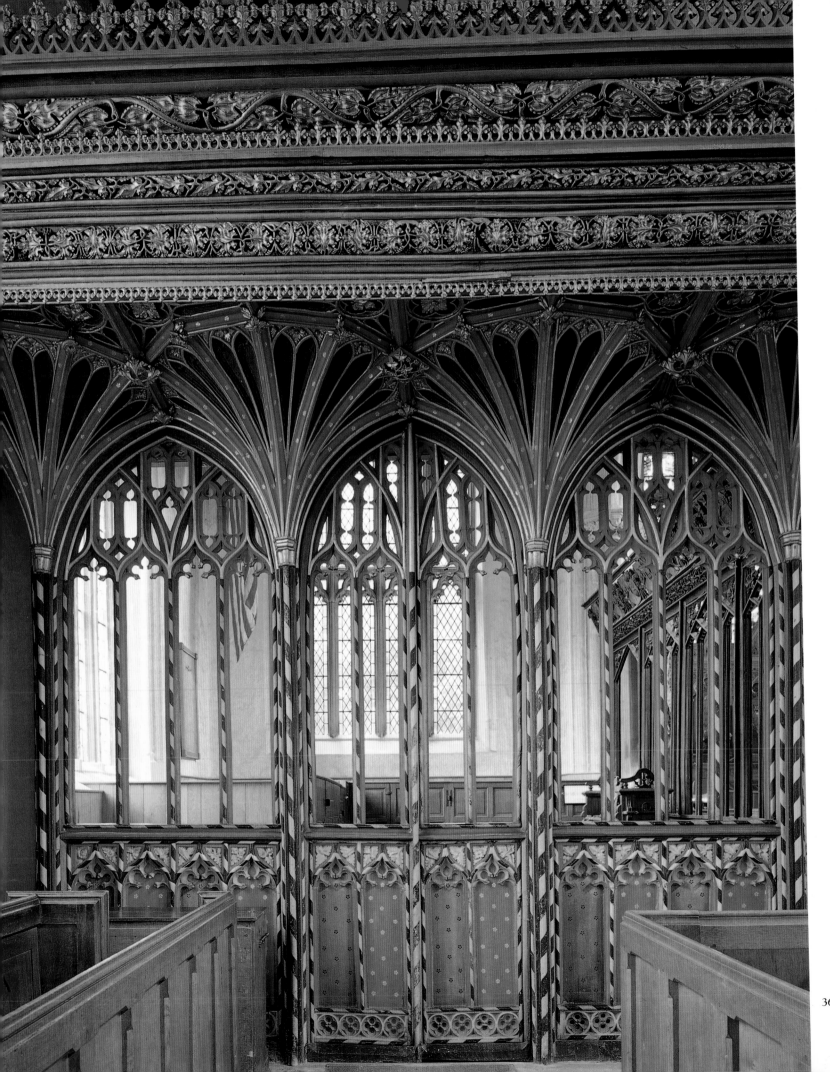

Colour plates 33–40

33 A painting, The Virgin and Child in a Church, *by Jan van Eyck, from the very end of the Middle Ages makes explicit the way in which a church was seen literally as the house of God. Inside the nave of a typical late Gothic church, the Virgin, crowned with a sparkling diadem of gold and gems and supernaturally out of the human scale, stands in front of her own image on the rood screen. Through a doorway we can see an angel conferring with the priest at the high altar.*

34 *A monstrance, a vessel for displaying the eucharistic host, in Toledo Cathedral (1515–24). It is the masterpiece of Enrique de Arfe, a German goldsmith working in Spain. Throughout the Middle Ages, architecture was the dominant art, lending its forms to furniture, sculpture and jewellery. This wonderful object is imagined as a miniature building, covered with niches, gables, tracery and tiny figures of saints and angels. The details repay prolonged scrutiny.*

35 The Miracle of St Giles, *by an unknown Flemish painter of about 1500. King Charles Martel, seen on the left, had refused to confess a sin, but asked St Giles (at the altar) to pray for him. In response to the saint's prayer an angel descended bearing a paper on which the king's sin was written and he received absolution. What is particularly interesting about this painting is that the artist has used the high altar of St-Denis, outside Paris, as his setting. The golden retable and the cross above it were already in the church at the time of Abbot Suger in the mid-twelfth century. Suger had no qualms about the possession of jewels and precious objects in the service of the Church. To him they symbolized God's glory and were a way of transporting the mind to heavenly things.*

36 *The richness of medieval church interiors is now hard to recapture. Sometimes stained glass survives, sometimes wall-paintings, sometimes sculpture – almost never the whole ensemble. This painted screen, retaining its original colours though restored, is at Cullompton, in Devon.*

37 *St Mary's Church at Fairford, in Gloucestershire, has miraculously kept its complete set of stained-glass windows. They culminate in the great west window which shows the Last Judgment. In the centre aureole sits Christ, surrounded by angels and saints. Beneath him the Archangel Michael weighs souls, consigning the blessed to Paradise (on the left) and the damned to Hell (right).*

38 *Bourges Cathedral embodies all the characteristic qualities of early French Gothic – its emphasis on height, the logic of its linear structure and (in this case) the richness of its coloured glass. But Bourges is in some ways untypical. It has double aisles: here we are looking from the inner south aisle towards the east end. To the left and in the foreground are the immensely tall piers of the nave arcade, with triforium and clerestory above them. On the right we can see that the aisle itself, almost uniquely in Gothic architecture, has a three-storey elevation of its own, with subsidiary arcade, triforium and clerestory; beyond that is the outer aisle.*

39 *Canterbury Cathedral creates a similar impression of verticality. The architects of the English Perpendicular style excelled in the creation of towers, and that of Canterbury, known as 'Bell Harry', is among the most splendid. The work of John Wastell, it dates from 1490–1503.*

40 *The masons who built the cathedrals are commemorated in one of the panels of stained glass at Bourges. Above it is a scene from the story of Dives and Lazarus.*

The majesty of God

FOR MOST PEOPLE in the Western tradition of Christianity the Gothic style is the Christian style *par excellence*. This attitude was given strong support in the nineteenth century – notably by Pugin – and the large majority of churches in the Gothic style have indeed been built since 1800. The medieval originals, still richly present in Western European countries, began to appear in the middle years of the twelfth century in northern France. It is peculiarly a Latin style: Byzantine ecclesiastical structures which have been Gothicized – and there are examples in Greece, Cyprus, and the Holy Land – owe their additions not to the inspiration of Orthodox patrons but to the Frankish knights who, as a by-product of the Crusades, occupied them for a few decades. When modern people think of a church, they tend to think of pointed arches, stained glass, and a spire: all are hallmarks of Gothic. So greatly has the Gothic representation of the church entered into Western popular spirituality, in fact, that the earlier claim of the nineteenth-century Gothic Revivalists, that Gothic is the authentic embodiment of Christian truth, has achieved a kind of fulfilment.

There have been many attempts to relate the Gothic style to basic religious and theological beliefs. The structural assembly of different components through a unified design intended to strain upwards to a higher understanding has seemed, to some, an embodiment in glass and stone of medieval Scholastic philosophy. The apparent dissolution of matter attained by the replacement of massive walls with great screens of glass has appeared, to some others, to represent an emphasis by later medieval spirituality on the transcendent elements within Christian theology. Those who believe that 'the spirit of the age' always has a reasonably uniform existence in the aesthetic and cultural accomplishments of a given society have certainly found in the Gothic style a proof of their contentions: here is the sublime expression of 'the age of faith'.

Yet there are major difficulties about the acceptance of any of these propositions. The first is that the cultural and religious ethos which produced both the Romanesque and the Gothic styles did not demonstrate any particular discontinuity that would account for the appearance of a new architectural movement. Gothic grew out of Romanesque without any culture shock. The rediscovery of Aristotelian intellectual categories, which lay behind Scholastic logic, preceded Gothic, and did not, anyway, have any special implications outside the world of theological and philosophical learning itself. Even if it could be said that Gothic structures, more than Romanesque, demonstrated a 'Scholastic' respect for unity derived from diverse categories, the same could hardly be said for Gothic decorative designs. Gothic buildings, like the decorative modes of the contemporaneous metalwork, tapestry, illuminated manuscripts or secular stone-carving, were all, indeed, produced in response to the same taste of the élite within Western society – a taste which later became known as 'Gothic'. This, furthermore, was not a 'spirit of the age' at work, for the élite were too narrowly defined, and their judgment in aesthetic matters too subject to fashion and emulation, to indicate the pervasive presence of a more deeply laid intellectual scheme or outlook. The Gothic style spread from France and England

In every medieval town, the largest building was the church, rising above the rooftops with its gable and spires. This detail is the view seen through a window in a fifteenth-century altar-piece.

Opposite: the octagon of Ely Cathedral. In 1322 the Norman crossing tower fell down. Instead of rebuilding it, the abbey authorities decided to demolish what was left of the crossing piers and turn what had been a square into an octagon by building diagonal walls across the corners, and to cover it with an ornate glazed lantern of wood, through which light floods into the interior. This painting by Turner, Interior of Ely Cathedral, *dating from 1796 conveys the experience of being inside this unique space better than any photograph. On the right is the choir, rebuilt at the same time as the octagon; on the left, the first bay of the old Norman transept.*

147

Drawing for a window of Prague Cathedral by the master mason, Peter Parler, c. 1353. Our knowledge of the way a medieval architect set about designing a church is scanty, especially for the earlier period. From the fourteenth century onwards a number of drawings like this survive.

Opposite: design for the spire of Ulm Minster, Germany, by Matthäus Böblinger, 1482. Only half of it was actually built before work stopped. In the mid-nineteenth century Böblinger's drawing was rediscovered and the whole spire completed.

to the rest of the Western world because a relatively small number of abbots and bishops and civic dignitaries chanced to travel around, to admire new buildings, and to copy them at home.

The change to Gothic also coincided with the end of the great age of Christian expansion in Western Europe. The next was not to begin until the development of the Spanish and Portuguese colonial empires in the sixteenth century, the emergence of an independent United States of America in the eighteenth and nineteenth and finally the greatest of all expansions, the evangelization of Africa, largely in the twentieth. By the twelfth century Western Europe was almost entirely Christianized, and the northern invaders, indeed, had been absorbed so effectively that in the Norman achievements of the Romanesque style they had already made a great contribution to Christian civilization. In most countries the division into parochial districts was almost complete. More local variations in religious use, in terms of custom, patronage and ecclesiastical jurisdiction, existed by this time than is often realized; yet the general pattern of European unity was still well established. The lands were covered with a network of small churches, and at the main centres of Christian life were the great Romanesque cathedrals and Benedictine abbey churches. Increased wealth throughout society, and especially in the hands of corporate bodies and the emergent merchant classes, was beginning to make funds available for the rebuilding of church structures.

The arrival of the Gothic style coincided with their enterprise. There is a sense, indeed, in which Gothic is the style of emergent urban capitalism. The ecclesiastical dignitaries, the civic heads, and the noble patrons, who ordered the building of new cathedrals and churches to replace older ones destroyed by fire, or for some other reason, usually financed the operation very much in the way, for example, that the merchant adventurers of Venice were arranging their trading expeditions to the eastern Mediterranean in these same years. It was done, that is to say, with the help of bankers, with a system of shared liability, and with the acceptance of an element of risk. It is well known that Gothic cathedrals normally took anything up to a century to complete; but the reason did not lie in the painstaking craftsmanship or poor technical skills. The delay was caused by the original arrangements made for the financing of the venture coming apart through some accident of the market. Thus the ability of a city to build a cathedral did not really depend on its inherent wealth, but on its expertise with the available financial resources. Amiens, for example, was good at the matter, and Cologne was far less successful. Yet the first was a small city and the second large and economically very advanced. When the economies of most European countries went into recession, in the fourteenth century, the building and repair of the great cathedrals and abbeys, and of the humbler parish churches, went into decline; with the economic revival in the later fifteenth century, large-scale building projects, at central and at local level, resumed: the result was the Flamboyant style in France and the Perpendicular in England, both extremely expensive variations of Gothic because of their decorative qualities.

There has also been a strong current of thought, much assisted by Ruskin, that has found in the Gothic style a true communion between the inherent genius of the individual craftsman – stone-carver, mason, carpenter – and the labour of his hands. In Gothic, it has been contended, an authentic folk spirit is resident, and in a great Gothic building we see an expression of the noble dignity of inarticulate virtue. The contrast, of course, was with the supposedly depersonalized labour of industrial society. But this view, too, is difficult to maintain. Gothic cathedrals were not the work of a community, expressing in stone their collective

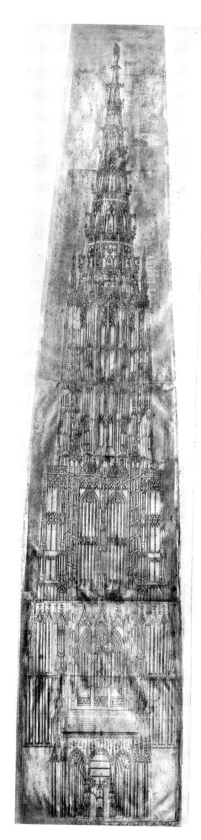

sense of religious identity. They were the work of individual building experts, many of whose names are still known to us. Some became wealthy and influential, and travelled around Europe tendering for jobs and, if successful, organizing professional work-forces – usually also itinerant – to carry them out. Sometimes they were organized into lodges, or professional clubs of skilled men. Even the decorative elements of Gothic, the mouldings, capitals, crockets, and so forth, were designed by professionals. This is a long way from the romanticized image, projected by Ruskin, and now commonly believed, of a simple craftsman

A French manuscript of 1448 casts useful light on building methods. The church on the right has been started at the east end, according to usual practice, and the chancel is finished and already in use. The nave is being constructed of brick faced with white stone, with the doorways (being carved in the foreground) in a darker stone.

149

Beauvais Cathedral (right) and Cologne (opposite) represent the culmination of the Ile de France Gothic which in many ways set the style for the rest of Europe. Beauvais was begun in 1247, Cologne in 1248. In both the architects aimed at extreme height and extreme lightness, every available surface being glazed. Beauvais, in fact, went too far; its high vault collapsed soon after it was built.

In England, the fourteenth century saw the emergence of the Perpendicular style, a variant of Gothic that had no equivalent in the rest of Europe. Above: Saffron Walden Church, Essex. Even more than ever before, lightness and openness seem to be the desired qualities, though with a corresponding loss of any sense of mystery.

expressing untutored genius through the skill of his unconscious art. Perhaps the most famous of the great master-builders were the Parler family, who came originally from Cologne, and one of whom built the great Gothic cathedral of Prague in the years after 1356. What is true of the major churches is almost certainly true also of the minor ones, though here documentary evidence is generally lacking. Parish churches, too, appear to have been very often the work of professional builders, who may, in some cases, be identified by peculiarities of detail.

Towards the end of the Middle Ages, and as the Gothic style passed into its later phases, this was especially notable. In most north European countries earlier churches were replaced by Gothic structures between the twelfth and the fifteenth centuries, and the astonishing uniformity of styles indicates not only the power of emulation but the widespread employment of professional builders. Churches, in fact, were built in much larger numbers than would have been required. Small villages put up enormous structures, which, even accounting for subsequent shifts of population, could never have been filled. Towns built churches almost side by side in staggering profusion. Here, too, is another key to understanding the extent of the spread of Gothic: churches were built in honour of the beliefs and aspirations of a society, not merely to provide shelter for worship, and the Gothic style happened to be in vogue when the increased wealth of a settled population allowed a more ambitious expression of those essential values. To afford the best craftsmen was a matter of local prestige. It has been estimated that in England, between a third and a half of the 11,000 churches listed as of architectural or historical importance are in the Perpendicular style – the later English version of Gothic – which, with its wide windows and delicate balances, most required professional builders.

The sketchbook of Villard de Honnecourt, compiled between 1220 and 1235, was at one time thought to contain working drawings of a practising architect. This now seems unlikely, but Villard, if not a professional, was certainly an informed amateur. This sketch shows the exterior and interior elevations of a large aisled church. On the left, the aisle wall with buttresses, then the aisle roof and then the clerestory. On the right, the main arcade looking through the arches into the aisle, then the gallery or triforium and finally the clerestory from inside.

These considerations ought not, however, to distract attention from the essentially religious nature of the Gothic style. But it is necessary to state that the religious inspiration was not an expression of any particular aspect of ecclesiastical organization or theological understanding, any more than the style represented, in itself, a particular political or social order. It was adopted because, like preceding styles, it acquired popularity with patrons and could be regarded as essentially Christian. Symbolism took a large part, as symbolism had always done. The desire to associate the geometric proportions of Gothic taste with Christian truth was no greater than the link, for example, made by the Early Fathers of the Church between numerical and spiritual categories. In the Gothic era, in fact, some symbolism of Romanesque structures was actually discarded. Transepts had evolved out of the *porticus*, but were later symbolically associated with the Cross of Christ; in the Gothic style, and especially in France, transepts tended to lose their independence and in some places scarcely extended beyond the lines of the aisle walls. But the principles of proportion were vital to Gothic structures. Architects and patrons devoted enormous energy to contriving exact geometric means of rendering in stone what they projected as the order and majesty of God. A Gothic church was intended to represent the mathematical perfection of the Creation.

Although the pointed arch was the first sign that an experiment in architecture was impending, it is not itself the chief feature of the Gothic style. Pointed arches had been constructed in Romanesque buildings in Sicily and in Burgundy. They were used, before that, in Islamic architecture in Spain. But as an obvious enhancement of the leading tendency of Gothic to point upwards, to evoke transcendence, the pointed arch had great utility. Height was very self-consciously sought; in France the vaults were occasionally suspended almost 150 feet above the naves. In England, by contrast, Gothic churches were longer, and not as high. The effects are quite different, but it is not clear that there was any ideological reason for the different emphases of the two countries, whose close political connexion, in the Plantagenet state, did not anyway encourage diversity. Everything about a great Gothic church was intended to point upwards. Internally, the lofty naves and pointed arches achieved this effect in two ways. Arcades were no longer punctures in the walls, but processions of slender columns rising up to triforia and to clerestory windows; the piers themselves were faced with groups of shafts or colonnettes, some of which, in the English tradition (though not the French) were made of coloured Purbeck marble. Capitals began to disappear, so that the grouped shafts rose directly up to the vaults. The whole building thus seems to strain upwards, in an almost organic progression from the earth to the sky – the plant motifs of much of the Gothic carving and ornament adding to the effect. Naves have sometimes been described as being like processional ways through a forest of trees.

The second main cause of the impression of transcendence is the light itself. Gothic buildings were intended to dematerialize in the sense that the larger windows, for which allowances were made by the buttresses and by the general engineering of the structure, filled the upper parts of the lofty naves with light. Unlike the relatively dark interiors of Romanesque churches, Gothic ones were from the start intended to use light itself as an essential ingredient of their spiritual message. As the style developed, the amount of glass increased, the stone supporting structure became more slender, so that eventually the Gothic church became a kind of skeleton of stone, with as much of the necessary supporting work hidden away as was possible. At its most daring this effect can be seen at the Sainte-Chapelle, built in Paris for St Louis in 1248, as a shrine to cover some

sacred relics of the Saviour's Passion. So much is glass, and so little seemingly stone, that the church has the appearance of a kind of enormous glazed bird cage. The use of light is not an accident of Gothic engineering skills. The effective founder of the new style, Abbot Suger, actually wrote about his intention of increasing luminosity.

But there must be a reservation here, as well. Coloured glass had been set into the narrow windows of some Romanesque churches; now, in the twelfth century, with the larger Gothic lancets, it was used more widely. The great screens of glass that eventually came to fill the walls of Gothic churches did not admit clear light, but brilliantly coloured light. In later developments of the Gothic, when windows were even larger – as in the English Perpendicular style – glass was less brilliantly coloured, and admitted more light: perhaps as an economy, since vignettes of coloured glass set in panels of clear glass are the least expensive way of filling the huge expanses which the large windows offered. The early and middle periods of Gothic, however, used rich and dark colours as important ingredients of the overall effect.

The Sainte-Chapelle, in Paris, was among the most lavish and expensive Gothic churches anywhere. It was built by Louis IX of France (St Louis) to house the Crown of Thorns, a relic he had bought from the emperor in Constantinople. Its sculpture, polychrome decoration and stained glass have survived largely intact.

Above left: two details from the glass of Chartres Cathedral showing scenes from the life of Christ: Noli Me Tangere and the Crucifixion.

The 'Jesse Window' of Dorchester-on-Thames Abbey, Oxfordshire. The genealogy of Christ, depicted as a tree growing from the body of Jesse, the father of David, is common enough in Christian art, but the idea of representing the branches of the tree as the tracery of a window is very rare.

There is a clue in this to the whole Gothic scheme, for the coloured glass was like the precious stones of the New Jerusalem, or, more immediately, like the rich encrustations of translucent stones and glass used in the decoration of shrines and reliquaries. There is a sense in which the Gothic church was the construction, on a massive scale, of a jewelled casket to house the treasures of spirituality. The effect of the coloured glass in a large cathedral can only have been general: a dazzling show of rich light for its own sake, for the glass was sometimes so dark as to render the interiors only slightly less dark than Romanesque buildings. It can never have been possible for the coloured glass of the clerestory windows to yield their narrative messages to the observers below. Yet in parish churches the coloured glass was used to convey the Christian view of the world in a manner which deliberately combined the astonishment of the people at the splendour or technique of the glass itself with doctrinal instruction.

Due to later destruction, through accident or for ideological reasons (both Protestant theological distaste and the lack of respect for Gothic art by men of the seventeenth and eighteenth centuries), not a great deal of early coloured glass survives. There are some well-known examples, like the 166 Biblical panels in the cathedral of Chartres, and the twelve windows of early thirteenth-century glass, showing the miracles of St Thomas Becket, at Canterbury Cathedral. St Mary's Church at Fairford, Gloucestershire (England), has a complete set of late medieval glass, put into the church around 1500. It is of extraordinary quality and very well preserved, with twenty-eight windows in all. The church itself is in the Perpendicular style, with large windows allowing a continuous narrative of the Biblical story, all depicted against an English background, so that the Temple of Jerusalem appears as a Gothic cathedral. The window of the Last Judgment (number XV) shows, at the centre, Christ in Majesty seated on a rainbow above a ruby-red earth, glowing in its last destruction. The dead rise from their graves and are directed towards their eternal rewards or punishments – some, at the behest of blue devils, are led into hell. The window is especially interesting, in the present context, for showing the oven in hell into which some of the lost are thrown; for it is the blast-furnace of a glassmaker's workshop, and beneath it is shown the mill in which the materials for making the glass were ground, with its cogs and wheels worked by a red devil with hair like flames and with yellow eyes. Priests must have brought their parishioners from miles around for occasional visits to the church, to be instructed in the awesome mysteries of the faith. The Fairford glass is almost certainly English, and not French, and as the parish was under royal patronage it is likely that the glassmakers of Westminster had some hand in the work.

Early Gothic windows had been narrow pointed arches. As the taste for coloured glass developed, and as windows expanded in size through the dematerialization of walls, stone tracery was developed to divide the windows and give them strength. Originally 'plate tracery' pierced the stone wall between two lancets, but before long 'bar tracery' was introduced – a stone fretwork which not only allowed great advances in the use of coloured glass for narrative purposes, but which also had a profound effect on Gothic decoration in general. From the windows the tracery spread to the rest of the church – to screens, blind arches, vaults, canopies, and tombs. Sometimes the tracery of windows could be of extraordinary complexity, and occasionally, as at the abbey church of Dorchester-on-Thames in England, it incorporated stone sculpture. The windows of the sanctuary in this church are in the Decorated style of English Gothic and show the Biblical scheme of Redemption. The 'Jesse Window' on the north side has stone tracery depicting the stem and branches of the tree of Jesse, on which stand the sacred figures of the prophets and kings of the Old Testament,

The roof of St Peter and St Paul, in Knapton, Norfolk, seems to flutter with angels' wings. The image of heaven above our heads, ready to receive the blessed after death, had never been so vividly or so simply stated.

Jesse himself, a mutilated Virgin and Child, and the Magi bearing their gifts. The glass of the window is a confused reconstruction from diverse fragments.

One of the most characteristic features of the Gothic style is the ribbed vault – stone roofs supported by prominent intersecting arches. It was almost certainly the technical developments – including the addition of external buttresses, which led to the ribbed vaults – that allowed the walls of churches to lose their Romanesque mass, rather than predetermined aspirations about the vaulting itself which led to the design of the walls. But whatever the order, the result was the seeming miracle of the Gothic vault: a great weight of stone held up, high above the church, by slender piers whose own grace and diminishing substance is emphasized by the clustered shafts that encompass them. Ribbed vaulting appeared at about the same time, around 1100, in both England and France, as a natural development of the Romanesque style. Like the pointed arch, therefore, it seems that its incorporation as an essential of Gothic came from within existing architectural ideas, and was a development rather than an external infusion. By the second half of the twelfth century the ribbed vault had spread to many other parts of Europe. Generally stone vaults were a feature of the cathedrals and great abbey churches; in parish churches, where the cheaper wooden roofs were still usual, stone vaults were sometimes found in porches which had upper chambers – as in the later Gothic 'wool churches' of the wealthy parts of England, where available stone and money from the cloth trade provided the means, even on a small scale, for the extravagance of stone roofing.

Wooden roofs, however, could achieve astonishing effects and their construction, as in the hammerbeam roofs, displayed sophisticated technical knowledge about stress and plasticity in materials. In some places, especially in England, wooden roofs were decorated with gilded carvings of angels, intended to represent the permanent witness of the hosts of heaven to the sanctity and mystery of the rites in the church below. A splendid example is the fourteenth-century church of St Peter and St Paul at Knapton in Norfolk. Here the roof is over 70 feet long, and was built in 1503 of Irish oak. The roof was restored in the 1880s by Gilbert Scott, and the lowest rank of angels is modern, their extended wings, shown as though in flight, clearly inspired by the double hammerbeam roof, built in 1500, at St Wendreda at March in Cambridgeshire.

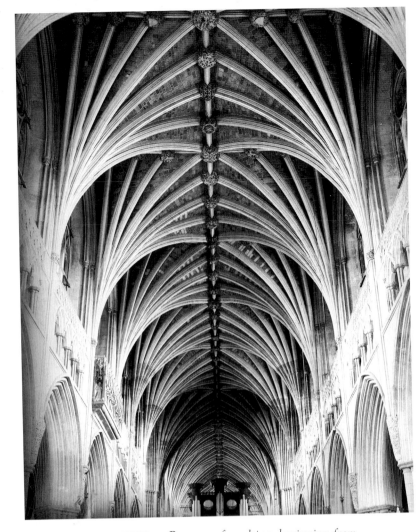

Patterns of vaulting, beginning from structural premises, became one of the major elements in the aesthetic of the Gothic style and in the emotional impact that it makes on the spectator. And it seems to be no mere figment of the romantic imagination to see stone vaults as having a particularly religious character. Hardly any secular buildings had them. Here are shown a handful of the immense number of variants. Above left: Notre-Dame, Paris, with in the nearest bay sexpartite vaults, a form which preceded the more usual quadripartite. Above: Exeter Cathedral – an early tierceron vault, a step towards purely decorative patterning. Left: Schwäbisch Gmünd, a late example, the ribs no longer even pretending to have a function.

Above: King's College Chapel, Cambridge, showing the last great innovation of English Gothic, fan vaulting. Right: the choir of Prague Cathedral, by Peter Parler. Below: Lübeck parish church, Germany, a 'star' vault of the early fifteenth century.

The Crusader church of St Anne, in Jerusalem. Built in a simple, early French Gothic style, it has the unusual feature of a dome over the crossing.

The stone-ribbed vaults of Gothic churches were sometimes decorated with carved bosses. These were highly coloured, and many still are today, though the painting is inevitably a modern restoration. An example is the fifteenth-century ribbed vault of the nave of Norwich Cathedral. The 225 bosses, like the glass of Gothic windows, recount the Biblical story of the creation and redemption of humanity. They have great folk charm, especially the depictions of Noah and his family looking out from the ark, surrounded by patient animals; of a stone-mason constructing a pier; of three lost souls gazing wistfully out of the jaws of hell. Not all Gothic ribbed vaulting was as graceful or as ornamental as this. Gothic roofs could be ruggedly massive, almost Romanesque in their bulk and weight.

The structures put up in the Holy Land by the Crusaders sometimes showed Gothic in this manner: light was less important, insulation against the great heat a greater priority. Crusader churches have an austerity and mass that, while true to all the tenets of classic French Gothic, form a distinct type. The crypt of St John at the coastal city of Acre has a roof supported by enormous columns. These rise from the central space of the chamber to a heavy ribbed vault. All the Christian buildings of the city – which had been the last to fall to Islam, in 1291, with the fall of the Latin Kingdom – were dismantled by the Ottomans in the sixteenth century, and the crypt was only recently rediscovered, amazingly intact, beneath the ruins of the Turkish fortress. Originally thought to be the crypt of a chapel of the Hospitallers, it is now regarded as a dining hall: Gothic crypts, rare in Europe, were, however, built in the Holy Land following the local custom of subterranean dwelling in the summer months. The Crusader church of St Anne in Jerusalem has a crypt, but it is not Gothic. The church was built over the shrine marking the traditional birthplace of the Virgin, and the crypt derived from earlier churches on the site. The Crusader church above is widely recognized as the most splendid of all the Gothic structures of the old Latin Kingdom. It has three aisles, each leading to an apse, and a transept. There is also a dome. Gothic domes usually contained Italian features, but the dome of St Anne's is not Italianate; it is without a drum, and is set with windows to light the interior. The entire building, despite its massive qualities, has a simple austerity which suggests a sort of grace. The roof of the nave is of groin vaulting outlined in white stones.

So characteristic of the Gothic style is this type of stone vaulting that it was carried to the New World by the Spanish conquerors. The ecclesiastical architecture of Spanish America is overwhelmingly Neo-classical and Baroque, but there are a few extraordinary examples of late Gothic vaulting. The church of S. José in San Juan, Puerto Rico, has a series of vaulted ceilings designed by the Dominican friars who built the church in 1532. The original cathedral of San Juan was built in 1520 and destroyed in a hurricane; the building which replaced it in 1540 has four chambers with ribbed Gothic stone vaulting.

If the architecture of the Holy Land and the late Gothic of Latin America showed an austere and simplified version of the style, it was nevertheless the religious orders in Europe who first pioneered an unadorned form. The Benedictines had been early promoters of the Gothic style in England and France. In England, in fact, the unique relationship between Benedictine monasticism and the cathedral establishments, where the abbey church and the cathedral were the same building – as at Canterbury, Ely, Durham, Norwich, Winchester, and elsewhere – had lasting consequences for cathedral styles in general.

But it was the reformed orders, and particularly the Cistercians and the mendicant orders, the Dominicans and the Franciscans, who in the thirteenth century began to strip Gothic of the excess of ornament that had by then appeared, in order to create a church style suggestive of the vocation of poverty.

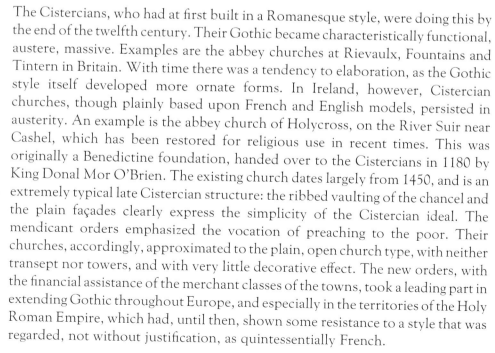

Many abbeys and priories, though ruined, have escaped later alteration and preserve a powerful atmosphere of their original purpose. Left: Rievaulx Abbey, Yorkshire, a Cistercian foundation built in the thirteenth century. The Cistercian movement aimed to purge monasticism of the luxury that had begun to compromise its ideals. In Ireland the abbey of Holycross (above) has been restored and is now occupied again by monks. The chancel, seen here with its fine reticulated window, dates from the fifteenth century.

The Cistercians, who had at first built in a Romanesque style, were doing this by the end of the twelfth century. Their Gothic became characteristically functional, austere, massive. Examples are the abbey churches at Rievaulx, Fountains and Tintern in Britain. With time there was a tendency to elaboration, as the Gothic style itself developed more ornate forms. In Ireland, however, Cistercian churches, though plainly based upon French and English models, persisted in austerity. An example is the abbey church of Holycross, on the River Suir near Cashel, which has been restored for religious use in recent times. This was originally a Benedictine foundation, handed over to the Cistercians in 1180 by King Donal Mor O'Brien. The existing church dates largely from 1450, and is an extremely typical late Cistercian structure: the ribbed vaulting of the chancel and the plain façades clearly express the simplicity of the Cistercian ideal. The mendicant orders emphasized the vocation of preaching to the poor. Their churches, accordingly, approximated to the plain, open church type, with neither transept nor towers, and with very little decorative effect. The new orders, with the financial assistance of the merchant classes of the towns, took a leading part in extending Gothic throughout Europe, and especially in the territories of the Holy Roman Empire, which had, until then, shown some resistance to a style that was regarded, not without justification, as quintessentially French.

Gothic spires. Limburg-an-der-Lahn, in Germany (above) is still close to Romanesque in its proportions, but Freiburg-im-Breisgau (above right) soars transparently upward in the manner of Ulm (p. 149). Below: the humble wooden spire of St Giles at Ickenham, Middlesex, added to an earlier church in the fifteenth century.

The interior of Gothic churches strained upwards: the diaphanous walls, the soaring clusters of columns, the floating vault above. But the exteriors of churches were intended to produce the same impression of height and transcendence. The effect of light, in contriving this, was less reliable than within, however: the mystery and brilliance of the jewelled coloured glass could not help here, and even the pointed arches of the windows pointed less obviously to the heavens when viewed from without. Instead, the Gothic builders depended for the upward movement of their structures on buttresses and pinnacles, and above all on towers.

A tower was a feature which could elevate the spirit towards the celestial realms even in a humble parish church, where soaring vaults were too costly for the resources of the parishioners and patron. It is important to realize that the function of Gothic towers as belfries was entirely secondary. They were essentially decorative and symbolic. Like the obelisks of ancient Egypt – which were adopted by the Popes for that very reason, and dispersed by them throughout Rome – the towers were monumental structures which pointed to the heavens. The Gothic development of the spire showed this most obviously: spires clearly have no structural function. In Ireland, where Gothic churches were sometimes built to replace older buildings on Celtic monastic sites, the existing round-tower belfries, still intact and functioning at the time, were retained and towers added to the new buildings for purely decorative purposes. This was the case, as may still plainly be seen, at St Brigid's Cathedral in Kildare. Here the round-tower belfry (of perhaps the eleventh century), with a Romanesque doorway, stands beside the cathedral, a building of the mid-thirteenth century (extensively repaired in the mid-fifteenth) which replaced the earlier, and notably large, cathedral founded in honour of St Brigid and her nuns. Cruciform in shape and in the Early English Gothic style, the central tower has solid qualities, topped, during the restoration by George Edmund Street (between 1875 and 1896) by the Irish-Norse stepped battlements which also, around the same time, replaced the original conical top of the round-tower. Where a church could not afford a tower, small belfries were often added to a gable or roof. The former is common in France: a good example is the small Chapelle Notre-Dame de Rocamadour in the Breton town of Camaret-sur-Mer. The latter is common in England: at the fourteenth-century village church of St Giles at Ickenham, in Middlesex, the bell-turret was added in the fifteenth century to the west end of the nave roof.

Gothic towers sometimes displayed massive qualities. When authentic French Gothic styles began to penetrate German territory, a certain Romanesque massivity also somehow persisted. This is clear in the cathedral of Limburg, built between 1211 and 1235, whose several towers and spires surmount a hill above the River Lahn in a dramatic gesture of Gothic triumphalism. Yet although unquestionably Gothic, and owing much to the cathedral of Laon, the twilight of the Romanesque still seems to flicker across the outline and general shapes of the building. The enormous range within the development of the Gothic style is seen at Freiburg-im-Breisgau, where the delicate tracery of the spire, dating from the thirteenth century, has ethereal, insubstantial qualities. In Scotland, similarly, there is a huge contrast between the western towers of St Machar's Cathedral in Old Aberdeen, of the fourteenth century, with their solid stability (though owing much to restoration), their battlemented appearance, and their short spires, and the elaborate crown spire of St Giles Cathedral in Edinburgh, of the fifteenth century, looking brittle and almost metallic in its structure. English spires were

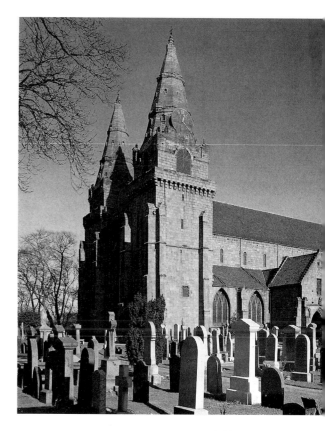

Above right: the three spires of Lichfield Cathedral, Staffordshire. Multiple spires were very often intended for Gothic cathedrals but few of them achieved more than two.

Scottish contrasts. The spire of St Giles Cathedral, Edinburgh (right), is one of a handful of late Gothic examples shaped like a crown. Far right: the squat and solid spires of St Machar's, Aberdeen.

graceful and slender, as at the cathedrals of Norwich and Salisbury, or the triple spires of Lichfield. Irish Gothic towers, like some of the Scottish ones, had a fortified appearance caused by the use, in both countries, of stepped battlements. Most famous of these, and rightly so, is the tower of St Patrick's Cathedral in Dublin, built by Archbishop Minot following a great fire in 1362. It rises 150 feet, and is topped by a spire, 101 feet in height, added in 1749.

Towers and spires were undoubtedly the largest and most extravagant of Gothic decorative effects. Something must also be said, however, about Gothic sculpted ornament, and especially about the employment of organic images in tracery and elsewhere. As plants grow upwards to the light, so the perfect decorative device of a Gothic building, with its upwards thrust, is foliage. This began to be used extensively in carving in the thirteenth century, when buildings almost seemed to come alive with the entwined vegetable and animal carvings. The effect is at once both spiritualizing and earthy. The ordinary and familiar world of nature is transformed into an ascending ladder as the decorative mouldings and capitals direct the gaze upwards; at the same time the writhing masses of interlaced vegetation are touched by a primitive, almost pagan symbolism. The figure of the 'green man' of the forests often appears in Gothic carving: a frank survival from a half-remembered world of pagan mythology,

There is an affinity between the Gothic style and the forms of nature which made foliage carving, from the very beginning, a specially appropriate ornament for the architecture. In England foliage reached its most inventive and naturalistic peak around the year 1300. Above: roof boss from the cloister of Norwich Cathedral, a head showing through leaves like the 'green man' of popular rustic myth. Right: the stylized leaves of early French Gothic, Reims, c. 1240.

Opposite: 'the leaves of Southwell', capitals in the vestibule to the chapter house of Southwell Minster, Nottinghamshire, where the English sculptors achieved the perfect balance between artistic convention and natural observation. Here the plants are hawthorn, maple and buttercup.

found in some representation or other throughout the whole of the European world. In some sense the foliated images of Gothic decoration remind us that, beneath the surface, the descendants of the barbarian invaders of Europe retained elements of their pagan heritage. In another sense, they speak of the transfiguration of the natural world by Christian truth, a demonstration of the worship of God by all living things in a riotous display of natural vitality.

Perhaps the most celebrated of the foliage carvings are the capitals and gables of the chapter house and entrance passage at Southwell Minster in the English Midlands. These date from around 1300, and consist of numerous variations of the leaves of oak, hop, vine, ivy, maple, buttercup, and others, all treated with a crisp realism, and attaining a surprising symmetry in their overall effect. The Lady Chapel at Ely Cathedral, similarly, has splendid (but alas mutilated) carvings of seaweed and leaves, set among the pinnacles of the gables and ogee arches of the wall arcading. The work here was done in 1321. The addition of Lady Chapels to churches in the later years of the thirteenth century, and in the first half of the fourteenth century, indicated an increasing devotion to the Virgin. Their decoration offered great scope to Gothic craftsmen in their most elaborate years of development.

Sta Maria della Spina (Our Lady of the Thorn) stands like a jewel-box on the river bank at Pisa. It was built in 1323 as a shrine for a thorn from the Crown of Thorns. In the elaborate tabernacles that surround the roof on all sides are statues of saints by sculptors of the Pisan school such as Nino Pisano.

Chancel screens and rood lofts also began their popularity at this time, and attained their greatest phase in the fifteenth century. These, too, became the occasion, even in the simplest parish churches (where the work was in wood rather than in stone) for the display of elaborate tracery and naturalistic carvings of foliage. The purpose of the chancel screens was similar to that of the iconostasis in an Orthodox church: it was to separate the mysteries of the sanctuary and choir from the place of assembly – the nave – where non-religious communal activities sometimes occurred.

Gothic decoration is probably seen in its most concentrated expression in the little church of Sta Maria della Spina (Our Lady of the Thorn) on the banks of the River Arno in Pisa. It is a Gothic gem, with two gables at one end and three small spires at the other; the whole rich with Tuscan polychrome marble decoration. The church was reconstructed in the Gothic style in 1323. Its external walls (which support a wooden roof) are a forest of pinnacles and sculpture, giving the little structure, indeed, the appearance of a reliquary.

What will have emerged from this description of the leading characteristics of the Gothic style is the great diversity that existed within it. There were also, of course, chronological developments, which have now to be outlined, and the evolution of regional variations. That it is in origin a French style need scarcely be said; that it was also the work of individuals of genius (rather than the more diffuse emanation of a communal sense) requires some emphasis. First, in his work on the cathedral of Sens, between 1130 and 1164, Henri Sanglier reduced the size of the transept, produced a three-storey nave whose arcades were beginning to show a reduction of massive bulk, and employed ribbed vaulting. Second, and more significantly, Abbot Suger's reconstructions at the Benedictine church of St-Denis near Paris, between 1140 and 1144, introduced the essential ingredient of Gothic: his ambulatory in the *chevet* of the church had vaults supported by slender columns. His purpose, as he explained in his own account of the work, was to increase the interior light of the building, and he used coloured glass, also, to achieve his effect. It was the beginning of true Gothic, the replacement of the heavy walls of the Romanesque, with the lighter structures which allowed the penetration of the church by filtered luminosity. Because St-Denis was the burial place of the Capetian dynasty, innovative work done here was bound to be emulated elsewhere; and as an enormous amount of ecclesiastical reconstruction took place in the rich basin of the Ile de France in the second half of the twelfth century, the example of St-Denis was rapidly copied.

In the great cathedrals that followed, and especially at Noyon, Laon, and Notre-Dame in Paris, there was something like a competition to increase the height, to raise the ribbed vaults ever more spectacularly above the naves. Choirs were lengthened, to accommodate the contemporaneous increase in the size of cathedral chapters; transepts either disappeared altogether (as at Senlis) or were left as minor residual appendages (as originally at Notre-Dame). The nave of Notre-Dame rose to 112 feet. At Laon, a cathedral which exercised a particularly strong influence on the styles of others, the five towers dissolve at the upper levels into colonnetted honeycombs, through which the light penetrates, giving the impression not only of upward thrust but of immateriality. These towers were completed in the 1220s. Notre-Dame in Paris was also widely copied. It was started in 1163, and it was at first supposed that the increased height of the building could be supported by wall piers sited within the structure of the roof. This was, on later reflection, thought to be insufficient, and flying buttresses were

The east end of the abbey of St-Denis was rebuilt by Abbot Suger between 1140 and 1144. Here the Gothic style came fully into its own. The upper parts were rebuilt in the later Middle Ages but the arches and the aisles with their vaults remain intact. The windows were once filled with stained glass embodying Suger's mystical philosophy of light and colour.

added to the outside in 1182. It was the first use of flying buttresses, which were to become such a Gothic trade-mark, on this scale. Between 1250 and 1270 the transept was extended, and enormous rose windows built on the end walls of each arm.

By the very end of the twelfth century 'High Gothic' had already developed in France, and its leading monument was unquestionably the cathedral of Chartres. The old Romanesque structure here was destroyed by fire in 1194. A miraculous survivor of the flames was a relic of the Virgin which had made the small city a pilgrimage centre; the city was also the home for a number of trading enterprises, and so Chartres was possessed of enough wealth, and sufficient financial knowledge, to plan a grand successor to the old cathedral. The choir and nave were completed by 1220, and by 1230 a transept had been added. The three storeys of the interior elevation were each of equal height, thus contributing to the effect of upward tension; the flying buttresses outside were patterned with a kind of arcading; seven towers were planned (though in the event only two were ever built). The glass, which is still such a feature of the building, was probably no more splendid than that in other contemporaneous French cathedrals, but it has survived, where other examples have not, and so may still bear witness to the extraordinary quality of French expertise in stained-glass techniques. Chartres

Above: Notre-Dame, Paris, the east end and the façade of the south transept. The east end, begun in 1163, is a clear demonstration of the way flying buttresses lean against the walls at crucial points to support the heavy vaults inside. The transepts belong to a later phase of building (1250–70) characterized by elaborate radiating tracery, and known as the Rayonnant style.

Opposite: the west front of Laon Cathedral, northern France. Although the twin-towered façade became standard in French Gothic, no two examples are the same. That of Laon has no parallel in the way it plays with depth and angularity. Most extraordinary of all are the tabernacles set diagonally to the corners from which peer the unexpected faces of oxen, a memorial to the beasts who had dragged the masonry blocks to the site.

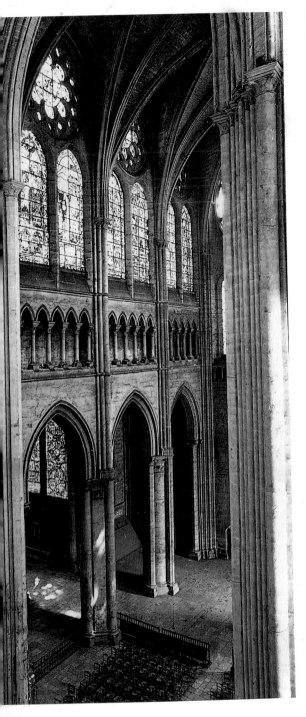

influenced a generation of ecclesiastical structures, among them the great cathedrals of Reims and Amiens, both begun in the first decades of the thirteenth century.

Height, again, was a major preoccupation of High Gothic. The vault at Chartres reached 125 feet; at Reims it is 131 feet and at Amiens 138 feet. The cathedral at Beauvais, the last great building directly inspired by Chartres, and constructed between 1225 and 1272, had a vault which soared to 144 feet, resting on slender piers. But aspirations were ahead of technology. In 1284 the vault collapsed, and it took forty years to repair the damage. Romanesque buildings were always collapsing; Gothic ones had a better record, but it is still as well to realize that, despite the often astonishing skills of their technicians, less was understood about stress and tension in materials by Gothic builders than is sometimes assumed.

The cathedral at Rouen was rebuilt after a fire in 1200. The new structure was

Amiens (above and right) and Reims (opposite), both under construction throughout most of the thirteenth century, represent the classic high point of early Gothic. The precise and satisfying logic of their structure has tempted historians to draw parallels between Gothic architecture and scholastic philosophy. Just as the axioms, syllogisms and distinctions of the Summa Theologica fit inexorably together to prove God's existence, so the piers, shafts, vaulting ribs and flying buttresses of the cathedrals seem with similar inevitability to demonstrate his glory.

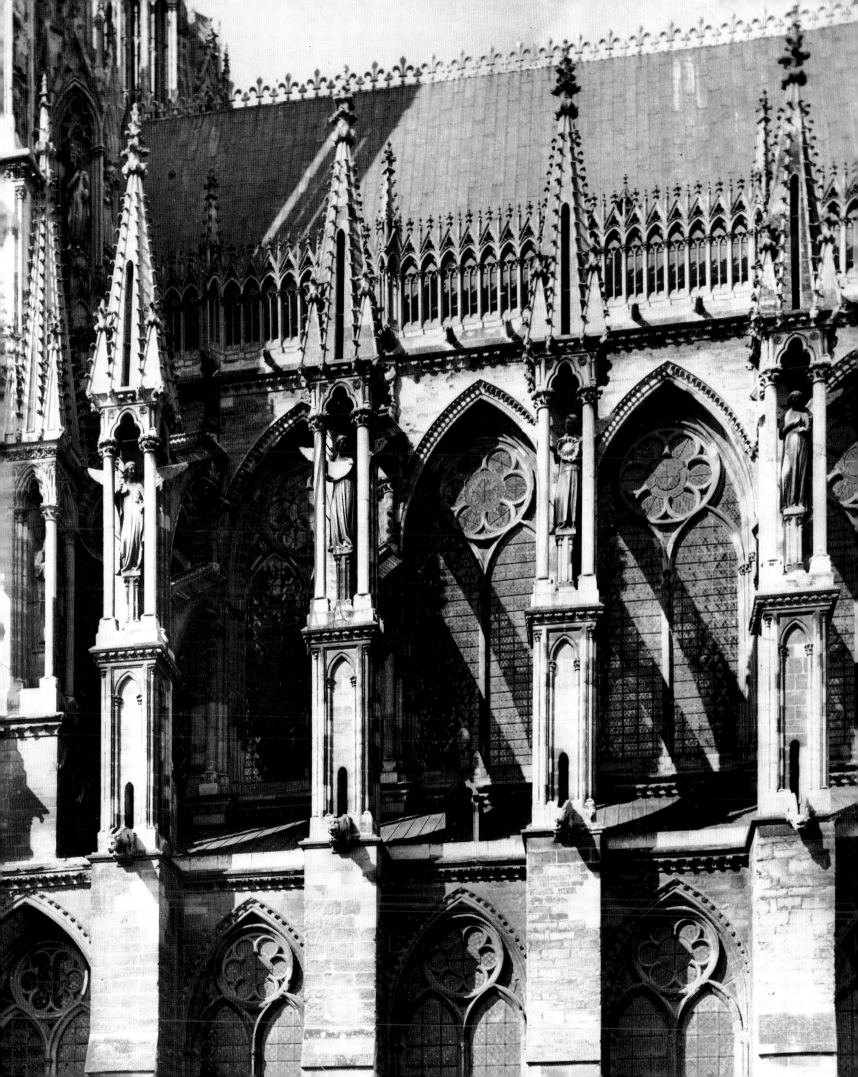

The nave of Strasbourg Cathedral is another contemporary of Amiens and Reims, though its proportions are lower because it had to conform to the Romanesque choir and transepts.

the work of Jean d'Andely, in a – by then – conventional Gothic style. The transept at Rouen, however, reflected the influence of a new development. Around 1230 what came to be known as the *Rayonnant* style began to appear, first, perhaps, in the reconstruction of the Benedictine church of St-Denis (completed in 1281). The leading characteristic of this phase was further dematerialization, the extension of windows as glass screens between the church and the world, the continued dissolution of walls. Strasbourg Cathedral, built between 1237 and 1276, became something of a model for other religious buildings in the Rayonnant mode. Because, for economy, the foundations of the Ottonian cathedral were preserved, the new cathedral was wider than most French ones in the Gothic style. Flying buttresses of great sophistication were designed to guarantee the additional weight of the vaults. The last phase of French Gothic, developed in the fourteenth century, is usually called the *Flamboyant* style, because its characteristic extravagances of tracery and pinnacles are thought to suggest the upward leap of flames. Like its predecessors, it soon spread to other parts of Europe, and, outside France, it was often characterized by an aisleless type of church building. Towers in the Flamboyant style were particularly intricate, like the north-west spire of Chartres Cathedral, added in 1507.

The country closest to France in the evolution of the Gothic style – a consequence of close political connexion, at least in the early and more formative years of Gothic – was England. In England, however, there were some important innovations, and here it has been conventional to divide the Gothic phases into three: the 'lancet' or 'Early English' style, nearest to early French Gothic; the 'Decorated' style, with parallels to, but really separate from, the Rayonnant; and the 'Perpendicular' style, a later English development with no discernible external equivalent. It was the reconstruction of Canterbury Cathedral, following the fire of 1174, which brought French Gothic to England. The architect was a Frenchman, William of Sens, and he had completed most of the choir before an accident (he fell from the scaffolding). His successor, William the Englishman, redirected the work. It remains the most striking as well as the most emulated importation of the early French Gothic into England.

In the last decades of the twelfth century it was the Cistercian orders who perhaps did most to spread the Gothic style in England, yet it was the great cathedrals, often with their Benedictine association, which are the chief glory of the Gothic in England. Almost at once English features – the use of Purbeck marble and vaults with ridge-ribs – began to appear, as in the choir of Lincoln Cathedral, begun in 1192, and the west end of Peterborough Cathedral, started in 1190. In no case, however, do English variations of the Gothic appear to reflect local political, social, cultural or economic conditions. They were what they seem to be: developments of a style for its own sake, to produce work which would be admired and copied by others (as it was), and which would bear witness to God's glory. Early in the thirteenth century, from 1230 to 1240, the west front of Wells Cathedral was built. It marked one of the most successful of the English innovations – the construction of an entire façade as a vast screen to contain statues of the saints. About half of the original 340 figures still survive. Similar west fronts were built at Exeter and Salisbury; and at Peterborough the façade was divided into three colossal pointed arches, with the rows of statues placed above them.

The English cathedral nearest in spirit to the Rayonnant style was Westminster Abbey, as reconstructed by Henry of Reynes in the mid-thirteenth century. Like the French originals, the nave aimed at narrow height – in contrast to the English liking for wider and longer churches. York is the greatest

French influence on English Gothic architecture came in two waves, exemplified by Canterbury (above) and Westminster (above left). The choir of Canterbury Cathdral was rebuilt after a fire by a French architect, William of Sens, between 1174 and 1185. Its sexpartite vaults are the most obvious French features. Seventy years later Westminster Abbey was designed, probably by another Frenchman, borrowing many of the characteristics of Reims.

The west front of Wells Cathedral (left) owes nothing to France. Built in the mid-thirteenth century (the towers were added later), it is a giant screen for exhibiting sculpture, but without the unity and dynamic energy of Reims or Amiens.

At the very end of the fifteenth century a 'New Building' was added to the Romanesque abbey church of Peterborough. It took the form of a retrochoir or enlarged ambulatory encircling the old choir, and made use of the fashionable fan vaulting that we have already encountered at King's College, Cambridge (p. 157). By now the ribs have lost all functional justification and are merely decorative patterns.

representation of the English Decorated style; the nave was begun in 1291 and the choir in 1361. The nave of Exeter Cathedral (started around 1310), another great example of the Decorated style, has a massive vault which, almost more than any other, suggests the tree-like nature of mature Gothic decoration.

Some have found the last phase of English Gothic, the Perpendicular, almost dehumanizing in its cage-like symmetry. It in fact reaches the maximization of the balance of glass over stone in the walls of church buildings, and the result is an infusion of lightness and space. There is a certain austerity about the style, perhaps in reaction to the contemporaneous French Flamboyant modes. There is also a mechanical quality about it, a repetition of decorative effects and a flatness of the wall surfaces. The best surviving examples are the choir of Gloucester Cathedral (1337–1350), where a Perpendicular stone cladding was applied to the eleventh-century walls, which remain concealed behind, and the nave of Canterbury Cathedral, designed by Henry Yevele (1379–1405). King's College Chapel, in Cambridge, is famous for the splendour and scale of its fan vaulting – another Perpendicular invention. Here the vaults were designed by John Wastell and built between 1508 and 1515. As in other Perpendicular buildings, the huge though delicate mass of vault seems to be supported by almost nothing but glass, so large are the windows and so narrow the piers of the external walls. The enormous buttresses, necessary for this effect, are disguised at base as chapels. Smaller in scale, but no less striking, are Wastell's fan vaults (1496–1508) in the 'New Building' at the east end of Peterborough Cathedral. The final development of those vaults, and the culmination of the English Gothic style, came with the pendant vaults, seen, perhaps, in their most perfect form at St George's Chapel in Windsor.

National variants of the Gothic style do not, elsewhere in Europe, really disclose *national* characteristics as such: they are, again, articulations and developments of style, not reflections of currents of opinion within either Church or State. Very few Gothic features anywhere can be attributed, for example, to changes in liturgical use, or to differences or shifts in the understanding of the Christian religion itself. Where a particular version of Gothic was adapted or developed by a court or a social class it did not really represent a 'court' style, and so forth, in the sense that the Gothic itself reflected features of the court or its aspirations, or disclosed in stone and glass something of its values. It showed, on the contrary, that style and fashion were related, and that Gothic was adopted because it had elsewhere acted adequately as the vehicle of the prestige of authoritative bodies, and was the style, among available historical styles, that in their day most seemed to offer honour to God and to express his glory. The very internationalism of Gothic, despite the regional and national variations, bears witness to its compatibility with very different ideals of government and understandings of Christianity. For beneath the universal aspirations of medieval society, enormous variations existed in particular countries. Gothic was adopted in them all.

Gothic was not really accepted in Germany until the 1230s, almost a century after its genesis in France. It was thus adopted in a mature form. The use of brick construction, both in the main church building and in the vaults, was, as in Scandinavia and Italy, quite common. The French pursuit of height was demonstrated most dramatically in the choir at Cologne Cathedral, begun in 1248, on the model of Amiens. Here the vaults eventually reached 141 feet above the ground; but the choir was the only part of this ambitious scheme to be put up in the Middle Ages. The rest of the structure was completed, on the basis of the original designs, in the nineteenth century.

In Italy, the Gothic style had many different local expressions. 'Venetian Gothic' specialized in brick, with enormous blank walls, as at the Dominican church of SS. Giovanni e Paolo, begun in 1246, and the Frari church, built between 1250 and 1443. In both cases the expanse of brick is offset by round windows, and in both cases, also, the gable at the west end is topped by three small perforated spires. Similar in its blank brick elevation to the two Venetian churches is the church of S. Domenico in Siena (dating from the fourteenth and fifteenth centuries); here the massive size of the building serves to emphasize, and to give a strange grandeur, to the absence of external decoration. The Franciscan preference for unobstructed churches was, in Italy, represented by the churches of S. Francesco at Assisi itself, and at Bologna, both dating from the mid-thirteenth century.

Florentine Gothic, like its Romanesque predecessor, showed a disposition to incorporate polychrome marble panels and horizontal banding, which the citizens, ever conscious of their classical predecessors, supposed a fitting witness to their continuity with the splendour and prestige of the Roman past. The Dominican church of Sta Maria Novella, begun in 1279, has polychrome rib vaults: we are further here from the French origins of Gothic than anywhere. The Duomo of Florence, begun in 1296 by Arnolfo di Cambio, has walls both internally and externally rich in marble panels, and a campanile, designed by Giotto (1334) in the same marble polychrome fashion. The audacious octagonal dome, which dominates the skyline of the city, and was intended to, is like nothing else in Gothic architecture: the dome had originally featured in the 1366 plans for the cathedral, but the techniques available at the time were not adequate to cover so large an area, and it was not until the fifteenth century that Brunelleschi's masterpiece solved the problem. It may not, as has now become apparent, have solved it for good. Recently discovered cracks, and the 'laddering' of the dome upwards from its base, have now elicited fears about the stability of the entire structure.

The cathedral of Siena, which belongs to the same family as Florentine Gothic, was in fact a not entirely successful adaptation, begun in 1226, of a

Italian Gothic evolved no consistent style. The brick façade of the Frari church, in Venice (above left), is Gothic only in its decoration, e.g. the portal. Milan Cathedral (above) uses forms from north of the Alps but its proportions have no parallel there; its west front was not completed until 1858 and incorporates classical windows.

At Assisi, the Upper Church, built in the thirty years following St Francis's death in 1226, has none of the soaring height of northern Gothic. It relies on painted decoration, including frescos by the school of Giotto.

Siena Cathedral is a picturesque hybrid of Gothic and Romanesque forms, made memorable by its domed hexagonal crossing and its use of striped coloured marble. It was begun in 1226. Towards the left is the famous pulpit by Giovanni Pisano.

Romanesque building to contemporary taste. It is a mass of dizzy banding and polychrome marble. The cathedral of Milan, on the other hand, is the best known and perhaps the most successful of the Italian versions of French Gothic. Started in 1387 according to the designs of Simone da Orsenigo, and built in several stages amidst intense discussion of its style, Milan Cathedral does not display many Italian features. Its richly ornamental and pinnacled exterior, in pink and white marble, owes as much to the nineteenth-century finish (it was eventually completed in 1858) as it does to the original scheme.

Gothic in Spain coincided with the reconquest of the peninsula from the Moorish occupation. This meant not only that a lot of Gothic churches were built but that they have distinctively triumphalist qualities. The great thirteenth-century cathedrals of Burgos, Toledo and León reflected the French Rayonnant style, though the first two retained hints both of surviving Romanesque and of Islamic art. The political and commercial success of Catalonia in the fourteenth century allowed the financing of some Gothic churches of extraordinary quality – like the cathedral of Barcelona, which has the spaciousness of an open, unobstructed church, and the superb church of Sta Maria del Mar, also in Barcelona (begun in 1328), with its lofty vaults and slender supporting piers. The fifteenth century in Spain was dominated by the late Gothic style known, after Isabella of Castile, as 'Isabelline'. Its monumental characteristics were nevertheless typically Spanish in their eclecticism. The great cathedral of Seville, started in 1401 by pulling down the mosque which occupied the site – but leaving the tower to serve as a campanile – is the largest Gothic church in the world. The influence of the French Flamboyant style is clear, and the international team of craftsmen and decorators who worked on the structure have all left distinctive elements of the many European versions of Gothic. It is a self-conscious, and enormous, essay in grandeur. As the most dramatic tower in Spanish Gothic, the cathedral of Saragossa, built between 1505 and 1520, displays astonishing intricacy.

Portugal's later version of Gothic surpassed all others in its extensive use of decoration. What became known as the 'Manueline style', after King Manuel of Portugal, started to make its appearance at the end of the fifteenth century. Though obviously owing something to the Flamboyant, its originality lay not in any structural development but in ornamental richness. Entwined fronds of seaweed, recalling Portugal's maritime enterprise, and barley-sugar and rope-like columns, cluster around archways and gables in a controlled profusion of elaborate stone carving. At its most extensive, in the Dominican church of Our Lady of Victories at Batalha, its effect can be overwhelming. The original church was a burial place of the kings of Portugal, begun in 1388; adjacent to it is almost a second church constructed in the Manueline style at the end of the fifteenth century. Even with royal patronage, and the prestige of being a national shrine, the decorative luxuriance of Batalha outran resources, and the new extension was never completed. Portuguese Gothic, like Gothic elsewhere, but in an exaggerated manner, eventually exhausted itself in excessive decoration.

León Cathedral (above), begun 1255, is French in its structure but eccentric in having its two towers separated from the body of the church. Seville Cathedral (left), begun in 1401, is the largest in area of any Gothic church in the world.

The 'Unfinished Chapels' attached to the monastery of Batalha, in Portugal, were to have been a huge octagonal mausoleum with chapels opening off it, but work stopped and it was left unroofed.

6 Permanent Truth: churches of the classical Renaissance

THE GREAT CHANGE that came over European culture in the fifteenth century and which is known as the Renaissance was a complicated process which is still sometimes misunderstood. The Renaissance, it is said, was the Age of Humanism; the Middle Ages was the Age of Faith. But it would be a mistake to see one as somehow more secular and less Christian than the other. The idea that the ancient world (which meant basically the literature, sculpture and architecture of Greece and Rome, since none of the other arts survived) could in certain respects enrich Christianity was neither new nor unorthodox. St Thomas Aquinas had used Aristotle in writing his *Summa*. What was new was the close and careful attention given to the original texts and monuments and the spirit of emulation that began to possess at least a small élite of scholars and patrons.

In no sphere of activity was the change more noticeable than in church building. Barely a hundred years separate King's College Chapel (p. 157) from St Paul's, Covent Garden (p. 195), but they belong to different worlds. The change was equally abrupt in all countries where Gothic had been the prevailing manner of building. Only in Italy, where classicism had never relinquished its hold, is it possible to see continuity.

Italian humanism as applied to churches had two strands. One was the adaptation of the classical orders (Doric, Ionic, Corinthian) to the design of Christian churches. This was not unduly difficult, but it could only be carried to a certain point. Unlike temples, they had to have naves, aisles and choirs, and the results were always unmistakably (and consciously) modern and not ancient. It was a question of vocabulary rather than form.

The other humanist strand was geometry. Renaissance thinkers, inspired by Platonists, were in love with geometry, which they saw as the demonstration of absolute truth, and therefore as a valid and important aspect of our knowledge of God. (God, said Galileo, wrote two books, the Bible and Nature, and we should learn from both.) In architecture, the circle, being the perfect figure, was a living symbol of God's perfection. Circular churches, or churches based on designs that were symmetrical in all four directions, fascinated Renaissance architects. It is no accident that the dome on a circular drum, a form without classical precedent, was to become as closely identified with Renaissance ecclesiastical architecture as the ribbed vault and the spire had been with Gothic.

For captions to colour plates 41–43, see p. 181

43

Colour plates 41–43

41 Sta Maria della Consolazione at Todi is the most perfectly realized Renaissance church, but it is a mystery. Who really designed it? According to the documents, its architect was the obscure Cola da Caprarola, but the inspiration behind it must surely have been Bramante's St Peter's, which had just been begun. Its symmetrical plan is justified by its being a pilgrimage church, made to house a miraculous image. It took a hundred years to build and the dome was probably meant to be hemispherical, not pointed.

42 Interior of St Peter's, Rome, as depicted by Giovanni Pannini. The decision to demolish Constantine's venerable basilica and replace it by a vast new church built in the revived classical style was symbolic at many levels. Politically it marked Julius II's new image of the papacy as the heir of Imperial Rome. Architecturally, it signalled the triumph of Renaissance values at the very centre of Christendom at a time when, outside Italy, they were no more than a minority interest.

Bramante's first design, of 1506, was for a centralized church like a very much larger version of Sta Maria della Consolazione. His successor, Michelangelo, also favoured a symmetrical design. But the Church authorities on the whole opposed it for practical reasons, because a centralized church could not accommodate large congregations and was inconvenient for processions and ceremonies. In the end, after Michelangelo's death, the clergy had their way and St Peter's was finished with a nave. Exactly the same controversy, with the same result, was to mark the building of Wren's new St Paul's, in London.

The nave, as finally completed, was designed by Carlo Maderna in the first years of the seventeenth century. Its main features, its scale and proportions were inevitably conditioned by Michelangelo's crossing, the space under the dome seen in the distance in Pannini's painting. The decoration is in a richer Baroque style in keeping with Maderna's own time. At the centre can be seen Bernini's huge baldacchino which stands over the tomb of St Peter.

43 The ideological content of architecture is often made more explicit in painting than in real buildings. Mantegna's Circumcision may be compared with van Eyck's Virgin and Child in a Church (pl. 33), separated in date by only about fifty years. Both use the architectural setting to comment upon and reinforce the religious message, one Gothic, the other classical. Mantegna places the sacred scene in an ancient Roman setting, since Christ was born into the Roman world and the capital of Christendom was to be Rome itself. At the same time, the Old Covenant, as set forth in the Old Testament, is evoked in the lunettes, with their reliefs of the Sacrifice of Isaac and Moses descending from Mount Sinai with the Tablets of the Law.

Permanent Truth

WHILE MOST OF EUROPE, and certainly all of northern Europe, remained faithful to the Gothic style for ecclesiastical buildings, new intellectual currents stemming from the 'rebirth' of ancient Roman culture came to the surface in Italy and were eventually to produce decisive changes everywhere. The architecture and decorative styles of the Renaissance are usually divided into the 'Early' phase, of the fifteenth century, the 'High' Renaissance, of the sixteenth, and a rather individualist enrichment, associated particularly with Michelangelo, known as 'Mannerism'. That the new styles were for a century restricted virtually to Italy is not surprising, for what they expressed was a rediscovery of the splendour of classical architecture – and of Rome, not Greece – which itself derived from the general respect of Christian humanist culture for the learning of the ancient world. It has sometimes been supposed that the rise of humanism was due to the emergence, in the major Italian trading and commercial centres, with their ducal patrons, of a class of lay scholars, less inhibited by ecclesiastical requirements than the men in holy orders who had before retained an exclusive control of educational endeavour. But this is scarcely a full picture: it ignores the importance of great university centres, like Padua, in the cultivation of the new learning, for these were centres closely under clerical supervision; and it ignores, also, the knowledge and admiration of the classical world available to medieval scholars before humanism began to have its appeal. The rediscovery of human capabilities, which was at the centre of the new learning, was not pagan, either. It was a thoroughly Christian intellectual outlook which no more subscribed to the notion of human moral autonomy than the scholarship of the ancient world had done – where men were forever governed by the capricious inclinations of the divinities. What it took from antique learning was a world picture of harmony, balance, and proportion. Even the sometimes random requirements of the gods operated within a universal framework of order which men could recognize.

In 1447 Tommaso Parentucelli became the first humanist to ascend the papal throne. But humanist learning did not sweep the Church; it tended, indeed, to division – some centres of scholarship adopting the new intellectual and cultural outlook, and promoting its advocates, and others, which did not, conceiving a considerable hostility for what appeared to them as alien modes of thinking at variance with the received, and by then traditional, scholastic thought. These divisions eventually helped to produce those successions of organic disintegration known as the Reformation. Initially, however, humanism presented itself more as a cultural view of the world, and the place of man in it, than as a theological scheme with implications for the doctrine of the Church itself.

It was this view of the world that Renaissance church buildings were intended to express. That the style of architecture was borrowed from pagan antiquity was not a problem: Christian humanists, like many of the Early Fathers of the Church, were conscious of a providential continuity between the classical values and Christianity. God, they believed, had prepared mankind for the reception of Christian truth by the learning and order of preceding pagan civilization – of

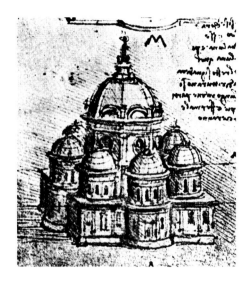

Leonardo da Vinci's notebooks give a remarkably clear insight into the mind of a Renaissance architect. His plans for centralized churches seem to be pure intellectual games, unrelated to any project for real churches. How they were to be used was of less interest to him than the symmetrical relation of their parts.

Opposite: the Pazzi Chapel, in the cloister of Sta Croce, Florence, was designed by Brunelleschi around 1430. Building continued after his death and there is some doubt about his responsibility for the structure as it now stands. Its proportions are based on a meticulous system of ratios, which are displayed graphically in the interior. The façade is unfinished and it is not clear how the upper storey would have looked.

183

Greece and Rome – just as he had employed the Jewish people in a particularization of religious knowledge. The ground was made ready for Christ by the thought of the Greek Sophists as well as by the material genius of Roman organization. In Italy, as had been clear throughout the Middle Ages, the cultural identification with the Roman inheritance had always remained strongest. The citizens of Florence and Rome saw themselves as in a direct line of succession from the collapsed Roman order; in Venice the formal links with the Byzantine Empire preserved there, too, a comparable sense of a recognizable ancestry in the Roman world.

The humanism of the fifteenth century, being an intellectual movement, was the work of small groups of outstandingly gifted men; it was in no sense a general reflection of 'the spirit of the age' or of any larger movement in society. These men began to envisage churches which looked like the pagan temples; which were, that is to say, embodiments of the permanent truths given by God to the ancients and disclosed in structures where the genius of men themselves was expressed on a human scale and with a calm sense of proportion and design. God, above all, was seen to have made a world with discoverable patterns of symmetry and order, and these could be, as they had been by the ancients, rendered in actual buildings. Thus the humanists set out to study surviving Roman buildings, of which there were still a large number in Italian cities. What they found was neglect and decay, and this gave an urgency to their mission of recovery. Eugenius IV used the influence of the papacy, in the mid-fifteenth century, to restore many of the monuments in Rome. This work did not halt the depredations permanently, however, and it was a later pope who authorized the removal of the bronze coffering from the Pantheon to be melted down for the baldacchino in the new St Peter's.

The architects of the Renaissance did not fully understand the Roman buildings they sought to copy, and whose principles they were so anxious to admire. Their knowledge of Greek structures, and their interest in the Greek world, was minimal – a curious feature, in view of the respect being paid by contemporaneous humanist scholars to Greek literature. They looked at Roman buildings with the eyes of Vitruvius, even though he had lived and written in the reign of Augustus, before, that is to say, the best buildings of ancient Rome were put up. From Vitruvius, however, they acquired a theory of proportion which seemed to correspond to their own; he had rendered reality, as they wanted to do, in terms of mathematical quantities harmoniously related. Men could then be set in a context in which their capabilities and reason could operate. What was sought was calm serenity on a human scale. Thus the Gothic architecture of the day, with its soaring attempts at dematerialization, was seen as a kind of barbarism; a return had to be made to the rounded arch, the coffered roof, the barrel vault, the symmetry of the Roman models, where men could be at harmony with the mechanics of the world around them. Churches had to look like pagan temples, for the divinity responsible for order was the same. In his great work on architecture, *De Re Aedificatoria*, Alberti, who was a priest, freely referred to churches as 'temples' and to the divinity being honoured as 'the gods' – in good Ciceronian style. He was among the first to try to make existing buildings resemble temples by adding façades which recalled the splendours of ancient pagan structures.

The number of churches constructed in revived classical styles during the Italian Renaissance was not large, and the styles themselves owed as much to an increase in secular building as they did to ecclesiastical patronage. The new commercial wealth, the relative order of the Italian city-states and the temporal

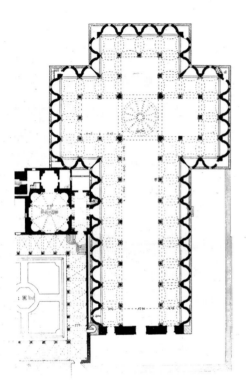

Brunelleschi's Sto Spirito *shows the architect trying to apply Renaissance geometry to the traditional church plan with its nave, transepts and choir. He rationalizes his design by making the aisle run all the way round the church (he originally wanted to run it across the west end as well). A system of niches also encircles the building in place of traditional chapels.*

possessions of the papacy, and heightened expectations to domestic convenience or dynastic grandeur, made this the first great age of the urban palace and the rural villa. The preceding burst of Gothic building, even in Italy where the Gothic style had not extended roots as vigorous as in the north of Europe, also pre-empted the possibility of large-scale church construction. Yet there were some religious influences encouraging the adoption of Roman-style buildings, and those derived principally from the impulses for Church reform which characterized the Counter-Reformation and which received their authority from the Council of Trent (1545–63). It was a period of general ecclesiastical renewal, with an emphasis on disciplined living by the clergy and closer attention to the performance of religious obligations. The Council insisted on preaching as a major feature of the latter, and church building, in consequence, tended towards hall-type structures, without arcaded aisles if possible, so that large congregations of believers could hear and see the preacher.

Similarly, the adoption of a centralized design, often on the basis of the Greek cross, assisted preaching audibility. The central plan also seemed more faithful to classical models, supporting the dome which now, once more, became an essential part of a church. Side-chapels, instead of open arcades, meant that altars were available for the clergy to say Mass. There was some ecclesiastical debate about the placing of the high altar in a centrally planned church – whether it

Sto Spirito, Florence, looking towards the altar. Brunelleschi's details, such as the capitals and entablature, are often closely modelled on antique originals, but the building as a whole is not based on classical precedent. Its closest parallel is with Early Christian basilicas like S. Paolo fuori le Mura (p. 25).

185

The dome that Brunelleschi added to Florence Cathedral between 1420 and 1434 stands midway between two ages. Its form, conditioned by the medieval octagonal crossing on which it had to stand, is Gothic: eight ribs meeting at a point. But the brickwork technique was an innovation worked out by Brunelleschi and the ornamental details, especially the cupola on the top, are purely classical.

should be directly beneath the dome, or in the eastern limb of the cross. In practice, however, the size of congregations required the adoption of Latin cross plans, by simply extending one of the arms of the Greek cross to form a nave – as, eventually, at the new St Peter's in Rome. Centrally planned churches were also favoured by Renaissance architects because they recalled the *martyria* of the classical world, and again suggested a continuity with Roman civilization.

Some of the earlier Renaissance buildings, like Brunelleschi's Sto Spirito and S. Lorenzo in Florence, were on the Roman basilican model, so reviving an adopted Christian style which had only just gone out of fashion in Rome itself. The most important influence in applying the spirit of the Council of Trent to church building and decoration was that greatest of ecclesiastical reformers, St Charles Borromeo, Archbishop of Milan, advisor of popes, and the figure who dominated the third session of the Council. He lived between 1538 and 1584, and so his life spanned the seminal years of the Reformation. His determination to purify the Church of the abuses which had given added credibility to the Protestants' rejection of Catholic doctrine extended to detailed observations about the structures of church buildings. In 1577 he produced *Instructiones Fabricae et Supellectilis Ecclesiasticae*, a handbook of instructions to the clergy about churches, from which a number of architects, also, derived some inspiration. His emphasis, like the emphasis of the Council, was on preaching as a means of securing pure doctrine.

The first architect of the Renaissance was Filippo Brunelleschi, whose solution to the problem of the dome at the cathedral of Florence secured him, as he knew it would, enduring fame and admiration. That solution, however, with its ribbed structures, was still essentially Gothic. Brunelleschi's importance as a Renaissance architect derives from churches built in a style which he believed was a faithful recovery of Roman models. He lived between 1377 and 1446, and practised metalwork and sculpture before turning to architecture. He visited Rome with Donatello and there made an extensive study of classical building techniques; his dome for the cathedral of Florence was influenced by the Pantheon. Back in Florence, then rich with the financial and entrepreneurial expertise of the Medici, Brunelleschi received a number of commissions which gave him the chance to experiment with the knowledge gleaned from his Roman researches. It is important to notice, however, that he did not, any more than subsequent Renaissance architects, see himself as an innovator: instead he sought to restore. His knowledge of Roman buildings was incomplete, and he managed to confuse the Greek orders, but he regarded himself as returning to a perfect model, not adopting the styles of a past model to different uses. The Roman structures of the Renaissance were thought of as in themselves uniform and complete; it was unthinkable that they should be extended or adapted in any way, as Gothic buildings freely were. A classical building expressed in structural form a mathematical perfection, a design of God, which men could discover by the divine gift of reason and the guidance of ancient wisdom.

Brunelleschi's first two Florentine churches were basilicas in the Latin-cross shape. S. Lorenzo, built in the 1420s, following his reconstruction of the Old Sacristy, has a square crossing, and arcades of semicircular arches supported by Corinthian columns. The square crossing is reproduced in a series of four units which make up the nave, thus producing a design of balance and symmetry, a simple mathematical wholeness. The church of Sto Spirito, similarly, comprises a series of squares, with a Corinthian colonnaded nave. It was begun in 1436 but remained uncompleted at the time of Brunelleschi's death. Both these basilicas had flat nave roofs (neither of which was actually built while Brunelleschi was

Right and far right: the Old Sacristy of S. Lorenzo, Florence. Here Brunelleschi was able to carry out many of the ideas that preoccupied the Renaissance architect. It is symmetrical in all four directions and articulated by refined classical orders. Above it rises a hemispherical dome.

living), and so remained faithful to the roofing of the Early Christian (and the pagan Roman) basilicas. In both churches, also, the side-bays contain chapels. There was a great austerity about the interior design and decoration of Renaissance churches, and this is seen in Brunelleschi's Old Sacristy at S. Lorenzo. Here there are some wall medallions and niches with frescos, but the general effect is of subdued tonal qualities. The Pazzi Chapel at the church of Sta Croce, begun in 1430 and continued during Brunelleschi's later years, shows the same sort of subtle colouring. Both buildings are central squares beneath domes. The Pazzi Chapel illustrates the increasing Roman influence in his later years, with its entrance dome recalling the Pantheon – perhaps the work of a student of Brunelleschi's, seeking to remain faithful to the master's intellectual progression at the time of his demise.

It was after Brunelleschi's death in 1446, in fact, that the other great architect of the Early Renaissance began to practise. Leone Battista Alberti, who lived between 1404 and 1472, was born in exile and the family did not return to Florence until 1428. There he met Brunelleschi. He was not, by training, an architect, and a few years later became a civil administrator in the service of the papacy. Alberti was a typical Renaissance man: he had studied several branches of knowledge and was proficient in a number of cultural accomplishments. Like Brunelleschi he studied Roman buildings, but unlike him his preoccupation was not with the mechanics and effects of Roman styles but with the ideas he supposed they expressed. In 1432 he went to Rome and studied the buildings of antiquity with the guidance of Vitruvius. The eventual result – published in the mid-1440s, before he had any practical experience of construction – was his *De Re Aedificatoria*, a work greatly indebted to Vitruvius, composed according to the same principles, and influential with the men of his day. Here Alberti explained the Vitruvian theory of proportion, and the importance and significance of symmetrical design, as evidence of the divine presence in the creation. It was Alberti who was to produce churches which decisively changed the future of religious buildings.

Alberti's façade to his church of S. Andrea, Mantua, is an enlarged version of a Roman truimphal arch. The same motif is used as the basis for the interior elevation which similarly consists of alternating arches and solid bays.

In 1458 he added a façade to Sta Maria Novella which is in dramatic contrast to the Gothic of the body of the church. It is a series of green and white marble panels – the Florentine hallmark – of exact symmetry, with pilasters and rounded arches arranged in two levels. The façade is a decorative device: it does not relate to the interior shape of the church, and Alberti in fact solved the problem of the lower roofs of the aisles by a means which was later to be widely copied, and to become a design feature in its own right, even when there was no problem of different roof heights to overcome. He added enormous scrolls to disguise the termination of the aisle roofs. They roll towards the pedimented top of the nave. This idea, so audacious and yet so effective, was to be employed in the façades of hundreds of Baroque churches. It also appeared in a number of Renaissance churches, too. The church of S. Agostino in Rome, for example, by Giacomo de Pietrasanta, has graceful scrolls taken from Alberti's great original in Florence. Alberti was even more inventive – if it is possible to describe the revival of an antique style as 'inventive' – in his church of S. Andrea in Mantua, which he designed in 1470. This was a direct and successful attempt to build a Christian church in the manner of monumental Roman architecture. Ten years before, he had designed S. Sebastiano in Mantua, with a centralized Greek cross plan clearly copied from the Roman tombs and early Christian *martyria*. S. Andrea has a façade based upon an enormous Roman triumphal arch surmounted by a temple-like pediment, and inside the elevation consists of a series of smaller triumphal arches leading into side-chapels. It is a huge building, with no aisles, a domed crossing, and coffered barrel-vaulted ceiling plainly inspired by the ancient roof fragments Alberti had seen in Rome. This roof, in fact, was the largest barrel vault constructed since Roman times, and its influence was very great, as may be seen at the new St Peter's in Rome, built in the next century.

It was in Rome that the greatest achievements of the High Renaissance took place. The architecture filled contemporaries with wonder, as it was intended to do, and made successive generations marvel. However, there have always been a few dissenters: Pugin described St Peter's basilica as 'vilely constructed, a mass of imposition. Bad taste of every sort seems to have run riot.' The decision to pull down the venerable church built by Constantine over the tomb of the Apostle was not taken lightly, nor was it uncontroversial. The great church was very dilapidated but not beyond repair. The breathtaking decision was taken at the court of Julius II, whose pontificate, from 1503 to 1513, saw the High Renaissance at its most brilliant, with Bramante, Raphael and Michelangelo all employed in commissions issued by the papacy. With the other great churches of antiquity now in Islamic hands – the Holy Sepulchre in Jerusalem and Hagia Sophia in Constantinople – Julius was determined to cover the tomb of St Peter with a magnificent church which would replace them both as a centre of Christian pilgrimage and a symbol of the ascendancy of the papacy in Christian history.

To achieve this he turned to Donato Bramante. A painter before he was an architect (quite a usual progression in the Italy of the time), Bramante was born in 1444. Early in the 1480s he was in Milan working for the Sforzas. The city still had a number of surviving early churches with central plans based upon the Greek cross, and these clearly influenced Bramante. In 1499 he arrived as an exile in Rome, after the fall of Milan to the French, and, like Brunelleschi and·Alberti before him, he began to make a detailed study of the ancient buildings. His earliest architectural work in the city included the cloister at Sta Maria della Pace; then he received the commission for the building which established his reputation and which was to exercise enormous influence over Renaissance church design. A chapel to mark the traditional place of St Peter's martyrdom was financed by the

In the mid-fifteenth century Alberti designed a façade for the medieval church of Sta Maria Novella, Florence: a Renaissance solution to a Gothic problem. His device of a pedimented centre with scrolls masking the transition from high nave to lower aisles was to be imitated widely in the years to come.

Bramante's first work in architecture was a fantasy (opposite) preserved in the form of an engraving. It shows a church, or temple, planned as a Greek cross, four equal arms inscribed in a square. What is particularly interesting is that it seems to offer the possibility of being prolonged in the viewer's direction, hinting, as it were, at a longer nave attached to a classically symmetrical crossing, exactly the situation that occurred at St Peter's.

189

The 'little temple' (Tempietto) which Bramante built to mark the site of St Peter's martyrdom, S. Pietro in Montorio, has resonances that unite pagan and Christian worship. It is at the same time a Roman round temple (its model is the Temple of Vesta, not far away) given Christian attributes (e.g. the frieze of liturgical vessels) and a tomb, again a Roman type taken over by the Early Christians as a monument to the martyrs. It is also one of the purest exercises in Renaissance geometry, the approach to God through the perfect forms of Nature.

Spanish crown and Bramante produced his perfect little rotunda, the Tempietto of S. Pietro in Montorio, some time in the first decade of the sixteenth century. It is in the form of a Roman temple, with a completed circle of colonnades in the Doric mode. The building was in some measure an adaptation of the Temple of Vesta at Tivoli (where the columns are Corinthian, however). The Doric columns used were authentic ancient Roman ones. A frieze above has incised representations of the Christian liturgical vessels. Roman temples had similar friezes with pagan cultic emblems. The surmounting dome, though not the original, perfectly completes this harmonious building in its symmetry and symbolism. For it recalls, also, the *martyria* of the early Church, which were usually in the rotunda form, and is, in effect, a monument to the Renaissance ideal of combining Christian truth with the external splendour of ancient Roman religion. The Tempietto was not a place of worship but a shrine, hence its small scale. It was originally designed to stand at the centre of a colonnaded court, which was never constructed, and with a small chapel in each corner. In Bramante's scheme, therefore, he anticipated some of the features of his new St Peter's.

Bramante received the commission for St Peter's from Julius II in 1506. What he then began to build, over the tomb of the Apostle (temporarily protected, after the demolition of Constantine's basilica, by the construction of a small chapel) was an enormous *martyrium*. It was in a centralized Greek cross plan, with a huge dome, and the whole building was conceived on a monumental Roman scale. It was, indeed, the largest structure built since antiquity and was intended not only as a triumphalist assertion of the glories of Christian truth but as a vindication of the glories of the ancient Roman inheritance as well. Yet Bramante plainly experimented as he went along, and, as later became apparent, the massive supporting piers for the central dome were not massive enough, and had to be enlarged, first by himself and then by his successors. When Bramante died in 1514, the central crossing had been constructed. Some confusion followed. Bramante's guiding plans were indecisive in some crucial particulars, and alternative plans allowed for the conversion of the Greek into a Latin cross, thus allowing the accommodation of far larger numbers of worshippers and pilgrims. In the end this change was made, and the result was the nave of St Peter's extending out from beneath the dome to the west. It is hardly surprising that these difficulties arose. A structure on this scale was outside the experience of those actually creating it. But it meant that the architects who followed Bramante – and these included Raphael, Peruzzi, Antonio da Sangallo and Michelangelo – had a formidable task on their hands.

Michelangelo succeeded Sangallo in 1546, and until his death in 1564 he worked on the completion of the basilica, according to a design which was not radically different from Bramante's. There had been some intervening problems which were not architectural or structural: the sack of Rome in 1527, and the permanent problem of financing the enormous undertaking. In Michelangelo's time the walls were carried up to a uniform height, and the plans for lesser domes were abandoned. At his death the base of the great dome had been reached, but no work yet begun on it, and it remains unclear whether Michelangelo himself envisaged a rounded dome, like the Pantheon, or a pointed one, like Brunelleschi's famous solution at Florence. As completed by Giacomo della Porta and Domenico Fontana, between 1586 and 1593, the dome was nearer to the Florentine model, probably because it had proved itself by remaining intact, and the finer points in the details of its construction were known.

St Peter's basilica, as eventually completed, surely justifies Julius II's daring decision to tear down the Constantinian predecessor. It evokes, still, the

atmosphere of an ancient *martyrium*. Beneath, in the grottoes, are the tombs of the popes; above is the cupola, filled with light. The domes of Byzantine churches are intended to enclose the space in which Christ and the heavenly company descended to earth; the dome of St Peter's evokes a calm grandeur in honour of Christ resident, already, in the world, and in honour of his servants who have laboured here in his service. The scale is gigantic, but the effect very human.

Michelangelo's architectural work was part of a distinct phase, evident from around 1520 to the end of the century, known as 'Mannerism'. It was scarcely a school: the architects concerned were too individualistic, and their work has left a much more ambiguous legacy. Michelangelo was a crucial figure in this version of Roman classicism because his work in Florence, in the 1520s, was emancipated from the canons laid down by Vitruvius and followed, as they thought, by preceding Renaissance architects. There is, in Mannerist work, a greater sympathy for decoration – witness Michelangelo's frescoed ceiling of the Sistine Chapel in Rome, done between 1508 and 1512. Michelangelo lived between 1475 and 1564 and was primarily concerned with sculpture. His buildings, therefore, were in some sense an extension of his preoccupation with materials and forms, and he was prepared to adapt the classical styles in a way which preceding Renaissance architects were not.

St Peter's took more than a hundred years to build and several great architects left their mark upon it. The original conception was Bramante's, but the personality that comes through most clearly is that of Michelangelo. To him are due the overwhelming sense of mass, the grandiose exterior elevations (here we are looking at the choir and one transept) and the superb dome set on a drum of coupled columns. In Michelangelo's design the dome would have dominated every view, but Maderna's nave, seen here on the right, defeated this effect from the direction of the façade.

Apart from St Peter's, Michelangelo built no other churches, though he made designs for some, all with centralized plans, and converted the Roman Baths of Diocletian into Sta Maria degli Angeli. His other major ecclesiastical work was the Medici Chapel, or New Sacristy, attached to S. Lorenzo in Florence. This exactly matches Brunelleschi's Old Sacristy (p. 187) but is conceived in Mannerist rather than Renaissance terms: tension instead of harmony – the niches seem to press against their frames, the frames against the spaces they occupy.

Nevertheless, there were often rather fine points of departure, and his Medici Chapel at S. Lorenzo in Florence was fully Roman, with a coffered dome, based upon the Pantheon, over a severe square building. The chapel was completed in 1529. It has strong sculptural qualities, with blind niches and an austere, plain apse containing an altar. Sculpted figures, heavy with symbolism, predominate, as they were intended to. The subdued atmosphere is not sepulchral, however, but calm; this is a place to appreciate the symmetry and balance of harmonious forms. Here is a memorial to mankind at his most reasonable, and everything is comprehended. This was one of very few churches built in the Mannerist style, but there was one other important one, also by Michelangelo, and conceived in his last years – Sta Maria degli Angeli in Rome, the conversion of the Baths of Diocletian into an undecorated monastic church. The church, as seen today, is largely the work of Vanvitelli in the eighteenth century. Giulio Romano's cathedral at Mantua, completed in 1545, has a rich interior more characteristic of Mannerism, with six aisles, some with flat wooden coffered roofs and some with coffered barrel vaults. The side-chapels, similarly, are also coffered, and half of them are covered by small domes.

One of the most influential of all the Renaissance builders of churches was Giacomo Barozzi da Vignola. He was born in 1507 in Bologna and died in 1573, and was most celebrated for his design of classical villas, and especially of the Villa Giulia in Rome. But his four churches were also important and one of them, because it was the mother church of the Jesuits, produced echoes wherever there were Jesuit churches – throughout the Christian world, in fact. He designed the Gesù, in Rome, in 1568, under a commission which specifically required him to pay attention to the needs of preaching. For this, he resorted to Alberti's S. Andrea at Mantua, and built a large church with a huge barrel-vaulted nave and side-chapels. The façade, with its two storeys of pilasters, its upper pediment, and its scrolls, designed by Giacomo della Porta in the 1570s, also owed a debt to Alberti. Like most Renaissance churches, the Gesù was originally sober within, its qualities being monumental rather than decorative. The rich painting and marble seen in the church today are sixteenth- and nineteenth-century embellishments. The church is in the form of a Latin cross, and in the left transept is the tomb of St Ignatius Loyola himself. It is not clear that the founder of the Jesuits would have approved of the enormous monument of silver and lapis lazuli. The silver, however, is now only plate, since Pius VI was obliged to melt down the original statue of Loyola in order to pay off Napoleon.

Vignola also built oval-shaped churches. These are usually associated with the Baroque style, but the earliest ones were designed by Renaissance architects, and so they may also be credited with the first real alteration in church plans for some centuries. Vignola was the pioneer, with the Roman churches of S. Andrea in Via Flaminia and S. Anna in the Vatican, both designed in the 1550s. There was no liturgical or religious purpose, and though oval churches certainly had acoustic advantages, the purpose of their construction was aesthetic rather than practical.

The ideological element so central to Renaissance church design – the expression of the Vitruvian theory of proportion, and the association of Christianity with classical Roman religious monumentality – was articulated most exactly by Andrea Palladio, who lived between 1508 and 1580, and who is, like Vignola, best remembered for his villas. Palladio studied classical buildings

Vignola's design for the Gesù in Rome, the headquarters of the Jesuit order, was to prove one of the most influential in the whole of church architecture. Begun in 1568, it consists of an apsed choir, shallow transepts and a longer nave. The heavy barrel vault needed substantial buttressing, but instead of building traditional arcades with buttresses on the exterior, Vignola placed his buttresses inside, using the spaces between them as chapels and dispensing with aisles altogether. The result is compact, functional and suited to the Jesuits' requirement for a large preaching hall. The façade, added later by Giacomo della Porta, adapted Alberti's Sta Maria Novella design (p. 189) and set the pattern for the standard Baroque church façade of the next century.

Andrea Palladio was a contemporary of Vignola but he remained largely immune to Mannerist influence, adopting a more classical style that aligns him with the early Renaissance. The façade of his S. Giorgio Maggiore in Venice (above) is an ingenious combination of two Roman temple fronts, one high reflecting the central nave, the other low reflecting the side aisles. Il Redentore (above right), his other Venetian church, achieves a similar effect by similar means, the giant order of the interior defining the nave and crossing and, at the far end, closing off the high altar from the monastic choir behind.

in Rome, where he arrived in 1541, and on this and subsequent visits made drawings of the ruins, just as his predecessors had done. In 1570 he published a treatise setting out his belief in the mathematical basis of the created order, and the divine nature of proportion and harmony. Two of his churches in Venice were intended to adapt the pagan temple style to Christian purposes, and to embody in material form the harmonious scales which lay at the basis of creation. S. Giorgio Maggiore (1565) and Il Redentore (1577) have façades which are based upon temple fronts. At S. Giorgio a high pediment rests upon four large columns and is a version of a classical temple. Behind this, however, is another temple front, broader and lower, whose pediment is hidden beneath the taller front. At the Redentore three pediments have been made to interlock. The plans of both churches are highly unusual. They are neither Greek nor Latin cross in shape, nor are they basilican. Instead there are naves with side-chapels, prominent altars, and choirs beyond. The reason – and it is the reason why these splendid churches have not been copied – lay in the special purpose for which they were built. S. Giorgio is a Benedictine foundation which needed a choir for the monks but also a large space for the annual visitation of the Doge of Venice and the choir of S. Marco. Il Redentore also received a comparable visitation: an annual thanksgiving for deliverance from the great plague of 1576. Palladio believed, however, that in general, and in principle, the central plan was the proper one for churches. The interiors of both these churches are plain; their effect, in anticipation of Baroque devices, depended upon the directed entry of light. Both are buildings of subtlety and grace.

Relatively few churches were built under the inspiration of Italian Renaissance styles in the rest of Europe, and when classical structures did become popular they were usually in the Baroque manner. These Renaissance buildings, intended by their designers to be so sober, only became popular in versions which were characterized by their decorative extravagance. The earliest influence of Renaissance art, in fact, was decorative rather than structural, first in France and then elsewhere. The Reformation had the effect of cutting England off from the inspiration of Catholic ecclesiasticism, and the same was true, in varying degrees, with other north European countries where Protestantism received official endorsement. In those places Gothic styles achieved an extended life. Even in Catholic Europe, Renaissance architecture, as it began to infiltrate, had a greater impact on secular than on religious buildings. There were some great exceptions, like Granada Cathedral and the royal monastic church at the Escorial in Spain (built from the mid- to the later sixteenth century).

Yet England was not untouched by the influences coming from Italy with the visits of individual artists and craftsmen. Thus the tomb of Henry VII in Westminster Abbey, by Pietro Torrigiano, completed in 1518, is in a fully Italian Renaissance mode; but it is set in a chapel built in Perpendicular Gothic. England had to await the work of Inigo Jones, who had been to Italy and seen the Renaissance buildings, before it had an ecclesiastical structure in a Renaissance style. But that was in the first half of the seventeenth century, by which time the Italian models Inigo Jones had seen and appreciated were a century old. His church in London's Covent Garden, St Paul's, completed in 1633, and the massive portico he added to the west front of Old St Paul's Cathedral (1640), later destroyed in the Great Fire of London, were indebted to the classical revival in Italy.

Most copies of Renaissance church buildings outside Italy have been more recent and were completed in the nineteenth century or later still; sometimes they only hint at the originals. The Sanctuary of the Beatitudes on a hillside overlooking the Lake of Galilee is a case in point, though a particularly beautiful one. The serene white and grey church, built in 1938 by the Italian architect Antonio Barluzzi, has a cupola set upon an octagonal base whose classical simplicity would perhaps be recognized by the Renaissance designers of churches. And so the traditional place of Christ's most hallowed teaching is marked by the latter-day representation of an architectural style originally intended to demonstrate an affinity between the pagan virtues and Christian truth.

Some later churches in Renaissance-Classical or Mannerist styles achieved notable distinction. The Brompton Oratory in London, opened in 1884, was designed by Herbert Gribble with the deliberate triumphalism of a Victorian Catholic convert. It was Newman who had founded the Oratory of St Philip Neri in Birmingham in 1848, and Father Frederick Faber who was charged with the setting up of the London house. Behind the division of the community of priests there lay extensive differences of view, however, and Faber's London Oratory was always intended to be – and always was – far more Italianate in devotional style and general ultramontane atmosphere. The present Oratory church, though built twenty years after Faber's death, is yet a monument to his spiritual genius. It evokes a kind of Mannerist Italian severity and dignity, with its pedimented west front, high-pitched dome, and (a surprising feature) concrete vaults.

The dome of the cathedral at St Paul, Minnesota, in the United States, is another successful modern adaptation of the Renaissance mode. Completed in 1915, and constructed in local granite, its enormous, crown-shaped dome rises to just over 300 feet and is surmounted by a lantern which suggests the influence of St Peter's in Rome. Elsewhere in the external appearance of the building there are *appliqué* decorative details rather far removed from the original Italian inspiration, and owing, indeed, something to French nineteenth-century classicism, but the building remains almost overwhelmingly successful as a latter-day version of Renaissance spiritual style.

The Renaissance came to England in the person of Inigo Jones. His church of St Paul's, Covent Garden, begun in 1631, takes the Palladian model but deliberately reduces it to the simplest terms. This eighteenth-century painting by John Collet shows it before it was damaged by fire and slightly altered in the rebuilding. The great doorway under the portico is in fact a sham; the church is entered from the other end.

7 Seen and unseen worlds: the Baroque synthesis

By the middle of the sixteenth century, the new values of the Renaissance were accepted throughout Europe, and with them the new architectural style. But from now on it is not possible to speak of Western Christendom as a unity. The Reformation had split it into two camps, characterized by different interpretations of Christian doctrine, different cultural outlooks and different demands of ecclesiastical architecture.

One of the issues upon which the Protestants felt most strongly was that of 'idolatry': many of them rejected images altogether and most were opposed to the representation of the supernatural in material form. Their churches accordingly tended to be plain and sober, and (since they placed greater emphasis on the Word than on the sacraments) centred upon the pulpit rather than the altar. Catholics, in reaction, emphasized those very aspects of their faith that most offended the Reformers: the intercession of saints, the holiness of relics, the power of the Church to bind and loose and the central miracle of the Eucharist.

Baroque art is essentially Catholic. Using the legacy of Renaissance forms, it turned what had been an intellectual scheme into an emotional experience. Where Renaissance churches had embodied clarity and order, those of the Baroque employed every device of art and illusion to transport the spectator into a visionary world in which the skies open, the saints descend and the holy mysteries are displayed in life-like painting and sculpture. It is impossible to discuss a Baroque church purely as architecture; without the contribution of the other arts, it ceases to exist. Nor is it easy to say where one art ends and another begins. What seems to be structural may be manufactured in stucco. Distinctions between the elements of the building, so important to the Renaissance architect, are deliberately confused, so that walls undulate and spaces flow into one another; *putti* fly out from capitals and pediments to lead lives of their own; frescos continue the architecture into fictitious depths; painted figures emerge into three dimensions; angels hover without apparent support.

Baroque began in Rome in the early seventeenth century with the generation of Maderna, Borromini and Bernini. The preference for centralized church plans persisted, often using complicated geometrical shapes such as ovals and stars. In the course of the later seventeenth century the Baroque style spread throughout Italy, assuming distinctive regional forms in Sicily, Venice and Piedmont, and in the early eighteenth was taken up with enthusiasm in Spain, Germany and central Europe. In Spain it is characterized by density of decoration (exported and intensified in Spanish America), in Germany by lightness, exuberance and a sort of playful gaiety.

Underlying all this artistic creation was the strong theological energy of the Counter-Reformation, an energy that produced striking innovations in every aspect of the Catholic Church, from preaching to the liturgy, from music to education.

For captions to colour plates 44–55, see p. 209

45

50,51

52

53

54

Colour plates 44–55

44 The pilgrimage church of Die Wies ('the meadow') in Bavaria
was built by Dominikus Zimmermann from 1746 to 1754. The
pulpit is a typical Baroque composition, with flying putti lifting
the curtain, two others above holding episcopal regalia and
another on the top with the Tablets of the Law. On the panels
are allegorical figures of Hope, Faith (holding the cross, the
chalice and the host) and, around the corner, Charity. Above the
preacher hovers the dove of the Holy Spirit. The actual structure
is broken up and concealed beneath strange crustaceous forms,
garlands, shell-like shapes, gilding and tiny mirrors. Beyond is
the high altar, conceived in a similar style and lit by windows set
back behind pillars of artificial blue marble.

45 Andrea Pozzo's ceiling fresco in the Jesuit church of S. Ignazio in
Rome takes perspective illusionism as far as it can go. Around
the edges of the picture one sees the real architecture of the
church. Pozzo takes this as his starting point and continues it
upwards for another whole storey where it ascends in arches and
cornice open to the sky. On the sides are groups labelled Asia,
Africa, America and Europe, representing the Jesuit triumphs in
these continents. The centre is devoted to St Ignatius, the founder
of the Jesuits, being received into Paradise.

46 The interior of the Gesù, Rome, in 1639. Vignola's late
Renaissance or Mannerist interior (see p. 193) was transformed
into something far more Baroque by decoration and painting.
This view, by Andrea Sacchi, shows it adorned for a festival
celebrating the centenary of the Jesuit order. On a dais in the
middle stands the Pope, Urban VIII, surrounded by cardinals.

47 Bernini's 'Cathedra Petri', St Peter's throne, is at once a
reliquary (inside it is an ancient chair traditionally said to have
been used by St Peter), a proclamation of papal power and a
theological statement. At the bottom stand over-lifesize statues of
four Doctors of the Church, Saints Ambrose, Augustine,
Athanasius and Chrysostom. Above it two putti hold the keys
committed to the Apostle by Jesus and the triple crown; while, at
the top, illuminated by a brilliantly contrived piece of Baroque
stagecraft, is the dove of the Holy Spirit surrounded by a flurry of
angels and more putti writhing in an ecstasy of adoration.

48 The high altar of the church of St George, Weltenburg, Bavaria,
by the brothers Cosmas and Egid Asam. St George, on horseback,

is silhouetted against a bright light that comes from unseen
windows at the side. On the right is the princess he is rescuing;
on the left, stricken by his flaming sword, the dragon. In such
works as this, church art comes closest to Baroque theatre.

49 The Assumption of the Virgin, at Rohr, also in Bavaria and also
by the Asam brothers. The Mother of Christ is borne aloft by two
angels. Here the supports are so well concealed that the whole
group does indeed seem to float in the air.

50 The sacristy of the Charterhouse in Granada, Spain. Here every
pretence that each part of a classical order has a defined function
is given up: pilasters, bases, capitals, cornice – everything
disappears in a frenzy of lines, edges and deep mouldings. The
style is associated with the Churriguera family; this example,
begun in 1727, is by Luis de Arévalo.

51 At Toledo Cathedral, the vault of one bay of the ambulatory
behind the high altar was taken out by Narciso Tomé and
replaced by coloured glass, the opening surrounded by sculpture in
stucco. Facing it is another sculptural composition, seen here,
glorifying the Blessed Sacrament and partly visible from the altar
on the other side.

52,53,54
Catholic churches in Central and South America are the heirs of
Spanish Baroque, taking the style even further in the lavishness of
their ornament and the intensity of their passion. Top left: the
Plaza de Armas and cathedral of Cuzco, the ancient Inca capital
of Peru. Lower left: S. Jerónimo, Tlacochahuaya, Mexico,
formerly a Dominican church, with its painted organ and naive
figure of an angel. Right: the chancel of S. Francisco Acatepec,
Mexico, built about 1730, bristling with saints, putti, foliage
trails and mirrors and all outlined in gold.

55 The chapel of St Januarius was added to Naples Cathedral in
the early seventeenth century and sumptuously adorned with
paintings and sculpture. The biannual liquefaction of the blood
of St Januarius still constitutes the central events of the
Neapolitan calendar. This painting, though made in the
nineteenth century, catches the Baroque atmosphere of such a
festival in such a setting. The blood itself, in a gold reliquary, is
being held up by a priest in front of the altar.

Seen and unseen worlds

THOUGH BAROQUE CHURCHES retained the architectural form of classical buildings – and were to that extent a continuation of the Renaissance mode – their purpose was quite different. They were not intended as expressions of an essential harmony between the virtues of the ancients and the calm Christianity of the later European world, but as triumphalist assertions of spiritual transcendence. The Baroque style represented a distinct religiosity: it was ideological in purpose. Though often referred to as the style of the Counter-Reformation it was not simply that, for the Counter-Reformation was itself far too complex a series of ecclesiastical and cultural impulses to have received an adequate representation in a relatively uniform artistic style. It was, it is true, overwhelmingly a Catholic style; later Protestant church buildings in the Baroque or Rococo manner are certainly to be found, and in some places quite abundantly, but they are rarely more than decorative emulations, just as some modern Catholic churches have been built in the Byzantine style. With Baroque there was a decisive shift in the centre of architectural intention: the earliest Baroque masters, like Bernini, still clung to the Renaissance notion that a building should represent the interior harmony of all classical forms, that it should express the symmetry and regularity of the human form itself. But with Borromini's strange genius the Baroque style moved quickly into another realm of interpretation. Buildings came then to be regarded as ways of breaking through the regularity and predictability of ordinary human affairs, and of the immediately observable world of the senses. They became, instead, anticipations of eternity, their sculptural forms and sometimes even joyous exuberance straining to pierce the existing realities and to allow the seen and the unseen worlds to intermingle. Much of the audacity of Baroque originality derived from the skilful contrivance of false appearances – wooden columns painted to look like marble, façades which curved like unfolded parchment, double-walls disguising the supports of domes, ceiling-panels cut away to allow tricks of light, and illusionistic paintings creating a sense of space and infinite perspective.

These devices were not employed merely to elicit dramatic response, though they certainly did that, and were, in the fullest sense, displays of what Bernini called *theatrum sacrum*. They were actually employed for the highest religious and theological purpose: they were a plastic and sculptural representation of the great Christian truth that the world of the senses is itself illusory if it is taken by humanity to exhaust reality. The finite understanding of men can conceive the splendours of eternity only through Revelation, and the experience of applied Revelation – as made to the fishermen of Galilee and to the little children brought to the Saviour – requires to be set in the context of a higher plane if it is to elicit the awe and religious ecstasy appropriate to the mystery of ultimate truth. The Baroque style sought to express the aspirations of a humanity straining upwards to grasp the treasures of a celestial order; all material reality is in a sense illusory, for though it conveys the patterns established by the Creator it suggests no active

The dynamic spiral of Borromini's spire on S. Ivo, in Rome, probably symbolizes the ascent to truth through learning. S. Ivo was the chapel of the university of the Sapienza.

Opposite: Bernini's Cornaro Chapel in Sta Maria della Vittoria, Rome. The group over the altar represents a mystical experience narrated by St Teresa. She dreamt that an angel came to her and pierced her side with a spear. On either side of the chapel, as if watching from the boxes of a theatre, sit members of the Cornaro family.

The chapel of St John the Baptist in São Roque, Lisbon. The whole chapel was designed in 1742 by Vanvitelli and Salvi and actually built in Rome before being dismantled and shipped to Lisbon. It is remarkable for the richness of its materials – columns of lapis lazuli, balustrades of verde antico and pilasters of alabaster.

spiritual work of itself, and needs to be arranged by men conscious of Redemption so that it discloses truth. The audacious contrivances of Baroque were attempts to represent this central scheme of things in dramatic sculptural buildings and in almost riotous decoration. The sense of movement evident in a High Baroque church (which in a Rococo building becomes a kind of divine joyousness) suggests the restless exuberance of humanity as it anticipates the splendours of eternity – caught in glimpses, through concealed use of light, and through painted representations of the saints in ecstasy, and of the heavenly society as it calmly beckons towards the glories that are to come. The church has become a sort of theatre for the drama of Redemption, in which the worshippers find themselves active participants.

So far was the Baroque style from the ideal – later attributed to Gothic architecture – that it should express local religious impulses that, in a revival of the practice of early Byzantium, entire church 'kits' were occasionally shipped off to satisfy the desire of particular patrons for Baroque splendour. The richly decorated little chapel of St John the Baptist in the Jesuit church of São Roque in Lisbon, for example, was actually built in Rome during the 1740s and transported to Portugal in crates. Baroque artificiality could scarcely go further.

The emphasis in the Baroque style was no longer on men's sin, but on their potential for salvation: figures are represented with grace and almost wistful aspiration, faces upturned to catch the light which shines from another world. The greatest painter of perspective illusion, the Jesuit Andrea Pozzo, who was active in the later decades of the seventeenth century in Rome, perfectly transcribed the essential theology of the Baroque style. At the church of San Ignazio in Rome he painted the ceiling of the nave with scenes from the labour of the Jesuits to evangelize the peoples of the world. Here may be experienced the ascending movement of the figures, in a kind of riotous ecstasy, towards a penetration of worldly life by the Saviour himself, holding his Cross, and extending a hand of blessing to St Ignatius Loyola, as the founder of the order leads his followers into the clouds of eternity amidst joyous exultation.

In some Baroque churches the same astonishing effects are produced by sculpted and stuccoed figures, which are used to reinforce the drama of the painting. Thus in the Capella di San Domenico at the church of SS. Giovanni e Paolo in Venice the extraordinary vitality of the ceiling fresco by Piazzetta (1727), showing St Dominic in glory, surmounts a cluster of sculptured dignitaries of the Church, their eyes raised upwards towards the vision of blessedness, though some of them look downwards as if to invite the worshippers beneath to join the heavenly assembly. Exultation, serenity, grace: the practitioners of the Baroque brought the mystery and the dignity of the life of salvation to the consciousness of ordinary men and women.

The sense that worldly existence is separated from the heavenly splendours by a mere curtain, which may be lifted aside to reveal the eternal world, gave Baroque churches transcendent qualities that some have rightly recognized as possessing affinities with the Gothic style. Sometimes there are even structural similarities, as in Francesco Borromini's chapel at the College of the Propaganda Fide in Rome, built between 1662 and 1664, with its diagonal ribbed ceiling, and its extensive use of glass in the walls. Borromini himself contended that his vaults were inspired by the ruins of ancient Rome, but the impression received by the observer is of a kind of flattened Gothic. The earlier Baroque churches retained the human scale of Renaissance buildings; some later ones began to show the skeletal, diaphanous features usually thought to be characteristically Gothic. This was especially true of churches in Germany, where the Italian genius of the

Left: Piazzetta's ceiling fresco of St Dominic in Glory, in SS. Giovanni e Paolo, in Venice. Figures standing on the edge of what pretends to be the walls of the church mediate between heaven and earth.

The ceiling of Borromini's chapel in the College of the Propaganda Fide, in Rome, is ribbed in a style that recalls Gothic. Borromini hated right angles. 'The corner', he said, 'is the enemy of architecture.'

In spite of its classical style, the royal chapel at Versailles by Jules Hardouin-Mansart (above) supports its vault by flying buttresses that are essentially Gothic.

origins of the Baroque style was more readily mixed with Gothic preferences. In France, too, the straining for height produced a 'Gothic' flavour to Baroque buildings: thus Jules Hardouin-Mansart's royal chapel at Versailles (1698–1710), with its soaring colonnade of Corinthian columns, and its flying buttresses.

In Piedmont (a major European country in the seventeenth century) the patronage of the royal house enabled Guarino Guarini to experiment with the structure of domes. The result was some brilliant and inventive Baroque architecture, characterized by ribbed and perforated surfaces. Both in the Chapel of the Holy Shroud in Turin Cathedral and in the church of S. Lorenzo, Guarini produced, late in the seventeenth century, astonishing intersecting ribbed domes whose Gothic resonances are immediately apparent. Bernardo Vittone, working in Piedmont in the eighteenth century, perforated domes and pendentives to allow the entry of light in dramatic profusion; the effect was to dematerialize his buildings. This, indeed, was the true common feature of the Gothic and the Baroque styles: not, really, the structural echoes but the ideological intentions.

Domes had been favourite features with Renaissance architects. During the age of Baroque they were equally popular but were treated differently – not as expressions of mathematical order but as openings into another world. This effect could be achieved most explicitly through painting, as at Ottobeuren in Bavaria (left), decorated in 1763, where the spectator looks from earth, represented by the continents, to heaven.

Sta Maria della Salute, built by Baldassare Longhena from 1630 to 1687, is dedicated to the Virgin as a thank-offering after the end of a plague which had ravaged Venice. The dome symbolizes the Virgin's crown.

Two domes by Guarino Guarini, both in Turin, dissolve the solidity of the architecture altogether, creating spatial effects without precedent. Left: S. Lorenzo, where a system of overlapping ribs leaves mysterious spaces lit by hidden windows. Right: the chapel of the Holy Shroud, in which superimposed segmental arches create the impression almost of a vortex.

Façade of Sta Maria della Pace, Rome, by Pietro da Cortona. Here the boldly dynamic curve of the porch is contrasted with the much more constricted curve of the upper storey, and both are set within the concave shape of wings on either side.

Below and below right: S. Andrea al Quirinale, by Bernini: the interior an oval nave opening into an apsed chancel, the exterior a massive classical portico sheltering a convex porch.

Baroque churches sought height and dimension, not by stretching the building upwards, as in a Gothic nave, but by illusion and false perspective and the use of light. Frequently the sculptural decorative effects and the painted surfaces were allowed to merge – a depiction in paint of the heavenly host spills out of its framed area and breaks into the spaces below; stucco *putti* riotously dissolve the formal barriers which ought to encompass a painted ceiling; altars and statues are softly lit from concealed windows to suggest that they exist in another world, just beyond the ordinary perceptions of man.

This last feature achieved its most exaggerated expression at Toledo Cathedral in Spain. Here, in the 1720s, Narciso Tomé removed a Gothic vault to provide a chapel for the Blessed Sacrament which was entirely defined by light. The *trasparente* is a typical moving assemblage of Baroque carved figures, caught in ecstatic adoration, flooded with yellow light from the perforation in the vault above, which is itself defined by carved figures of the inhabitants of heaven. The effect, as was intended, is not only one of profound awe at the mystery of the Sacrament itself but of the melting away of the present realities as the aspirant to faith contemplates the triumphant glories of the celestial host.

The sense of movement in Baroque churches is structural and not merely decorative, for the buildings themselves frequently departed from the rectangular or square shapes of basilica or Greek cross pedigree. Renaissance experiments with oval churches were now copied and developed in great profusion. Several oval spaces were sometimes interconnected to form the basic plan, and great inventiveness was shown in this, for the scenographic qualities of Baroque were enormously enhanced by the curvilinear surfaces that could be produced. The great master of the Baroque, Gianlorenzo Bernini, conveyed this to marvellous effect in his Roman church of S. Andrea al Quirinale, completed in 1670. Borromini showed how it is possible to vary a basic oval design to produce a church whose curved interior surfaces created spacial illusions: witness his S. Carlo alle Quattro Fontane in Rome, built between 1637 and 1641. This church also demonstrates another Baroque feature – curved façades, often intended to

Two influential façades by Borromini that make use of convex and concave shapes. Above: S. Carlo alle Quattro Fontane, Rome. Right: S. Agnese in Piazza Navona, Rome. The fountain in the foreground is by Bernini.

enhance the immediate urban landscape, though later (and especially in Latin America) copied in rural areas. Borromini's astonishing cupola and campanile at S. Andrea della Fratte have alternating convex and concave surfaces of brick rising between Corinthian pilasters. The undulating façade at S. Carlo was only completed in 1667, after Borromini's death. At the oratory of St Philip Neri Borromini created a brick façade in a wide concave form. Completed in 1640, it was probably the first curved front to be added to a building in Rome. Borromini's church of S. Agnese in the Piazza Navona has a wide concave front designed in the 1650s. Pietro da Cortona also built some curved façades in Rome whose distinction and popularity helped to establish the device as a leading feature of Baroque churches everywhere. His church of SS. Luca e Martina, built between 1634 and 1669, has a tall, two-storey convex façade; and his façade added in 1659 to Sta Maria della Pace exaggerates the convex form to the point at which it becomes a kind of oval section for the colonnaded porch at street level, with a convex upper storey rising above it.

Even more than the Renaissance church builders, the Baroque architects were concerned with the creation of total environments. The insides of churches were sometimes planned in relation to exterior vistas – as with the great front doors at Baldassare Longhena's Sta Maria della Salute at the mouth of the Grand Canal in Venice, built to celebrate the deliverance of the city from the plague of 1630. The

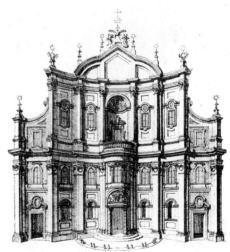

The façade of the oratory of St Philip Neri, the headquarters of the Oratorian order: another ingenious use by Borromini of a shallow concave curve contrasted with the convex shape of the central porch.

The high altar of Sta Maria della Salute, Venice (see p. 214), occupies a mysteriously lit space of its own opening off the central octagon.

façade is in the form of an enormous triumphal arch, and through the entrance the view of the main altar, carefully lit from behind, is uninterrupted and deliberately dramatic. The subdued tonal qualities of the interior, with grey walls and light-green glass, suggest a continuation of the Venetian urban environment: watery flat vistas. Raised upon a million wooden piles sunk into the mud of the lagoon, the Salute is in the shape of a crown, a tribute to the Queen of Heaven for her intervention on behalf of the citizens at the time of the plague. The huge dome is supported around its drum by massive and theatrical sculpted scrolls: the shape of the heavenly crown itself, above which is a statue of the Virgin, her head surrounded by a further circle of stars. Sometimes Baroque masters of architecture rearranged the immediate environment to provide a fit setting for existing religious buildings – like Bernini's famous colonnades in St Peter's Square, started in 1656, and intended to enhance the great basilica itself as the gateway to Redemption.

In other churches the notion of *theatrum sacrum* involved the employment of the immediate urban environment to produce dramatic scenographic effects. Thus Alessandro Galilei's massive façade added in 1735 to the basilica of St John Lateran (the cathedral of Rome) and surmounted by colossal figures of Christ and the Apostles, was intended to dominate the intersections of two main thoroughfares, and so point to the supremacy of the Church in the city. Thus, also, Cortona's Sta Maria della Pace in Rome, with its prominent convex façade, actually extends to right and to left, so that contiguous buildings are drawn into the plan of the church; and the two churches in the Piazza del Popolo in Rome, designed by Rainaldi, are inseparably integrated with the curving front of the great space enclosed within the piazza.

Baroque Rome was turned by successive popes into a vast theatrical setting for the sacred drama of the papacy. Left: the Piazza del Popolo, the principal entrance to the city from the north. The central street, the Corso, is ancient. The one on the left was laid out by Clement VII in 1525, that on the right by Leo X in 1518. The two churches already there were given matching façades under Alexander VII in 1658. Above: Maderna's façade of St Peter's with the huge oval colonnade of Bernini's piazza in front of it. Right: façade of the Lateran basilica, another Baroque addition to an earlier church, dating from 1735.

The pilgrimage churches of the German lands – a product of the cult of local saints in the seventeenth and eighteenth centuries – often made use of Baroque and Rococo styles to incorporate surrounding features of the landscape to startling effect. The most celebrated example of this is the Benedictine abbey of Melk in Lower Austria. The ancient foundation here, set upon a rock above the Danube, was completely rebuilt in the first two decades of the eighteenth century by Jakob Prandtauer, so that the large twin-towered church, and flanking monastic buildings, rise in decorative splendour, crystalline Baroque above a glassy river surface. Baroque planners also employed the classical concept of a 'sacred stairway' to give their churches the significance of a route towards the celestial realities. Most well known of these is undoubtedly the Spanish steps in Rome, designed by De Sanctis and constructed between 1723 and 1726 to link the wedge-shaped piazza below with the church of the Trinità dei Monti above. Though now the haunt of pickpockets and the vending place for 'folk-craft' ephemera, these magnificent stairs were originally intended to enhance the sacred presence of the church in the grandeur of the city beneath it.

Rather more liturgical in inspiration was the *Via Crucis* stairway in front of the Portuguese church of the Bom Jesús near Braga, built in the 1720s. The church itself was actually built last – in the 1780s: a twin-towered masterpiece by Cruz Amarante. The stuccoed walls of the stairway, topiary work, decorative obelisks and urns, begin to suggest the further classical idea of a 'sacred garden'. These particular steps were copied in the Portuguese overseas territories, notably

It was Baroque architects who discovered the dramatic possibilities of the staircase. Above: Via Crucis, *leading to the church of the Bom Jesús, near Braga, in Portugal; the steps are lined with small chapels containing tableaux of the twelve stations of the Cross, while the landings have fountains with allegories representing the five senses.* Right: *the Spanish Steps, Rome, a brilliant exercise in curves and counter-curves. The three flights and three landings allude to the Trinity, to which the church at the top is dedicated.*

beneath the church of the Immaculate Conception at Panjim (Panaji) in Goa.

The cult of saints was at the centre of Baroque spirituality, and Baroque churches are accordingly filled with carved, sculpted and painted representations of them. Smaller versions, in wooden statues covered with *gesso* and brightly polychromed, were kept in private houses as treasured possessions of the family – usually representing a central figure of Christianity, like the Virgin, or the personal saint of a member of the family, or a favourite with the particular locality. In folk religion the saints were expected to give actual help in daily labour, or in times of sickness and crisis, and the presence of the carved representation was intended to guarantee the immediate patronage of the heavenly society. The large versions in churches were decorated and carried in procession on the days which were by local custom, or by the calendar of the Church, specified in their honour. The height of the popularity of the Baroque style – in Europe, this was the seventeenth and eighteenth centuries, but in the Spanish and Portuguese colonial territories, even after independence, this

For the monastery of Melk, on the Danube in Austria, Jakob Prandtauer conceived the idea of setting back his twin-towered church façade, bringing forward the two arms of the monastic building (the library and the Kaisersaal), and connecting them by a lower transparent screen. The situation gives an effect of unparalleled splendour.

The Virgin of Guadeloupe is perhaps the most famous religious image in Latin America. In 1531 St Juan Diego, an Indian peasant, was directed by the Virgin – who appeared to him in the form of a native Mexican princess – to gather roses from a mountain-side in his cloak. When he later unwrapped them, there appeared, on the cloak, a miraculous representation of the Virgin. This event encouraged many local cults of the Virgin in the conquered territories of Latin America, and resulted in numerous shrines, some of Spanish and some of native Indian inspiration.

extended to the end of the nineteenth century – saw a revival of popular devotion to medieval saints, and to the saints associated with the ecclesiastical miracles of the florid spirituality of the Counter-Reformation. In Europe, and especially in Bohemia, many local saints attracted an enduring following. Chief amongst these was St John Nepomuk, martyred by King Wenceslas IV in 1393, his head surrounded by a star-shaped nimbus as he was thrown into the River Moldau. He was canonized in 1729, and many churches in his honour survive.

But it was in the Latin American world, and in the other countries of the Spanish and Portuguese expansion, that the cult of saints reached its most extravagant dimension, with the converted peoples of the great empires finding in the transplanted European saints some familiar associations with their own half-abandoned religious practices. The process of indigenization of popular Catholicism soon showed indications of syncretism: the 'idols under the altar' of the Latin American peasantry, and their carved and painted Christian saints with their sad Indian faces. In the Spanish empire, from South America proper and the Caribbean islands, to New Mexico, California and the Philippines, there was an astonishing iconographic uniformity, and the same can be said of the Portuguese world – Brazil, Goa, and Macau in particular. Everywhere the *santos*, or religious images, whether statues (*bultos*) or painted panels (*retablos*), followed easily recognizable conventions, so that a traveller entering a church in any one of these territories could instantly identify the represented saints.

In his study of the religious art of the Philippines, Fernando Zóbel de Ayala has categorized the representations of the Baroque saints as 'popular', 'classical' and 'ornate'. These divisions are not really chronological, for the crude peasant images, with their human charm and simple piety, were made in rural areas until almost the present day; and the more sophisticated and decorated carvings, sometimes even of European origin, were first produced in urban centres, like Manila, in the sixteenth century. Everywhere there is a strong preference for the saints who assist the poor in daily life. There is San Roque, with his dog by his side, pointing to the sores on his leg; the saint, who died in 1380, had fallen ill of the plague in a forest and had been fed by a dog carrying bread in its mouth. He is the guardian against disease. San Ramón Nonato, holding the monstrance with the Blessed Sacrament in one hand and the palm of martyrdom in the other, had worked among captives of the Moslems in North Africa until his death in 1240. He is the patron of midwives – a very necessary intercessor in view of the high infant mortality rate among the peoples of the Spanish colonial empire. San Isidro Labrador is shown with an angel (who once ploughed his field miraculously) and an ox. He is a particular favourite with peasant labourers and farmers.

Many of the saints seen in the churches are there because of the religious orders who spearheaded the missions in the New World: St Ignatius of Loyola in the Jesuit churches, St Francis of Assisi in the Franciscan, St Augustine in the Augustinian, St Vincent Ferrer (a popular preacher and miracle worker who died in 1419) in the Dominican. Sometimes the figures are nostalgic reminders to the colonial settlers or officials of their homelands: St Anthony of Padua, patron of Lisbon, with the Christ Child in one hand, or the Virgin of Montserrat, a favourite with the Catalonian sailors of Barcelona. Representations of the Virgin tend, also, to follow Iberian cults – La Reina de los Cielos, de los Dolores, and de la Consolacion, for example, and in the nineteenth century, the patron of the poor, Nuestra Señora del Rosario. An exception was the Virgin of Guadeloupe, whose radiance and Indian features were the first fruits of the indigenization of Christianity in the Americas.

Catholicism in general demonstrated a great consistency and uniformity in the colonial empires. This indicated the degree of Crown control, and the centralized authority of the religious orders who actually advanced the frontiers of Christianity. In the nineteenth century the disintegrating tendencies of the liberalism or urban secularism which accompanied the independence movements was arrested, in some measure, by ultramontanism emanating from Rome. Baroque was the normal style of building and decoration during this extraordinary and successful expansion of the Christian religion. It is thus to the Baroque churches of these lands that the observer must look to discover some of the most interesting and some of the most extravagant developments of the style. The resources of the new lands added a new richness to church interiors: the silver of Mexico, and the gold of Colombia and Ecuador, fashioned into glowing and ornate altars, and shining from the coffered ceilings of chapels. Decorative motifs were borrowed from the tropical environment: a riotous mixture of ferns and palm leaves, luxuriant fruits, sea-shells and fantastic creatures. Most distinctive of all, however, was the infusion of native artistic creativity. Originally, perhaps, the Spanish and the Portuguese used the splendours of the Baroque style to impress the conquered peoples with the power of their religion, but within a generation, already, the indigenous craftsmen were re-creating their own faith in the buildings which they decorated. The carved angels came to have Indian faces, the saints began to look like splendidly dressed rural peasants, and even the representations of Christ showed a man of toil and suffering, bent low as he carried his cross or displaying horrific and realistic wounds. There was no sentiment here, but only the earthy reality of the lives of the poor, offered up in the only way left to them to suggest a higher purpose.

The finest impression of this indigenized, popular Baroque may be seen at Cholula in Mexico. It was, before the conquest, a holy city, with some 400 shrines. Cortés demolished them all, and at over seventy or so of the sites he set up churches. Here the visitor may therefore see some perfect sixteenth-century Baroque, like the astonishing Capella Real, with its forty-eight domes, and the crowded interior of Sta Maria de Tonantzintla, with its stucco *putti* whose Indian features stare down in passive indifference. At nearby Puebla, 'the City of the Angels', the local craftsmen have for centuries specialized in polychrome tiles, and the Baroque churches of the area, like S. Francisco Acatepec, are enriched with tile cladding. Many of the domes of the churches of the city are covered with glazed tiles as well. The splendid cathedral is well known for its marble floors and columns and for the gold-leaf woodwork of its altars.

In Puebla, too, may be seen the convent of Sta Monica, dating from 1606, with its delightful cloister, faced with eighteenth-century Baroque tiles, and its church, which was rather poorly adapted to Neo-classical taste in the nineteenth century, but is still structurally very typical of Mexican Baroque. The convent was closed down by the government during the anti-clerical purges of the 1920s and 1930s, yet a few nuns survived in a hidden part of the building, reached through a secret doorway. The convent, for years run by the State as a museum of atheism, has in more tolerant times become a museum of religious art (the exhibits have remained the same, but the labels have been changed), and here may be seen some fine examples of Baroque church furnishings.

The cathedral of Mexico City itself, started in 1525, was largely built out of stones originally used in the Aztec temple on the site. It was rebuilt in 1573 and enlarged on and off until 1813, so that it is the largest, as well as the oldest, cathedral in Latin America. Inside, there is a celebrated and popular 'Black Christ', a miracle-working carving of the Crucifixion which attracts the devotion

S. Francisco Acatepec, in Puebla, Mexico. The façade is covered with brightly coloured tiles, a technique traditional in Spain but here carried to an extreme unknown at home (see pl. 54).

Detail of the interior of Sta Maria de Tonantzintla, Cholula, Mexico, c. 1700, crowded with ornament and with figures whose features suggest their Indian origin.

Right: the present cathedral of Mexico City, built on the site of an Aztec temple, was begun in 1573 on a huge scale and finished by 1667. The original intention was probably to have four towers, one at each corner. To the right is the Sagrario Metropolitano of 1769, in a style that has been christened 'ultra-Baroque'. Its details recall those of the Granada sacristy (pl. 50).

of the poor of the city. Annexed to the main structure, to the south side, is the Sagrario Metropolitano, built in 1769 in the 'Churrigueresque style' (after José de Churriguera) – an ornate façade recalling, as it was doubtless intended to do, the great west front of the cathedral of Santiago de Compostela.

To the north-east of the city is the great shrine of Guadeloupe, on a hill once venerated in the Aztec religion as the abode of an earth-spirit, a female fertility goddess. Here, in a happy continuity of faith, Our Lady herself appeared in 1531, shortly after the conquest of the city, to St Juan Diego, in a series of apparitions. Eventually gathering the roses she indicated to him in his *serape* – a rough cloak of cactus fibres – he took himself to the Bishop of Mexico. When he unfolded the *serape* it was found to bear the miraculous imprint of the Virgin herself. The *serape*, with its representation of the Virgin, looking like a young Aztec princess, may be seen to this day in the new basilica at Guadeloupe. The old basilica, a fine Baroque building, has had to be abandoned because of subsidence; a larger shrine was anyway required because of the thousands of pilgrims who came here every day to pay their respects to the Virgin and to seek an answer to their petitions. Nowhere in Mexico is Baroque spirituality so alive, even in the concrete modernity of the new church. The pilgrims cross the huge piazza on their knees to enter the shrine and light candles to the gentle Virgin with her Indian face and serene form, set amidst a radiating sunburst, her hands in prayer. Our Lady of Guadeloupe is the patroness of Latin America.

The typical Baroque church of the Spanish and Portuguese colonial empires has a twin-towered façade – bells were important for calling the illiterate peasantry to devotion and for warning against danger – and an external simplicity. The austere walls, often given colour-wash in the nineteenth century, provide no clue to the splendours within. The buildings often have rather massive qualities, even when their dimensions are actually quite modest: an indication of the large

masonry blocks used in their construction. This was for protection against collapse during earthquakes (for the whole Western seaboard of both North and South America comprises an earthquake zone), and was a device copied from the native populations, and especially from the Incas of Peru. In Lima, capital of Peru, and the seat of the Spanish colonial administration for the whole of the South American empire, the main churches show the size of these solid towered fronts. The cathedral, containing, in a glass coffin, the body of Pizzaro, founder of the city, was completely rebuilt following the great earthquake of 1746, and its huge, rather squat western towers are sentinels each side of a thoroughly Baroque entrance portico. Here the ornate carving, and the niches containing statues of saints, echo some of the other Baroque churches of the city – San Augustín, for example, with its 'Churrigueresque' façade, built in 1720. San Augustín was itself badly damaged in the earthquake of 1974. The church of S. Francisco is also notable for its massive west towers. This building, on the site of the first church of 1546, was completed in 1674. The interior has some wood-carving, both in the choir and in the altars of the fifteen chapels, which is of outstanding quality, and some breathtaking painted ceilings. Beneath the church are three descending levels of brick vaults; the catacombs contain the remains of the friars and some more recent burials, and are a kind of melancholy reminder to the visitor of the cycle of life and death. For above are the splendid ceilings, disclosing the heavens and penetrating the mysteries of eternity, and below are the decayed remnants of the citizens of the world, stacked in fearful vaults where scorpions emerge to feed upon the human debris.

In contrast to these chill depths is the delightful sanctuary of Sta Rosa de Lima. This simple, pink-wash, barrel-vaulted church, beside the River Rimac, is another example of the deceptive external austerity of the South American Baroque mode. It is a pilgrimage church, in honour of St Rose, who was born in Lima in 1586, and who died there, a Dominican nun, in 1617. Her ascetic life was offered in expiation for the corruptions of society, and behind the altar of her

Façades of two churches in Lima, Peru. Above left: S. Francisco (1669–74). The emphatic contrast between the powerful masonry of the towers and the ornately decorative portico is characteristic of Spanish America. Above right: San Augustín (1720), its central section even more densely filled with ornamental features, piled on top of one another until the eye has nowhere to rest.

225

The Franciscan church of Nuestra Señora del Pilar at Buenos Aires, Argentina (1716–32), by Andrés Blanqui, a Jesuit architect: a reaction against the excesses of Churrigueresque.

S. Francisco, Bogotá, Columbia, mid-sixteenth century.

church may be seen a Baroque showpiece: a large painting of the saint being received into Paradise. In the little rose-garden, beside the sanctuary, are the remains of the small adobe hut that she built, and it is said that the imprint of her hands may still be discerned in the mud walls. It was here that she received her miraculous visitations from the Infant Christ. St Rose is the patron of Spanish America and the Philippine Islands.

The technique of building in large blocks to lessen earthquake damage is nowhere shown to better effect than in the monastery church of S. Francisco in Santiago de Chile. Part of the walls of this church are red stucco, but beneath is massive masonry. Yet the church is a reproduction of the mid-nineteenth century, preserving the Baroque style and decorative effects of the original mid-sixteenth-century structure. It is now a national monument, containing, as it does, the statue of the Virgin brought to the city by Pedro de Valdivia, founder of Santiago, in 1541. Another late example of massive building techniques may be seen in the mission churches of California. The original structures here, established by Junipero Serra between 1769 (when the Franciscans took over from the Jesuits as the missionaries for the territory) and his death in 1784, were frail and simple shelters of wood and adobe. Buildings in stone blocks were introduced early in the nineteenth century precisely to lessen earthquake devastation. Thus the Mission at Santa Barbara, planned by Serra but actually established just after his death, in 1786, had to build four churches in two decades. Finally, following the earthquake of 1812, the old Mission church was constructed of stone blocks and survives to this day. A noble Baroque edifice formed by two massive and domed square towers, it was completed in 1820 (the second tower being an addition of 1833), yet perfectly preserves the Baroque style which had been stable in the Americas for three centuries.

It should not be supposed that all the churches of the Spanish overseas territories were so austere and massive in exterior appearance as those just considered. In many places buildings of great delicacy were built. Most of the old churches of Buenos Aires in Argentina were gutted by Perónista mobs in 1955, but one was spared, presumably because of its location beside the Recoleta necropolis. This is the church of Nuestra Señora del Pilar, a superb example of the Colonial Baroque style, whose pilastered façade of white and yellow stucco has simple forms yet somehow suggests an almost Rococo exuberance. The campanile echoes the same forms. The church was begun in 1716 by the Franciscans, and contains a fine wood-carving of San Pedro de Alcantara by the seventeenth-century Spanish master Alonso Cano.

In Bogotá, the capital of Colombia, there are some splendid Baroque churches with decorated exteriors. The cathedral hardly ranks among them, for, despite a rather grand pedimented façade in the Baroque mode, it is an odd mixture of classical styles, the result of more or less complete rebuilding in 1807. But the church of S. Francisco, which dates from the mid-sixteenth century, has a simple façade and large square tower whose subtle decorative effects actually achieve great delicacy. Inside the wood-carving of the high altar and choir stalls, done in 1622, is a spectacular display of triumphalist Baroque – not of riotous ascending movement, but of noble and ordered disclosure of religious dignity. The church also contains some notable paintings by Gregorio Vásquez, in particular his scenographic version of the Last Judgment. The European Baroque device of illusionistic perspective painting is not absent from South America, though examples tend to be modern adaptations. Thus in the cathedral of S. Juan de Puerto Rico – a building of 1540 heavily restored in the last and in the present century – there is fine ceiling painting suggesting false coffering and the clouds of heaven, but it is a modern restoration, completed in 1977. The cathedral is the resting place of Juan Ponce de Leon, founder of the Spanish colony and also the commander who pioneered the earliest Spanish and Catholic presence in Florida. It is also the less likely resting place of San Pio, a Roman martyr brought to Puerto Rico in 1862.

The Baroque churches of the Philippines are no different from those of the South American Spanish colonial empire, save for their exceptionally high numbers. They are found throughout the lush landscape of the extended archipelago, the crumbling stucco walls of the rural churches, with their colours faded by the tropical heat and humidity, seeming to merge with the vegetation itself. The more sophisticated structures were in Manila, but most of the older churches there were destroyed during the heavy bombardment of February 1945, when General MacArthur reclaimed the city from the Japanese, reducing most of it to rubble. One of the finest of the old Baroque churches somehow survived, however, within the wrecked walled city which was once the jewel of the Spanish empire. San Augustín is actually dedicated to St Paul, but as the main church in the city of the Augustinians it has always borne the name of their patron. Replacing two slightly earlier wooden structures, the church was built in a classical Baroque style between 1599 and 1606. Its foundations are shaped like the hull of a ship so that it would 'float' during an earthquake. There were twin towers, one of which was demolished following an earthquake in 1889. The façade, like Roman Baroque churches, has two storeys of columns, the lower Doric and the upper Corinthian, surrounded by a high-pitched pediment. The effect is one of grace and proportion, as the architect, Juan Macias, intended. The large rounded entrance door, of molave wood, consists of four panels with curved Augustinian symbols, and to each side are niches containing statues of Saints Peter and Paul. Just as in South America the converted Indians left traces of their culture in the decoration of the churches, so in the Philippines the Chinese craftsmen and labourers made their own mark. At San Augustín, there are four stone lions along the base of the façade, a reminder of the lions which guard the entrance to Chinese temples. Inside, the church is lined with fourteen chapels, each side of a Latin cross plan. The nave is covered by another example of Baroque illusionistic painting, and again it is a fairly modern emulation of Baroque originals, being the work of the Italian painters Dibella and Alberoni in 1875. Attached to the church is a cloister and the monastic buildings, begun in 1587, stand just before the church itself. The whole complex is a splendid reminder of the vitality of the Spanish Catholic diaspora, and the tenacity of its hold upon the affections of the varied peoples it drew into the Christian faith.

The religious expansionism of the Portuguese was no less extraordinary than that of the Spanish: witness the white glistening churches – in an early twentieth-century, last flowering of the Baroque style – which stick up with surreal abruptness out of the jungles of Southern Angola. In Brazil the Portuguese produced not only some superb Baroque churches but also an architect of genius. Antonio Francisco Lisboa, known as 'El Aleijadinho' ('the Little Cripple'), was similar to the Italian masters of the Baroque in that he was both an architect and a sculptor, and his churches accordingly have that sculptural quality which so distinguished the High Baroque in Europe. His greatest church is usually thought to be the basilica of Bom Jesús de Matozinhos in Congouhas do Compo. Baroque churches are found in greatest profusion in Minas Gerais, Bahia, and the old province of Pernambuco. Recife, the modern capital of the latter, is filled with delightful churches, each loved for particular statues of saints. The church of São Pedro dos Clérigos, completed in 1782, and noted because of a fine façade, has

São Pedro dos Clérigos at Recife, Brazil, by Manuel Jacome, hides an elongated octagonal nave behind its flat façade.

Façade of Santiago de Compostela in Spain: the structure of the towers is still recognizably Romanesque, but the whole front was covered by Baroque decoration in the eighteenth century.

The altar of St Ignatius in Old Goa, India, a city that flourished under Portuguese rule in the seventeenth century, when a whole range of Baroque churches was built. It was intended that Goa should be the starting point for the Christian conversion of the East.

illusionistic ceiling paintings. Perhaps the most splendid church in the city, however, is the Golden Chapel of the Third Order of St Francis. Begun in 1696 and finished in 1724, it is a treasure-house of rich gilded carving and fine painted panels. At Olinda, on the coast just to the north of Recife, and the older capital of Pernambuco, there are also many churches, convents and monasteries, of which the monastic church of São Francisco contains some splendid Baroque carving and painting.

The conversion of the East was projected to take place from the Portuguese territory of Goa on the western coast of India, and the great Apostle of the enterprise was St Francis Xavier. This famous Jesuit missionary visited Japan in 1549, and then, after a brief interlude in Goa again, set out for China in 1552. But he died on a small island off the Chinese mainland, and his work, still largely unfulfilled, was left to others. Traces of the Mission survive in the scattered Baroque churches of the East – of which the most magnificent outside Goa itself is unquestionably the seventeenth-century church of St Paul built by the Jesuits in the Portuguese colony of Macau. The main body of the church was destroyed by fire in 1835 and never rebuilt, but the surviving façade, with its pedimented five tiers of columns is a masterpiece of Baroque at its most audacious. As at San Augustín in Manila, Chinese symbolism has been incorporated: there are dragons carved into the stonework.

But it is Goa that contains what is perhaps the best concentration of Baroque ecclesiastical buildings anywhere in the world. After a couple of centuries of neglect, when the creepers of the surrounding tropical vegetation covered the disintegrating red laterite walls, and snakes were said to inhabit the churches, the structures of Old Goa, the Portuguese capital, have now been restored. The largest church is the cathedral, begun in 1562, as a mixture of styles, none of which are authentically Baroque. It has a Gothic-type exterior and an interior with classical features. But the church and convent of São Francisco, dating from 1661, is in Portuguese Baroque and contains some fine wood-carvings and painted panels. Begun in 1655, the church of São Cajetan is in a classical Baroque style, and was, indeed, modelled on St Peter's in Rome as far as the structure is concerned (with Portuguese Baroque models for its decorative effects).

The greatest church of the group, however, is the basilica of Bom Jesús, filled each day with pilgrims who come to see the tomb of St Francis Xavier. The body of the great missionary was finally returned to Goa in 1554, after resting for some years in Malacca; in 1613 it was enshrined in a silver and glass coffin (exposed for public veneration every ten years) in the Bom Jesús. The saint is miraculously preserved. The church itself was completed in 1605 and the simplicity of the interior contrasts with the sumptuous gilding of the carved altars. The tomb of St Francis is a huge sarcophagus, with the reliquary-coffin resting on its top, designed by the Florentine sculptor Giovanni Batista Foggini in 1688. The sacristy has a small reliquary containing a section of one of the saint's toes. In the anteroom is a delightful naive painting of St Francis standing on a beach preaching to the Indians, and in the foreground fish and other creatures of the deep lift their heads from the waves in order to hear his words.

The Baroque style was overwhelmingly Catholic. But there were some Protestant examples, and those in the Low Countries enjoyed a particularly inventive and successful transplanting to South Africa. The first resident minister of the Dutch Reformed Church arrived at the Cape in 1665, and the religious presence which issued from his labours came to be expressed in a distinctive Baroque-Rococo 'Cape Dutch' style: white stuccoed single-storey churches with undulating gables. What is thought to be the oldest surviving church in South

Africa, built in 1743 – the Old Roodezand Dutch Reformed Church in Tulbagh, Cape Province – is also one of the most delightful illustrations of the style. It has graceful Rococo plasterwork, with a gable surmounted by a scallop motif. The building has been restored and is now a museum.

In Namibia, the former German colony of South West Africa, there are some fine early twentieth-century Lutheran churches in faithfully exported Rococo. These show few signs of distinctive adaptation, yet are by any standards buildings of distinction and grace. The Evangelisch-Lutherische Kirche in the coastal town of Swakopmund, with its pilastered front, scrolled gable, and slender tower, is painted in a light yellow typical of the Rococo churches of Germany. It was built between 1909 and 1912.

Thus churches continued to be built in the High Baroque and in various localized folk Baroque styles until well into the twentieth century in the European overseas areas of influence. For many people in the Developing World, therefore, Baroque architecture expresses their normal idea of what a church is like. During the nineteenth century city churches in Latin America began to be built in the French Neo-classical mode, but this has never succeeded folk Baroque in the popular imagination.

In Europe, however, the Baroque style underwent some earlier developments. In Spain extravagant ornament became fashionable at the start of the eighteenth century: as seen in the fantastic crowded façades of churches built in the 'Churrigueresque' manner. Best known of these is at Santiago de Compostela, where the façade, of yellow granite, which was added to the Romanesque cathedral – the centre of the cult of St James and a favourite pilgrimage church of Europeans for centuries – was completed in 1749. The soaring grandeur of the twin towers is arrested at several levels by the weight of decorative devices.

In other parts of Europe the Baroque mode merged into classicism in a series of transitions and regional idiosyncrasies which make exact categorization hazardous. The work of Sir Christopher Wren in England, for example, was permanently influenced by his only visit abroad – to Paris in 1665 and 1666, where he met Bernini, who was working in the city at the time. There he studied the French Baroque buildings going up in Paris. It is difficult to describe features of Wren's architecture as anything other than Baroque, though his churches (of which he produced designs for no less than fifty-two in London, following the opportunity provided by the Great Fire of 1666) do not really fit the general European Baroque culture. His love of steeples was not a Baroque feature.

But it is Wren's great masterpiece, St Paul's Cathedral, which is a monument to his adhesion to a crucial Baroque characteristic: the love of sculptural illusion. Built between 1675 and 1710, the new St Paul's was a building of original genius. The charred Gothic remnants of the old cathedral, with its recently added classical façade, were completely dismantled, and Wren's replacement was triumphantly classical. Its greatest feature, the dome, is a Baroque set piece. Apparently raised upon false outer walls, which hide the buttresses, the huge dome of wood and lead actually encases a smaller inner dome, of brick and stone. Thus the observer within the cathedral looks up to a deceptive, rather flattened dome, in the belief that he is seeing the exterior higher structure – itself designed to be seen as part of a distant vista. The lantern and cross are raised upon an inner cone of brick, hidden between the exterior and interior domes. So Wren, who was trained as a scientist and knew well how to contrive his mechanical effects, produced an illusionistic building of great audacity which, in typical Baroque manner, he consciously fashioned to provide the centre of great urban scenographic drama.

Looking into the inner dome of St Paul's Cathedral, London, by Sir Christopher Wren. It rests on four mighty corner piers, but Wren disguises this fact by outlining semi-circular arches on the piers, so that the crossing space appears to be an octagon.

229

In the German regions of Europe the Baroque style, originally imported by Italian practitioners, was developed by some truly great architects, making southern Germany, Austria and Bohemia the second centres of Baroque church building. Johann Fischer von Erlach had studied in Rome and knew Bernini. His main work was in Salzburg and in Vienna, where, in 1705, he became architect at the imperial court. The royal church he built in honour of St Charles Borromeo in Vienna (the Karlskirche) was on an oval plan, as were some of his other churches. There is a large central dome, but the church is dominated by its west façade, where low towers frame a classical portico, and where two Christianized replicas of Trajan's Column produce a bizarre and unique feature. The odd proportions of the church, however, were the price to pay for its symbolic purpose. The Karlskirche is a monument to the ruling dynasty and was intended to evoke associations both with imperial Roman power and with the Temple of Jerusalem. It was completed in 1740. Fischer von Erlach's earlier churches in Salzburg were also in the grand Baroque manner, and his Kollegienkirche, completed in 1707, also contrives echoes of former imperial glory. These churches were too expressive of the distinctive genius of Fischer von Erlach to represent a particular variation of the Baroque style, however, and it is to Bohemia, and to the work of Christoph and Johann Dientzenhofer that it is necessary to turn to find a popular and much-copied evolving style. Numerous little country churches emulate their major work. In Prague Christoph Dientzenhofer's St Nicholas in the Mala Strana, built between 1703 and 1711,

Attached to the Asam brothers' house in Munich is their church of St John Nepomuk, a tour de force of decorative effects on a small scale. There is a carefully graded progression from the dark lower storey to the light ceiling, paralleled by the iconographic progression from the altar, through the painting of the Assumption of the Virgin to the Trinity at the top.

Right: interior of the mid-eighteenth-century pilgrimage church of Vierzehnheiligen, in Bavaria, by Balthasar Neumann. It is a complex plan with an oval at the centre. Here stands the ornate shrine of the Fourteen Saints, whose cult gave rise to the church.

shows his majestic ability to create interior vistas in a characteristic and triumphalist fashion. As the late Baroque became increasingly associated with Rococo decoration, the work of Balthasar Neumann became a major influence, radiating from Würzburg, where he lived from 1711. His marvellous pilgrimage church at Vierzehnheiligen, started in 1743 to commemorate a local folk miracle, has all the lightness and delicate colouring which the Rococo decorative styles, whether in churches or secular palaces, used to evoke a sense of joyous movement.

In Bavaria a comparable stylistic achievement was attained in the work of the Asam brothers, and especially in the church of St John Nepomuk, completed in 1746, and still one of the most delightful churches in Munich. Perhaps even better known is the pilgrimage church built by Dominikus Zimmermann between 1746 and 1754: the Wieskirche, on an oval plan and with a light and delicate profusion of stucco decoration in the Rococo manner. Rococo derived its name from the *rocaille*, and marks the restoration of organic decoration to the position it had achieved in late Gothic. Yet its lightness and seemingly carnival quality suggests, still, the essentially Baroque world in which the splendour of Paradise can be viewed from the perspectives of ordinary human existence.

The Karlskirche, Vienna, by Johann Fischer von Erlach. In this unprecedented design the architect combines elements from ancient and modern Rome (Trajan's Column and the dome of St Peter's) with a complex political and ideological programme.

8 Neo-classical sobriety: churches of the Enlightenment

PROTESTANT COUNTRIES had never been sympathetic to the underlying ethos of Baroque, and although its spatial and decorative complexities clearly intrigued many English and French architects, the churches they built could never be confused with those of Italy, central Europe or Spain. When, in due time, the Catholic countries themselves experienced a reaction against the emotional extravagances of Baroque, the two sides drew closer together again architecturally. Neo-classicism, as the new style has come to be called, was in one sense a return to the early Renaissance and the ancient Roman ideal, but this time it was more learned, more archaeologically accurate and more earnest. It also, for the first time, included ancient Greece among its models. The complete temple front, with columns and pediment, which had not been used in the Renaissance, now became common. An interest in pure geometry revived, but characteristically it was concerned less with dynamic curvilinear forms – the circle, the oval, the spiral – than with static rectilinear ones – the cube and the pyramid. Just as in the Renaissance, architects found it natural to approach God through the classical past and abstract order.

Gothic, Renaissance and Baroque churches can all be interpreted without too much difficulty as expressions of religious experience and of particular attitudes to Christian doctrine. It is less easy to do this in the case of Neo-classicism, which was essentially a stylistic rather than a religious movement. For the first time, architects consciously and deliberately *chose* a style, and it was not long before it became clear that the choice was a multiple one. The earliest Neo-Gothic churches are contemporary with Neo-classical ones. Soon there was to be no automatically accepted style of the age, and it was left to architects and patrons to decide what they preferred, irrespective of their beliefs.

For captions to colour plates 56–60, see p. 237

SUB INVOC. S. GENOVEFÆ D.O.M. A. FUN. EXCITAVIT LUD. XV

57

58

Colour plates 56–60

56 *Louis XV laying the foundation stone of the church of Ste-Geneviève, now the Panthéon, in Paris, 6 September 1764. This painting, by Pierre-Antoine De Machy, is not what it seems. The building had, in fact, hardly risen above the ground. What we see here is a huge model of wood and canvas erected on the site to give the king and the court an adequate idea of what it was going to be like. If one looks through the central door one sees the houses on the other side of the square. Louis XV stands in the foreground examining the plan with the architect Jacques-Germain Soufflot. On the extreme right can be seen a row of workmen dressed in white with a crane; they are standing on the lower courses of the south transept. On the left is the church of St-Etienne-du-Mont.*

57 *Canaletto's panorama of the City of London in the mid-eighteenth century, dominated by St Paul's and by the myriad towers and spires of Wren's other City churches. The relation of secular to religious buildings is still that of the Middle Ages. Even the steeples – a medieval feature adopted by Wren without classical precedent – are not so unlike what they would have been before the Great Fire of 1666.*

58 *James Gibbs's St Martin-in-the-Fields, London, was designed at a time, 1722, when the Baroque was in full swing in southern Europe, yet it remains cool and chaste, betraying only by its plaster decoration and the curved bays flanking the chancel that Bernini and Borromini have lived and died. Box-pews were normal in England, as were the galleries fixed rather awkwardly to the Corinthian columns to provide more congregational space. Unlike any Catholic church, the altar is virtually ignored. Everything is concentrated on the preacher in his high three-decker pulpit.*

59 *Christ Church, Cambridge, Massachusetts, was designed in 1761 by Peter Harrison. Made of wood and far simpler than St Martin's, it can nevertheless be seen as a colonial expression of the same principles. But the ambitious columns (they were originally Doric, changed to Ionic in 1826) support only a simple coved ceiling. Harrison's King's Chapel in nearby Boston is a closer approximation to Gibbs's original.*

60 *The church of Canova's native town, Possagno, in Italy, was certainly inspired by the great sculptor's Neo-classical taste, though whether he actually designed it himself is debated. It was begun in 1819. Its basic elements are drawn from the Pantheon in Rome (the body of the church) and the Parthenon in Athens (the Doric portico). Neo-classicism could go no further, though it is curious that the pediment lacks any sculpture.*

Neo-classical sobriety

CHURCH BUILDING since the Renaissance had occurred in a social context in which architectural and decorative styles were increasingly set by the requirements of secular taste and use. The construction of urban palaces for leading families, and of country houses for great landed magnates, at first began to rival, and then to overtake, ecclesiastical patronage as the most dynamic influence. In the Baroque age it was still true – due to the overseas expansion of Iberian Catholicism – that more churches than secular buildings were planned and constructed; but in the reaction to Baroque taste, from the later decades of the seventeenth century and through the eighteenth, the pace was definitely set by secular patrons. The return to the simplicity and relative austerity of classical buildings was made with little reference to religious ideas. Even in France, where ecclesiastical requirements continued, more than in other countries, to exercise a major influence in architectural development, the adoption of Neo-classicism can scarcely be said to have expressed any kind of reorientation of theological opinion or any sort of shift of emphasis in ecclesiological priorities. The inspiration for France, on the contrary, derived from the presence in Rome in the mid-eighteenth century, at the French Academy, of a group of scholars who first absorbed and then actively propagated the ideals of the Picturesque and the architectural models of Piranesi. In France, perhaps even more than in England, buildings came to be appreciated as part of a wider context, historical and cultural, as well as in the ordinary sense environmental.

At their most fanciful and lyrical, classical buildings were represented in pastoral landscapes, sometimes in ruinous decay, but always suggesting monumental qualities which indicated rather more of the grandeur and order of ancient pagan civilization than of Christianity. Where the Renaissance revival of antiquity had been inspired by the supposition that its virtues disclosed an essential affinity with the Christian religion, and where Baroque taste had used those classical forms to transcend the world of immediate experience, Neo-classicism found in the ordered and sober, even melancholy, sculptural shapes of ancient buildings a source of human autonomy whose relationship to the Christianity simultaneously professed by the men of the times was not clear. The fascination for geometric forms – for spheres, pyramids, and cubes, for example – which preoccupied the architectural visions of the French eighteenth-century designers Etienne-Louis Boullée and Claude-Nicolas Ledoux, had no direct religious associations and was a straightforward adoption of pagan symbolism. Theirs was the exploration of a species of Deistic rationalism, not a calm rendition of received Christianity in any recognized sense. The neo-classicism of the eighteenth century, indeed, had sepulchral qualities which were often hinted at in the British churches of the period and were sometimes most perfectly expressed in actual cemeteries. The Glasgow necropolis in Scotland, for example, is like a Neo-classical city on a diminished scale – a city of the dead in which the sculptural shapes of Greek and Roman buildings are lined up for the observation of the living in a manner which somehow manages to combine a sense of grace with a horrific and nightmarish evocation of decay. The two things, in fact, seem

Steeples after Wren could assume some bizarre forms. For St George's, Bloomsbury, London, Nicholas Hawksmoor reconstructed what he imagined to be the mausoleum of Halicarnassus, one of the Seven Wonders of the ancient world, surmounted by a statue of George I as St George.

Opposite: the interior of Ste-Geneviève (pl. 56) is meticulously classical in its forms, but Soufflot based his constructional methods on Gothic, supporting his heavy domes and arches on a system of buttressing and counter-thrusts. Unfortunately his calculations were wrong and soon after it was built the large windows of the ground floor had to be filled in with masonry to strengthen the walls.

St Mary's Catholic Pro-Cathedral in Dublin, begun in 1815, is continental in its stern classicism, perhaps as a deliberate contrast to the two Protestant cathedrals in Dublin, which were Gothic.

The Catholic church of St Hedwig, in Berlin, marks the beginning of Neo-classicism in Germany. It was designed in 1747 but not completed until twenty-five years later. Again the model is the Pantheon, Rome, but with the portico integrated as closely as possible into the circular nave.

to be essentially conjoined in Neo-classicism. The love of ruins set in an ideal landscape, as in the paintings of Nicolas Poussin or Claude Lorraine, points to the dissolution of human contrivances and yet also to the permanence of the beauty of the natural world.

A major influence in the development of the new taste was the excavation of the Roman city of Herculaneum, started in 1738, with the consequent revelation of classical ruins on a massive scale. The simultaneous rediscovery of Greek material culture offered an alternative to Roman antiquity which seemed, to eighteenth-century interpreters, to indicate more perfect because more austere forms, closer to nature. Out of this reorientation of thought came the Neo-classical vision: a combination of reason and order with pastoral innocence and rustic simplicity. The Doric columns of Greece were identified as symbols of a lost society which once embodied those ideals. Greek forms began to appear alongside Roman ones in buildings, secular and religious alike. The resulting sober, monumental structures, with their minimal adornment, had no external features which distinguished their use – banks, custom-houses, churches all looked the same.

In 1831, for example, the Anglican cathedral of St John was opened in Buenos Aires: the oldest non-Catholic church in South America, half of its cost met by the British taxpayer. Its massive columned west front is a perfect summary of the Neo-classical ideal. Did the vision of human reason set in an ideal natural landscape have any affinities with the 'Natural Theology' which became the orthodoxy of Protestant scholarship in the eighteenth century? It is difficult to know how to answer that question, partly because there was in some sense a shared cultural outlook of the age which must have seeped into both secular and religious endeavours, but partly also because Catholic theology, which was less indebted to 'Natural Theology' in the period, was cultivated by men in Catholic countries where Neo-classicism was just as strong as in Protestant ones.

This was the age in which parklands were laid out with mock classical temples as focal points, and in which Christian churches, built to resemble pagan religious structures, were called 'temples' as well. Pagan and Christian motifs were placed side by side: at the church of St Magnus the Martyr in the City of London, built by Wren, the clock is decorated with representations of Atlas and Hercules as well as of St Magnus and St Margaret. Everywhere there were flower garlands and wreaths, urns and cornucopia, styles and symbols thought appropriate in a salon were regarded as no less suitable in the plaster decoration of an altar-piece. Numerous attempts were made to reproduce the great portico of the Pantheon in Rome, and in many capitals local versions of the Pantheon were built in order to cultivate quasi-Christianized national halls-of-fame in the guise of churches. Even in the United States, with its constitutional separation of Church and State, L'Enfant's plan for Washington included a 'national pantheon or church', and a Greek Revival church was indeed built, according to designs by Robert Mills, only to be converted in 1867, just prior to its eventual completion, into the National Patent Office. It is now the National Portrait Gallery.

The inspiration for this sort of shrine came from the church of Ste-Geneviève in Paris, designed in 1755 by Jacques-Germain Soufflot, and itself intended to rival St Peter's in Rome. It was, in conception, intended to reflect the Neo-classical ideals of the French Academy in Rome, and the huge western portico was envisaged as a version of the Pantheon. The walls of the nave originally contained large windows which admitted great floods of light to the church, but these had to be filled in, for reasons of structural safety, in 1791. At that time, also, Ste-Geneviève was taken over by the revolutionary government and converted into a secular shrine to national heroes of France – the *Panthéon*. But Soufflot's attempt to combine the austere solemnity of the classical temple with the dematerializing light of Gothic, was to prove, despite the modifications to the original scheme, a widely emulated masterpiece of Neo-classicism.

Versions of the Roman Pantheon were often free adaptations, with Greek columns sometimes provided instead of Roman ones; everywhere, however, the intention was the same – the restoration of classical form without the enrichment of Baroque exuberance, a return to simplicity and to elementary shapes. In some capitals the Christianized Pantheon-like buildings achieved remarkable quality: St Hedwig in Berlin, by Georg von Knobelsdorff, completed in 1772; the Lutheran church in Warsaw, by Szymon Bogumil Zug, opened in 1781; St Mary's Pro-Cathedral in Dublin, the only work of the amateur architect John Sweetman, completed in 1815 with a Pantheon-inspired portico, and an interior based in part upon the church of St-Philippe-du-Roule in Paris. The fashion persisted: the church of the Immaculate Conception in Belgrano, a fashionable suburb of Buenos Aires, is a Pantheon-inspired rotunda, surmounted by an enormous and wide dome, begun originally by José y Nicolás Canale in 1865 and completed by Juan Buschiazzo in 1878.

The Pantheon-churches were commissioned for both Catholic and Protestant use, and since the papacy had anyway long since converted the great original into a Christian church there was an authoritative Roman precedent. Some Protestant churches, especially in England, went further, however, and boldly copied pagan tombs and temples as features of churches. St George's Church in Bloomsbury, London, by Nicholas Hawksmoor, completed in 1730, has not only a portico based upon the Pantheon, but a stepped tower, in the shape of a steep pyramid, and intended to reproduce the mausoleum at Halicarnassus. This astonishing fantasy is surmounted by a statue of King George I of England made to represent St George. St Alphege in Greenwich, also by Hawksmoor, and finished in 1718 (but with the addition of a tower by John James in 1730), is a huge pedimented temple, with urns along the roof. The façade is plain, with Tuscan

Nicholas Hawksmoor practised a version of Neo-classicism so personal and eccentric that some have been tempted to call it Baroque. These two churches are on the outskirts of London. The east end of St Alphege, Greenwich, (left) is based on a motif from late Roman architecture, which occurs also at Christ Church, Spitalfields, (above) but there serves as the ground storey of a spire which in its upper parts is pure Gothic.

The most extreme examples of Neo-Greek taste are the two sacristies of New St Pancras church, London, by H. W. and W. Inwood (1819–22). For no reason other than antiquarian enthusiasm they reproduced the caryatid porch of the Erechtheum in Athens, and not once but twice – there is a matching set on the other side.

pilasters. New St Pancras Church in Euston Road is a monument to the travels in Greece of Henry Williams Inwood. With his father he designed a church, built between 1819 and 1822, which incorporated almost exact copies of the porch of the Erechtheum from the Acropolis of Athens, and has a tower based upon the 'Tower of the Winds' from the Agora. In a still more intriguing tertiary emulation, the old Anglican cathedral of Cape Town, demolished in 1953, was a copy of New St Pancras.

It has been usual to regard the sober, unadorned, tonal qualities of eighteenth-century Neo-classicism as the natural expression of the religion of the 'Age of Reason', but there are reasons why this is not a very accurate thing to do. The age, for a start, produced a good measure of religious enthusiasm which, in the Protestant countries, spilled out of the conventional vessels of the established churches to reinforce and diversify religious Dissent. In Britain, especially, the chapels built by Dissenters in the eighteenth century were usually in the Neo-classical style, and many, with their modest scale and plain, box-like simplicity, actually had enormous charm. A similar simplicity, due to economic as much as to doctrinal reasons, reigned in the American colonies, as we shall see in a moment. Their nineteenth-century successors, often built in defiant competition with resurgent Gothic taste, were no less attractive – as seen to this day in the delightful Neo-classical chapels of Wales. At their most austere the Protestant Dissenters built simple one-room meeting-houses; the most austere of these are probably the Mennonite places of worship in Waterloo County, Ontario, in Canada. Yet occasionally Dissenting chapels displayed unexpected flair. The Old Unitarian Church at Bury St Edmunds in Suffolk, England, for example, has a brick façade with prominent scrolled reliefs which can only be categorized as Baroque. It is a reminder that the simplicity of Neo-classicism was not adopted by the Dissenters for economic reasons: Dissent was, in origin, characteristically a protest by people in middle sections of society, and the wealth available to them for chapel building, especially in the new industrial areas, was not inconsiderable.

Neo-classicism was a *style*, like other styles, and most of the churches constructed in the eighteenth and nineteenth centuries were emulations of other buildings. Within the established Churches, too, it is hardly true to say that Neo-classicism matched a sober version of Christian worship or religious understanding. It was certainly an era of marked Erastianism, but it is a later, clericalized view to imagine that lay-dominated religion was cold, formal, unadorned. Most countries underwent just such a clerical reaction in the nineteenth century, and in each the reformers represented their eighteenth-century predecessors as purveyors of a dry, formal religion, whose worship was suited to plain buildings and secularized decoration. This was how the ultramontane clerics in Catholic countries came to interpret their predecessors during the great nineteenth-century transformation of Catholicism into a centralized, Roman and Italian-orientated ecclesiastical machine. This was also how the High Church enthusiasts in England, associated with the Oxford Movement, came to depict the English Church of the preceding century as a desiccated inconsequence. Even in Russia, the popular revival of Orthodox spirituality in the nineteenth century represented the immediate past as a time of low religious temper and worship. Yet in all of these countries eighteenth-century Christianity had in reality shown plentiful fruits of authentic spirituality and enthusiasm. The cold formalism of Neo-classical church design did not represent a religious condition but an aspect of class taste. In most countries the Church was dominated by the ruling classes, either through government at the centre or through the local landed élite. They adopted Neo-classicism in their domestic architecture, in the great age of the

country house, and it was their extension of this taste to religious building which in many ways seems to account for the apparent religious sobriety of the age.

This also explains another aspect of Neo-classicism. It provided, in England and then in English colonial territories, the first really Protestant church style. At its most typical this was the pattern of the church as a square-shaped classical box with a pedimented front and – in a way the most characteristic feature – a tower with a steeple. Nothing could be less 'classical' than a Gothic steeple rising above a temple, but the English passion for this, starting with Wren and the reconstruction of the City churches after the Great Fire of London in 1666, created an ecclesiastical style which, especially in America, has become, after Gothic, the conventional idea of a church for most Protestants. Protestant Neo-classicism did actually have one important ideological purpose. Just as the mendicant religious orders in the Middle Ages had built churches like halls to facilitate preaching, so the Protestants required churches to be primarily 'auditory'. Wren himself, indeed, clearly distinguished between 'Romanist' churches, which were primarily for the offering of Mass, and the churches of the 'Reformed Religion', which were for preaching the Word. Since the churches which were to be rebuilt in London after the fire had to occupy irregularly defined sites still dictated by medieval street patterns, and since Wren was experimenting with Gothic and Neo-classical principles simultaneously, the result was a great variety both of shapes and of styles. But all of these churches were intended to produce light and unobstructed interiors, many with galleries to assist the worshippers in hearing the essential preaching. It was conventional for the sacrament of Holy Communion to be celebrated only four times a year in the Established Church of England (not until the High Church revival in the mid-nineteenth century were weekly – and in the Highest churches of all, daily – celebrations introduced), so the normal function of the building was the recitation of the offices and the preaching of sermons. This indeed was *theatrum sacrum*: with its square shape and galleries, and with a special gallery for musicians, the interior of the English Protestant church even looked like a theatre.

The earlier Nonconformist chapels of all denominations were almost invariably classical, partly to distinguish themselves from parish churches. Plain in style and modest in scale, they can nevertheless be architecturally satisfying. Above left: Saron, in Wales. Above right: the Old Unitarian church at Bury St Edmunds, Suffolk (1711–12).

243

Sir Christopher Wren, faced with the task of designing fifty-two new churches for the City of London after the Great Fire, showed seemingly inexhaustible powers of invention, so that no two are alike.

Above: St Mildred, Bread Street, a small church with an exquisite plaster dome on four arches. Built in 1682, it was destroyed in the Second World War. Above right: St Mary Aldermary of 1679–82, a deliberate exercise in New Gothic by Wren, with a version of fan vaulting. Right: St Stephen Walbrook (1672–77), the most complex and arguably the finest of all Wren's City churches. Its plan is a Greek cross inscribed as a square, its centre covered by a shallow dome on eight arches – perhaps a small-scale rehearsal for St Paul's Cathedral.

St Paul's Chapel, New York (right): the
Gibbs formula in the New World. Built
between 1765 and 1766 by Thomas
McBean, it has a French altar quite
unlike anything to be seen in England,
lending a touch of the Baroque to its cool
interior.

Below: the church of Great Packington
in Warwickshire by Joseph Bonomi
(1789–90) represents a highly original
application of Neo-classical principles.
Doric columns in the corners, complete
with their entablatures, support a plain
(admittedly un-Greek) groin vault.

While the Gothic style was being revived
as an exotic novelty, the old churches of
the English countryside went on being
used, stripped of their imagery, and with
the Tables of the Law installed beside the
altar instead of statues of the saints.
Right: Badley, Suffolk.

Chancels became at first very shallow – in contrast to the deeply recessed chancels of Gothic churches – and in some of the square-shaped buildings disappeared altogether. Organs became popular in the first half of the eighteenth century, and these too, though now popularly associated with religion, were originally regarded as an incursion of the world into the church. (Some instruments at the extremities of Christendom were exotic – like the famous bamboo organ in the church of Las Piñas, to the south of Manila in the Philippines, assembled by an Augustinian friar, Father Diego Cerra, in 1794.) Pulpits began to be moved into more prominent positions, and seating was arranged so that, regardless of other liturgical use, the church became an effective auditorium.

Class requirements demanded that these seats were in the form of high box-pews, each reserved and paid for by members of the congregation. The poor (or those of them who bothered to attend at all, and evidence now suggests that not very many did) were ushered into the galleries. Most of these box-pews were taken out in the nineteenth century, and all seats made 'free', so eliminating visible class segregation at worship. But a few have survived. Good examples can be seen in the Old Church at Parracombe in Somerset, where an almost perfectly preserved Georgian interior owed its continued existence to Ruskin's intervention: in order to save the whole building from the threat of demolition the great apostle of Gothic taste also secured the non-Gothic furnishings. St Petroc's Church has a musicians' gallery, too. Box-pews for important officials were sometimes very grand, as in St Paul's Chapel in New York City, built from 1765 to 1766, and containing two splendid pews originally reserved for the governor and other dignitaries of the colony.

However important preaching became in English Neo-classical churches, the altar retained a dignified separate existence, though not without some struggle. Archbishop Laud had instituted railed altars, but they had been abolished by Parliament in 1643, only to be returned again in 1660 with the Restoration settlement. It is a tribute to the surviving sacramental sense of Anglicanism, despite the infrequency of Communion, that altars were never again down-graded, as they had been after the Reformation, to movable tables, and Neo-classical churches all provided designated sanctuaries for them. As if to emphasize the Erastian constitution of the Established Church, however, it was also made obligatory, in 1660, for the Royal Arms to be displayed in churches. Interior decoration, in fact, became markedly secular, with marble memorial plaques and reliefs, in honour of dead notables, replacing religious painting or carving. Painted or plaster-moulded altar-pieces were often the only overtly religious decoration in the entire building whose atmosphere, otherwise, resembled the drawing-room of a country house, or perhaps, in less endowed parishes, a court-room. Painted tables of the Law – the Ten Commandments – often appeared on boards set up behind the altars, and in a surprisingly large number of places these survive to this day.

However, the towers and spires most clearly defined the distinctively Protestant nature of English Neo-classicism. Wren's inventiveness in this respect was truly astonishing, and his mixture of Gothic steeples attached to classical towers discloses his audacity. He intended that London should be a scenographic unity, a city of spires whose slender grace should encompass the majestic dome of St Paul's Cathedral. They still inspire wonder today, though what is now visible in many cases represents careful reconstruction following wartime damage of the 1940s. The classical proportions of the tower of St Lawrence Jewry, for example, which Wren built between 1671 and 1687, is largely just such a reconstruction,

Two Wren spires. Top: St Magnus the Martyr (1671–76) at the end of Old London Bridge and (bottom) St Lawrence Jewry (1671–87).

but it is a faithful one. There are slender stone obelisks at each corner, and a steeple made of fibreglass. At St Magnus the Martyr (1671–76), a pilastered square tower is surmounted by an octagonal upper storey crowned by a small dome which itself supports a tapered spire. This church, which once fronted the Thames directly, but is now separated from it as a result of the later eighteenth-century embankment of the river, seems to have inspired a number of others in London's Docklands. The idea that a tower or spire was essential to a Protestant church received legislative encouragement in 1711 when Parliament, in providing for the construction of fifty new places of worship, stipulated that there should be 'Towers or Steeples to each of them'.

Wherever Protestant Neo-classicism spread, towers and steeples appeared. Sometimes the sense of height was enhanced by 'pepper-box' constructions: storeys of decreasing size ascending to a small cupola or spire. Among the most celebrated of these is the fine tower of St Anne's Shandon, in Cork City, Ireland. Here a tower of 1722, with rounded windows, is topped by three diminishing storeys crowned by a gilt ball and a weather vane in the form of a fish. It is built of red sandstone on two of its sides, and grey limestone on the other two: an interesting tribute to the mixed sources of the materials, since the sandstone came from the nearby castle demolished in the siege of Cork in 1690, and the limestone from the Franciscan abbey on the North Mall. As the famous Cork poet Father Prout observed: 'Party-coloured, like its people; red and white stands Shandon steeple.' The church, in Protestant style, is extremely plain within, the decoration (if that is what it is) being in the form of funereal memorial plaques. Wherever English Protestants built churches throughout the growing colonial empire, plain interiors with memorialized walls are to be found. The Anglican cathedral of St Thomas in Bombay, designed by Gerald Aungier in 1672 and completed in 1718, is typical. It is an austere Neo-classical building in a city largely noted for the extravagance of its English Neo-Gothic architecture.

The greatest inspiration in the world-wide distribution of classical churches with towers and spires was probably the London church of St Martin-in-the-Fields, by James Gibbs, built between 1722 and 1726. The tower actually sits rather oddly behind a large temple portico, and was perhaps never meant to be viewed, as it is today, from a frontal perspective. When Nash laid out Trafalgar Square in 1829, St Martin's emerged from the small lane in which it was constructed, its tower doubtless originally meant to be seen rising above the rooftops. In many variations this tower and spire were copied in North America and in other areas of English settlement. Gibbs's influence was considerably enhanced by the publication of his designs for churches. By the nineteenth century a Neo-classical building with tower and spire was the normal style for a colonial church, and some very fine examples still exist. A number, like St Mark's at Niagara-on-the-Lake in Ontario, Canada, a structure of the first decade of the century, were subsequently Gothicized. St Mark's was remodelled by John Howard in 1843, when the spire was replaced by a Gothic tower, and the appearance of the church today scarcely reveals its true pedigree, so successfully was the transformation accomplished. Others preserve their original splendour. The convict-architect Francis Greenway designed the graceful St Matthew's Church in Windsor, New South Wales, Australia, completed at the end of the first decade of the century. Its tower bears a timber lantern and four large urns. Greenway's church of St James in Sydney, built in the 1820s, on the other hand, is notable for its temple-like pedimented façade and rounded windows.

It is in the United States, however, that the influence of English Protestant Neo-classicism is most obvious, and where some of the most impressive building

Gibbs's St Martin-in-the-Fields (1722–26) was one of the most influential of all church designs. Its combination of classical portico and steeple can be seen all over the English-speaking world.

St Anne's Shandon, in Cork, begun over the same period as St Martin's, is chiefly remarkable for its tall tower diminishing in stages at the top.

Benjamin Latrobe had been a pupil of Soane in England and his Catholic cathedral of Baltimore (above) is as distinguished as any Neo-classical church in his home country. Its circular nave, yet another offspring of the Pantheon in Rome, is defined by four wide segmental arches and four smaller semi-circular ones.

Above right: St Michael, Charleston, owes an obvious debt to Gibbs, whose designs were propagated by being published in book form. Its four-stage octagonal spire is particularly vigorous.

occurred. Peter Harrison, whose work was inspired by Gibbs, built the King's Chapel in Boston between 1749 and 1758. Its light and homogeneous interior, with free-standing Corinthian columns supporting a gallery, its canopied pulpit and box-pews, have on the whole survived in their original form. Always in the advance of fashionable Boston opinion, it was the first Congregationalist church in America to convert to Unitarianism, in the 1780s. Christ Church, across the Charles River in Cambridge, was designed by Harrison in 1761 for the Episcopalians. It shows how a building of wood faithfully incorporated the light and elegance of Neo-classicism – though it is rather less austere than many churches in the style. The smaller towns and rural areas of North America became richly endowed with timber-frame Neo-classical churches like this. The Royal Chapel of the Mohawks in Brantford, Ontario, is just such a simple wooden church, complete with modest west tower and small steeple. It is the oldest Protestant church in Canada, built in 1785 on land provided for the loyalist Mohawks who had supported the Crown in the conflict between Britain and the thirteen American colonies. Another transmitter of English Neo-classicism to America no less distinguished than Harrison – who also helped the style to become the vernacular of American religious building – was Charles Bulfinch. His New South Church in Boston, built in 1814, has a steeple based on Gibbs's model.

In the late eighteenth and early nineteenth centuries nearly every small town in New England built itself a church (usually several for different denominations), sometimes in brick, most often in wood, hardly ever in stone, with a classical portico, two rows of columns down the interior and a steeple based on Wren or Gibbs above the west end. A list of such churches would run into many hundreds. They are never mere copies, however. Conditions in Massachusetts, Connecticut, Virginia or the Carolinas were not those of the mother country, and a specifically American style is soon easily recognizable. St Michael, Charleston (begun in 1752), for instance, owes a good deal to Gibbs's St Martin-in-the-Fields, but has a simplicity and charm of its own. Further west, the Congregational church at Atwater, Ohio, has the same features reduced to more blocky and amateurish proportions. A later and much more elaborate example is the Catholic cathedral of St Louis the King in New Orleans, built in 1850, with two orders of columns inside (Doric and Ionic) and a delicate plaster ceiling.

Benjamin Latrobe's Catholic cathedral in Baltimore, completed in 1818, indicates that the style was Catholic as well as Protestant in America, and the cathedral, with its austere walls, large portico, and dome, shows some indebtedness to Soufflot's Ste-Geneviève in Paris.

An equally powerful influence, however, is the Greek Revival, a style that ran parallel to Neo-classicism during the first half of the nineteenth century. The Robert Mills design at Washington mentioned above is an example of this. Another is the same architect's Monumental Church at Richmond, Virginia (1812–14), with its powerful Doric portico, built to commemorate the victims of a disastrous fire when a theatre on the same site burned down. The First Presbyterian Church at Sag Harbor, New York, is a curiosity in uniting a Greek Revival interior with an exterior based on Egyptian forms. The Egyptian style enjoyed a vogue in the States in the nineteenth century, but was used only rarely for churches: the colourful interior of the First Presbyterian Church at Nashville, Tennessee, comes as all the more of a shock.

Just as Protestant churches had previously emulated the styles originally evolved in Catholic countries, so, with Neo-classicism, Catholics came to adopt ecclesiastical tastes at first distinctively Protestant. The Catholic cathedral at Cavan in Ireland, for example, which was built in 1942 (according to the design of Ralph Byrne), with its tower and spire set back from a pedimented portico, is something like an enlarged version of a Gibbs church. A particularly splendid example is the basilica at Fatima in Portugal, built in 1928 to accommodate pilgrims visiting the site of the apparitions of the Virgin in 1917. The three-storeyed tower, rising directly from the western front of the building to a height of 215 feet, dominates an enormous colonnaded square. Inside there are colonnaded galleries beneath a barrel vault of surprising delicacy. The gilded crown at the top of the tower, the attribute of the Queen of Heaven as the Immaculate Conception, is more distinctively Catholic than the architectural

Ralph Byrne's Catholic cathedral of Cavan, in Ireland, shows that Gibbs's example was still powerful after two hundred years. It was built in 1942, and presents essentially the same components as St Martin-in-the-Fields.

La Madeleine, Paris, is perhaps the most consistently Neo-Roman church ever built and its exterior comes close to being a replica of a classical temple. It was unlucky in its building history. Begun as a church in 1777, it was continued under Napoleon as a 'Temple of Glory', but (still unfinished) reverted to Christian use after 1815 and was not completed until 1842. It has no windows and is lit entirely through the roof. In the pediment is Christ the Judge, 17 feet high.

The belfry of the Zosima and Savvaty church at Zagorsk, Russia, was added between 1741 and 1769. To build a Neo-classical tower was a challenge, since there was no Roman model to copy. Here the architect has placed four self-contained classical pavilions, diminishing in size, on top of one another.

details of the building – which is, by any standards, a gem of the Neo-classical style. This modern, Portuguese, Neo-classical building owed much to south European Neo-classicism in general.

Classical taste developed in every country, often in ways quite unlike England. In France the most prominent church in this style is probably the Madeleine in Paris, begun by Vignon under Napoleon but finished much later: a cold and perhaps overscaled replica of a Roman temple. Smaller but more original is St-Sulpice in Paris, with its façade of 1733–49, influenced by St Paul's, by Servandoni. St-Philippe-du-Roule, by Chalgrin, of 1768, is sterner, more austere, closer to Greek models.

In Italy the flowing lines of Baroque subsided into the discipline of classicism without entirely losing an element of theatricality: for instance, the new façades added to S. Giovanni Laterano by Galilei and to Sta Maria Maggiore by Fuga. The only church designed by the great sculptor Antonio Canova is at Possagno in the Veneto (1819–30); it memorably combines a massive Doric portico with a body modelled on the Pantheon.

In all the Mediterranean countries the idea which gained currency in the north – that Gothic was somehow a religious style and classicism a secular one – never prevailed, and we find various forms of classicism (progressively adulterated with ornament from other sources) continuing to be used for churches to the end of the nineteenth century and beyond. French examples would include Notre-Dame-de-Lorette in Paris by Lebas, and – most bizarre and eclectic of all – Notre-Dame-de-Fourvières in Lyons (1872–96) by Pierre Bossan, where classicism, the Italian Renaissance and Byzantium come miraculously together.

In Russia, particularly at St Petersburg, Neo-classicism reached new heights. The cathedral of the Holy Trinity, by Ivan Yegorovich Stasov, completed in 1776, is notable for its splendid proportions. Russian towers in the Neo-classical manner were extremely graceful: the bell-tower of the Zosima and Savvaty church at Zagorsk, designed by D. V. Ukhtomsky and built between 1741 and 1769, for example, or the comparable tower at the monastery of the Caves in Kiev.

Neo-classical domes of all periods and in all places demonstrated a good deal of variation, and few are really distinguished in the way the dome of Ste-Geneviève in Paris is. Some are wide and austere, like the dome added to the Carmelite basilica of Stella Maris, on the side of Mount Carmel, in Israel. The whole conventual complex was rebuilt in 1836, following its demolition by the local Pasha in 1821, and the dome floats above a very unadorned and rather bleak range of buildings. It seems far removed, and not only geographically, from the robust and enormous dome of St Joseph's Oratory in Montreal, Canada, constructed in stages between 1904 and 1960 to honour Brother André of the Holy Cross order, whose pilgrim shrine this is. Somehow reminiscent of the Duomo at Florence, this is nevertheless a Neo-classical and not a Renaissance-style building, influenced, as is only to be expected in Montreal, by French models. The influence becomes very evident from the pedimented façade, where a flattened portico is surmounted by a huge semi-circular window. The church and the dome are so large that they dominate the skyline of the Westmount district of the city. How this gigantic structure contrasts, again, with another modern Neo-classical dome: at Quiapo Church in Manila, designed by Juan Nakpil and completed in 1935. This, too, is a pilgrim church, housing the statue of the agonized Christ bearing his Cross, the 'Black Nazarene', which was brought to the Philippines from Mexico in the seventeenth century. It is believed to have miraculous powers, and the faithful resort here in huge numbers every Friday.

The church has an exceptionally long nave and a very modest dome which yet achieves elegance and proportion with a stuccoed octagonal drum. The dome at the Franciscan sanctuary of Cana, on the road between Nazareth and Tiberias in Israel, was built in 1879 in honour of the first miracle of Christ in his earthly ministry. The church is Neo-classical with Baroque overtones, recalling Latin American Mission churches. The dome, however, is wonderfully proportioned and properly austere.

In England, which never experienced true Baroque, Neo-classicism was refreshingly un-doctrinaire, assuming individual and often eccentric forms that reflect the personalities of particular architects. Nicholas Hawksmoor built six London churches under the terms of the Act of 1711, and each is in its own way a masterpiece. To demonstrate English variety one need only contrast Hawksmoor's St Anne's, Limehouse (1724), or his Christ Church, Spitalfields (1714), with the grace and airiness of, say, John Nash's All Souls, Langham Place (1824), with its extraordinary two-tiered colonnaded rotunda surmounted by a Gothic spire, or with Sir John Soane's St John's in Bethnal Green (1828), with its curious pillared square tower and urns along the parapets of the roof. The variety was due in some measure to the genius of the architects, but in some measure also to the essentially eclectic nature of Neo-classicism. What had begun as a reaction to the artistic extravagance of Baroque, and a desire to return to the simplicity of the Greek and Roman originals, had matured as an unreconciled blend of Gothic and classical styles.

Put in another way, these two elements could be translated as Christianity and paganism. Few people (though Ruskin was one) saw any discrepancy between the style of a classical church and the Gospel that it represented. And indeed that Gospel had so transformed the style that the discrepancy had virtually disappeared. The large un-Roman windows were filled with glass depicting Old and New Testament subjects. The pediments carried large-scale sculpture (for instance St Paul's, London, or the Madeleine, in Paris) of crucial events in Christian history. Most un-pagan of all, a steeple – a medieval invention – usually rose calmly above the portico. The result was not contradiction but an apparently effortless harmony and grace.

Nash's combination of porch and spire for his church of All Souls, Langham Place, London, is a brilliant piece of town-planning, the focus of two vistas.

Sir John Soane brought an original, analytical mind to the problem of the Neo-classical church. Above: the west tower of St John's, Bethnal Green, London. Left: cut-away perspective, made to look like a romantic ruin, showing a galleried church with classical columns along the sides.

251

9 The Gothic Revival: liturgy, theology and architecture

MORE CHURCHES were built in the nineteenth century than in any corresponding period before or since. In Europe it was a time of rapid population growth, and in the rest of the world one of vigorous missionary activity. There was also a new ideological urgency. As Christianity came under attack with the development of scientific and social knowledge, the Churches re-examined their beliefs, some returning even more devoutly to established dogma and tradition, others attempting to liberalize their faith and adapt it to the modern world.

Architecturally, however, there was no 'nineteenth-century style', a fact that caused considerable anguish to many architects. The only choice open to them was the imitation of one or other style from the past. Neo-classicism remained popular, especially in France and America. Neo-Romanesque, Neo-Early Christian and Neo-Byzantine also had their supporters.

But the most dynamic of the revived styles was Neo-Gothic, which became identified with the 'Age of Faith', when, it was thought, Christianity was at its purest and strongest. The turning-point in the history of the Gothic Revival came with Augustus Welby Northmore Pugin. Before his time a Neo-Gothic church was a Georgian church in Gothic dress. Pugin went further. For him Gothic was the *only* Christian style and Gothic meant not just the church building but also the way it was used, its furnishings, vestments, images and liturgy, the rites that took place within it and the theology that sustained it. He became a Catholic, but his books, more influential than his buildings, gave Anglican Neo-Gothic a seriousness that it had lacked hitherto. The next two generations of English church architects were totally committed to Gothic. A whole new science came into being to ensure that they built correctly: ecclesiology.

Something similar was happening in Germany, where Goethe, in his essay on the master-mason of Strasbourg Cathedral, had given Gothic a nationalist dimension by claiming it as a specifically German style and stressing its independence of the classical tradition. The German Middle Ages became bathed in a visionary light, vividly conveyed in the castles of Ludwig II and the operas of Wagner.

If England's Gothic Revival was primarily religious and Germany's romantic, that of France was scholarly. Its greatest exponent was Eugène Viollet-le-Duc, architect and historian, restorer of many of France's medieval monuments and proponent of Gothic as above all a system of rational structure. American Neo-Gothic shared all these aspects, sometimes creating (in a land without medieval cathedrals of its own) ambitions to outstrip the Old World that were too vast to be realized.

The Gothic Revival was the channel through which a strong current of genuine religious fervour found expression. From the vantage point of the late twentieth century both the fervour and the churches that expressed it seem unmistakably Victorian and only remotely medieval. Perhaps there was a nineteenth-century style after all.

For captions to colour plates 61–71, see p. 265

63,64

65,66

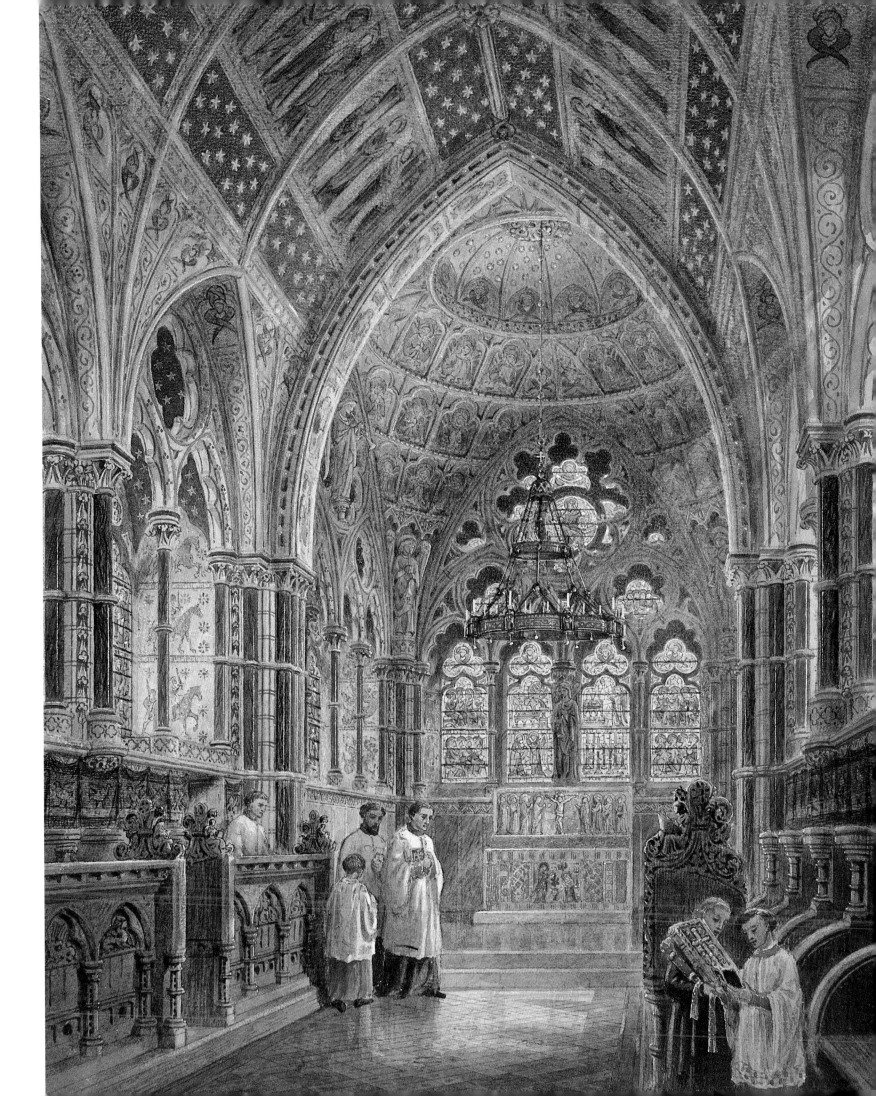

67,68

Colour plates 61–71

61 Karl Friedrich Schinkel's Medieval Town on a River re-creates an ideal Germany that existed mainly in the imagination of the Romantics. A king, in the foreground, dressed in red, riding under a baldacchino, is returning victorious to his capital. Painted in 1815, this was an allusion to King Friedrich Wilhelm III of Prussia, who had taken part in the defeat of Napoleon. The cathedral, which draws on elements from Reims and St Stephen's, Vienna, is not quite finished. Work still proceeds on the left-hand spire.

62 Designs presented to the Commissioners for New Churches in 1825 by Sir John Soane. The drawing is by Soane's draughtsman J. M. Gandy. The New Churches Commission was appointed in 1818 to provide buildings for the emerging industrial areas of Britain, where population had outstripped churches. Soane's projects demonstrate the adaptability of early nineteenth-century architects and their willingness to work in any style.

63 Reliquary of the Crown of Thorns, designed by Eugène Viollet-le-Duc and made by Placide Poussielgue-Rusand in 1862. Both Pugin and Viollet were imaginative designers of church plate in the Gothic style. This reliquary is not a mere copy of any medieval piece, but a free invention in the manner of a thirteenth-century goldsmith. It was made for Notre-Dame, Paris, which Viollet-le-Duc was in the process of restoring.

64 Truro Cathedral in Cornwall was one of the largest commissions ever given to a Neo-Gothic architect. It was designed by J.L. Pearson in 1879 and finished in 1910. Many of its features are taken from the early Gothic of Normandy but the way the body of the nave is brought forward of the two towers is an original stroke.

65 St Michael, by Edward Burne-Jones, in the church of St Michael at Froden, Wales, 1873. The firm of William Morris and Company was largely dedicated to the revival of medieval techniques and styles. But Burne-Jones, its chief designer of stained glass, was increasingly influenced by the Renaissance.

66 The church of Studley Royal, Yorkshire, by William Burges, built from 1871 to 1878. Like many of the most lavish Victorian churches, Studley Royal was the result of private patronage, in this case that of the intense medievalist the Marquis of Bute. In Burges he found an architect to match his enthusiasm and Studley Royal has everything that money and talent could provide: painted ceilings, coloured marbles, polychromed sculpture, stained glass, metalwork and ornately carved woodwork.

67 H. H. Richardson's Trinity Church, Boston (1872–77). Richardson's chosen style was Romanesque and at Boston he was able to use it with all the resources of Victorian opulence. The round arches and motifs such as the demi-columns and capitals are historical, but the plan, with its galleried transepts and wide crossing with lantern tower, and the amazing roof belong to his own time. The church contains both English and American stained glass of high quality. Choir stalls were added in 1902, pulpit in 1916.

68 Brompton Oratory brought the Italian Renaissance to London, and represented the ideological commitment of the London branch of the Oratory of St Philip Neri to the styles of the Counter-Reformation. The Oratory was designed by Herbert Gribble and built between 1880 and 1884. The interior as now furnished has a more Baroque appearance than in this drawing; over-lifesize Italian seventeenth-century statues stand along the nave.

69 It was the rise of new industrial communities in the nineteenth century that made the provision of new churches so important. This is the pit-head chapel of a mine in the Harz Mountains, evoking with its plain wooden benches and stove by the window an atmosphere of uncomplicated religious observance. It has been reconstructed, using items from various sources, in the Deutsches Museum in Munich.

70 The Sacré Coeur in Paris was built as a monument of expiation and renewal after the horrors of the Paris Commune of 1870–71. Its plan is a Greek cross with a high dome over the centre, its style Neo-Byzantine, chosen by its architect, Paul Abadie, because he had previously worked on the restoration of St-Front, Périgueux (p. 123), the most Byzantine church in France. It was an exotic choice, yet this strangely un-Parisian building has become almost a symbol of Paris.

71 Neo-classicism was not by any means replaced by Neo-Gothic on the Continent. Jacques-Ignace Hittorff's St. Vincent-de-Paul, Paris, of 1824–44, shows the style still capable of new life and new variations. Hittorff's two storeys of columns (Ionic below, Corinthian above) with flat entablature are separated by a wide frieze painted by Hippolyte Flandrin with a procession of saints. The clerestory windows are set back behind the upper columns, making the church inconveniently dark. The apse painting, by Picot, shows St Vincent de Paul kneeling before Christ and presenting children to him; the crucifix over the altar is by Rude.

The Gothic Revival

AFTER THE ORIGINATORS of the Byzantine style, it was probably the Gothic Revivalists of the nineteenth century who were the most precise and enthusiastic in seeking to make church structures correspond to what were seen as Christian ideals. The symbolic importance of various structural and decorative arrangements was debated at enormous length by the promoters of what became known as 'ecclesiology' – in the belief, almost certainly without authentic historical foundation, that the medieval practitioners of Gothic, and especially the actual masons and craftsmen, had invested a peculiarly heightened spirituality in their undertakings. Translated into the language of ideology this became the dogma, propounded especially by Pugin and Ruskin in England, by François René de Châteaubriand in France, by Pietro Selvatico in Italy, and by Gottfried Semper in Germany, that the Gothic style of architecture and decoration was distinctively Christian, and that it was, indeed the *only* proper style for ecclesiastical use. In England, something like half the existing churches were built in the nineteenth century, and a very high proportion of these were Gothic. It once seemed to Lord Clark, in fact, that the Gothic Revival was 'an English movement', though in later editions of his *Gothic Revival* he came, rightly, to modify this claim.

Interest in medieval history, often with strong nationalist motivations, lay behind new appreciations of Gothic which occurred in several European countries in the first half of the nineteenth century. In France the pioneer was Alexandre Lenoir, and the leading exponent was Eugène-Emmanuel Viollet-le-Duc, the restorer of Notre-Dame in Paris and the Sainte-Chapelle. In Prussia, Karl Friedrich Schinkel represented Gothic as the soul of German national self-consciousness. In Holland Petrus Cuypers was not only a purist restorer of Gothic churches but the builder of a number of his own, and also, like the English ecclesiologists, he became involved in the study and production of ecclesiastical furnishing. In Italy, characteristically, the revival of Gothic employed marble and polychrome cladding in the remoulding of older buildings – as in the façade of Florence Cathedral, begun in 1867 by Emilio de Fabris, or, more austerely, in the severe stone west front of the Duomo at Naples, by Enrico Alvino, completed in 1905.

A feature of the English Gothic Revival was the export of the style throughout the English-speaking world. The same can be said of the continental revivalists. Namibia was a German colony until it was occupied on behalf of the British in the Great War, yet German building styles have persisted and are, indeed, a characteristic of Windhoek, the capital. The Catholic cathedral of the tiny city, with its twin towers and spires, and its distinctive coloured glass, is typically German. The English Gothic Revival was itself influenced by continental Gothic in the mid-century, a shift which had behind it the authority of Ruskin's writings on Italian churches (*The Stones of Venice* was published in 1851–53), and the foreign travel, sketchbook in hand, of Gilbert Scott and George Edmund Street. Churches by William Burges were all in continental Gothic styles. Some of the great European Gothic cathedrals were actually copied in

For Caspar David Friedrich, Gothic architecture was like the mountains and the forests – a sublime symbol of God's presence. His painting The Cathedral is loosely based on a real building in Prussia, but he shows it lifted literally out of this world by a flight of angels.

Opposite: St Michael's, Mark Street, London, (1863–65) by James Brooks. Brooks specialized in providing large, cheap churches for working-class districts, which for that reason often achieve a stark dignity that is still impressive. St Michael's is made of brick (apart from the nave arcade) but is given visual interest by polychrome patterning. The floor-tiles, wooden roof and metal screens are simply but strongly conceived.

267

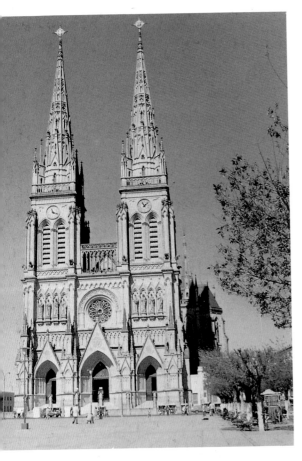

French Gothic provided the inspiration for the basilica of Luján in Argentina, designed by P. Salvaire and finished in 1890.

North America and in the areas of missionary influence overseas. St Patrick's Cathedral in New York City, built between 1858 and 1888 in white marble and stone, is based upon Cologne Cathedral in Germany; its twin towers rise to 330 feet. The twin-towered basilica at Luján in Argentina was inspired by Chartres in France. Luján is something of a national shrine, housing a miraculous statue of the Virgin brought to the district in 1630; each bay of the church is dedicated to a different province of Argentina. The existing Gothic structure, by P. Salvaire, was completed in 1890. The cathedral of Canton in China, built in 1863, is also based upon Chartres; its twin spires rise to 160 feet. The building was used as a warehouse during the Chinese Cultural Revolution but has now once again been restored to Catholic use.

Despite the widespread European incidence of the Gothic Revival, however, it is still true to say that its most ideological and scholarly inspiration was the work of Englishmen and of those under their influence in the English-speaking world. Thus, although the English Pre-Raphaelite school of art and design, which had a great influence on the Gothic Revival, was preceded by the Nazarenes in Germany, the styles of church decoration which spread throughout the world owed much more to Englishmen like Rossetti, Morris, Burne-Jones and Ford Madox Brown than it did to the Germans, to Cornelius or Overbeck. The passion for ecclesiology, too, stemmed from the English Camden Society, founded in 1839 by two Cambridge undergraduates, John Mason Neale and Benjamin Webb, in order to study Gothic architecture, ecclesiastical ornament, and liturgy. Within half a decade the Society had the patronage of two archbishops and sixteen bishops, and its influence in the revival of Gothic, and its stimulus to the High Church attitudes and ritual practices that accompanied it in some of the most dynamic developments, were enormous and often very exclusive. It was the Cambridge Camden Society and the succeeding Ecclesiological Society which insisted on an exact relationship between theological meaning, liturgical practice, and actual church structure. It was their influence that spread the still current belief – quite mythical – that Gothic architecture was the work of simple craftsmen of inherent spiritual genius in the Middle Ages, whose example had now to be followed in order to re-create authentic Christianity. It was their insistence, furthermore, that only the 'Decorated' style properly represented Gothic, and that all churches surviving from the past which chanced to reveal evidence of a 'Decorated' influence should be remodelled so that the whole fabric should be in the same style, which resulted in some very far-reaching suggestions. Neale once told the Ecclesiological Society that he would be willing to see Peterborough Cathedral utterly dismantled 'if it could have been replaced by a Middle Pointed Cathedral'.

Now the ideals of this movement were spread throughout the world by associations and church groups in direct emulation of the English model. Local ecclesiological societies were in existence, during the second half of the century, in the United States, Canada, Australia, and even in Sri Lanka and India. The link with the wider dissemination of Anglican Tractarianism was at first important. The early founders of the Oxford Movement – the High Church Revival – were not in any sense 'Ritualists'. Even the wearing of a stole by a priest, or lights upon an altar, could cause intense controversy in the 1830s and 1840s. But their successors succumbed readily enough to the whole panoply of Roman practices, and the ecclesiological societies actually had a restraining influence here, in requiring the enthusiasts to prove their actions by reference to medieval usage. Some had, before this, simply adopted the whole Italianate glitz without too great a concern about its historical origin. Thus Father Frederick Faber, on his visit to

Rome while still an Anglican clergyman, in 1843, came home with bags full of rosaries and devotional pictures and other religious requisites which owed nothing to the authentic past of English Christianity.

The Camden atmosphere was antipathetic to all that sort of thing: it sought the restoration of a real Gothic pedigree for English Church practice. Buildings, ornaments, and ritual, should all correspond to what once had been. In the English Roman Catholic Church there was a very considerable controversy about the theological propriety of Gothic ornament precisely because Italianate modes were thought to be more in accordance with Roman ultramontane discipline and outlook. In 1839, after conducting an enquiry into the spread of Gothic vestments in the English Church, the Prefect of Propaganda banned their use. The equally doctrinal Pugin, who was a Catholic convert, rapidly undermined the Roman authorities in practice, however, and the mid-century clash between the Gothicists and the Romans in the Catholic Church, which corresponded to two quite distinct styles of spirituality – the 'Old Catholic' party of traditional English piety, and the ultramontane sympathisers – for a time lurched eliptically in favour of the Gothic, in taste though not in ecclesiastical discipline. The signs of this were Pugin's Gothic churches of St George in south London and of St Chad in Birmingham (built in 1848 and 1841 respectively), both of which, on the restoration of the Catholic hierarchy in England in 1850, were to achieve the status of cathedrals.

To the Catholics and Anglicans who were involved with the revival of Gothic, therefore, the style had very precise religious purposes. There was no sense in which the Revival corresponded to an existing popular spirituality, or expressed the inherent instincts of ordinary people, as Pugin and Ruskin imagined. The Gothic Revival was certainly related to movements of artistic and literary opinion within the educated classes, and to what may be called a Romantic disenchantment with the material culture of industrial society. But it was the work of an élite. No doubt for many in rural areas, or for those living in the crowded new urban concentrations who could still remember their earlier rural context, the Gothic style evoked the normal form for a church. To such persons the Gothic Revival must have seemed unremarkable. That it became merely a *style*, however,

Two aspects of Pugin – the ideal and the reality. His church of St Giles at Cheadle, Staffordshire, of 1840–46, was, like Studley Royal, the gift of a munificent patron, the Earl of Shrewsbury. Pugin was able to employ all the resources of colour and ornament that he usually had to forego. Below: an illustration from his book Contrasts *(1836), showing his vision of an idealized and visionary Middle Ages.*

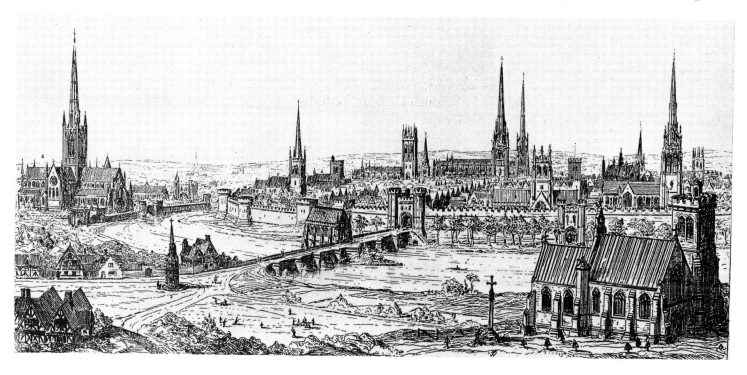

Charles Barry's church of St Peter at Brighton is an example of pre-Puginian playfulness – an ingenious design with the lower storey of the tower treated as an enormous portal – but with only vague connexions with real medieval architecture. It was built between 1824 and 1828.

outside the clerical coteries and the ecclesiological hot-houses, may be seen in its attraction to Protestant Dissenters. Even here, it is true, there were a few who offered ideological reflections upon Gothic taste: F. J. Jobson, a Methodist, wrote *Chapel and School Architecture* (1850) to apply Pugin's thesis, that Gothic and Christian were synonymous, to English Nonconformity. More modest Gothic structures also had the advantage of being cheaper to build, since brick could be used instead of the stone which was unavoidable for the pediments and columns of the Neo-classical styles. The use of iron, particularly, for internal galleries, reduced costs still further, and the Ecclesiological Society, anxious to point out that theologically correct churches still need not be too expensive, even produced a design for a Gothic church constructed completely of iron. Within Non-conformity the battle of tastes was largely won by the Gothicists, and throughout Britain the chapels began to be built in the Gothic style. To the ecclesiologists the style was inseparably related to deep chancels, rood-screens, liturgical refinements; to the Dissenters it was, in general, just a matter of adopting the new fashion of architecture.

There were two main phases of the English Gothic Revival, the first in the eighteenth century lasting until the 1840s, and the second, sometimes known as the 'High Victorian movement', which occurred between 1850 and 1870. Thereafter taste transferred to Arts and Crafts decoration and to the 'Queen Anne' domestic architecture of those such as Richard Norman Shaw. There was, of course, a real sense in which Gothic had never died out, and throughout the whole period of Neo-classicism old churches had been repaired by architects and craftsmen who retained a knowledge of Gothic building techniques. Most of their work was removed and redone by the restorations of the High Victorian architects, so there is little evidence to indicate how extensive it must have been. The restorers of the nineteenth century themselves exaggerated the extent of the decay into which ecclesiastical structures had fallen: the truth is that all buildings deteriorate very rapidly without regular attention, and between the end of the Middle Ages and the start of the nineteenth century most parish churches in England must have received periodic treatment. The skills never quite died out. It is true, on the other hand, that knowledge of the relationship of structure to ornament was imperfect.

The nineteenth-century Gothic enthusiasts insisted that the structural fabric of churches must be left undisguised, and that ornament should relate to it and not be applied indiscriminately or randomly. Gothic repairs before their time had not respected this canon, and nor had the architects who had continued to build in the Gothic style in the late seventeenth and eighteenth centuries. Thus in Wren's church of St Mary Aldermary, in London, the fan vaulting of the nave is a plaster imitation. Other architects who used both Neo-classical and Gothic tended to copy Gothic stone features in plaster, and their perception of 'authentic' Gothic architecture was in many other things to induce paroxysms of horror among the Victorian purists. Sir Robert Smirke built in both styles at the start of the nineteenth century; so did Sir Charles Barry, the creator, with Pugin, of the Palace of Westminster built to replace the one destroyed in the fire of 1834.

Gothic taste in the eighteenth century was largely secular. It was cultivated by men of leisure and intended to evoke an atmosphere rather than to express an ideology. It was a matter of contrived melancholy and the delicious thrill of perceived transience: a vicarious anticipation, in the parks and gardens of great houses, in little ruined temples and 'Gothick' follies, of the certainty of worldly decay. As a religious style, Gothic evoked Catholic sentiments, and in the Erastian religious and social culture of eighteenth-century England Catholic sentiments were, to say the least, suspect. But Gothic could nevertheless recall a distant past. Indeed, it is astonishing now to realize how even educated people of the time had little actual knowledge about the date of the surviving Gothic churches which covered the land. Many supposed them to be of Saxon origin; a notion reinforced by the conviction that Saxon political institutions had laid the foundations of English liberty. The taint of Roman Catholicism attached to the Gothic style was enhanced by Bishop John Milner's liking for it. Milner's liking was so great, in fact, that he even had his bedroom windows fitted with stained glass. He became Vicar Apostolic of the Western District – one of the divisions into which Rome had divided the English 'mission' for purposes of ecclesiastical discipline. After ordination in 1773 he had served in Winchester for a time, and it was there that he wrote about the Gothic style and even assisted in the design and construction of a Gothic chapel for Catholic use. The taint of Roman association was increased by Pugin, but, in the mid-nineteenth century, was decisively removed by Ruskin's influence within the intelligentsia. Ruskin was a thoroughly Protestant Englishman – to the extent that he was an orthodox Christian at all (rather than an ethical and artistic theorist who used the symbols and images of Christianity to convey his meaning) – and his praise of Catholic places of worship in Italy wiped away the lingering suspicions of Catholic medievalism and High Church Ritualism, which still encompassed the Gothic style for some.

Eighteenth-century Gothic had been Perpendicular in flavour: slender, insecure of appearance, tonal, and relatively clean of line. For secular purposes the model was Horace Walpole's reconstruction of Strawberry Hill, completed in 1753; its triumphalist peak was James Wyatt's extravagant Fonthill Abbey, built for William Beckford in the 1790s – and which was everyone's idea of Gothic grandeur until the very high and narrow tower fell down in 1825. There was a chapel at Fonthill, but its purpose was atmospheric rather than religious. Yet churches were soon to appear in a kind of Perpendicular Gothic which reflected the artistic sense which Strawberry Hill and Fonthill had popularized within the governing classes. Until approximately 1820 most new buildings in the Gothic style were houses for the gentry or gate-lodges for great estates. The very few churches that were built before then had considerable delicacy, however, and a splendid example is the Chapel Royal of Dublin Castle in Ireland. This was the work of Francis Johnston, and was completed in 1814. The stucco decoration (by Edward and John Smyth) and the ceiling (by George Stapleton) show how far from the Gothic postulated by the purists of the style this sort of building is. As was only to be expected of a church intended for the ceremonial use of the government, the decorative motifs are throughout secular rather than religious: the coats of arms of representatives of the British crown. The chapel was reconsecrated as a Catholic church in 1943, following the conversion of the Irish Free State into a republic. Later ecclesiastical buildings of this first phase of the Gothic Revival tend to exhibit clean lines and slender qualities very different from the 'Decorated' excess of the High Victorian churches. The movement for 'Church Extension' at the end of the Napoleonic Wars enormously stimulated English thought about church construction and the styles to be adopted. Both the clergy and the government were anxious to prevent the slide of the masses into a French-Revolutionary infidelity by providing more church accommodation in the extended urban areas. The Church was also worried by evidence of the multiplication of Dissent. As a result, the Church Building Society was established in 1818, with a good deal of prestigious support and royal patronage, and in the same year came the first of two Church Building Acts – the first providing a million pounds of public money for new churches, and the second, in

Francis Johnston of Dublin was one of those architects who worked equally happily in Gothic or classical. Top: his exquisite fan-vaulted chapel of Dublin Castle (1814). Bottom: design for a three-decker pulpit, still wholly Rococo in feeling.

1824, a further half million. This was to be the last occasion in England on which the government was to give direct financial assistance to the Church. The commissioners appointed under the terms of the legislation eventually built 214 new churches, 174 of them in the Gothic style. The official initiative elicited a wave of privately funded churches as well, and the great nineteenth-century expansion of church building was the result.

Some were very poor in their level of artistic or architectural achievement. Others, however, were really impressive – like St Luke's Church in Chelsea, London, set up by private Act of Parliament in 1819 and constructed, according to the design of James Savage, between 1820 and 1824. This church actually has a Neo-classical form, in the sense that it is an 'auditory' church, intended as a preaching hall; but with stone construction, Perpendicular tower, flying buttresses, and vaulted roof, it is authentically Gothic. It is very tall, the nave rising to 60 feet, and there were doubts, at the time of construction, about its safety. More modest churches in this kind of style were built in many places, and they sometimes disclose a quiet charm. Little Trinity Church at King Street East in Toronto, Canada, is a late example. It was put up in 1843 by Henry Lane, and at the base of the western tower and the flanking nave ends are three ogee-arched doorways, rising to crockets, the central one of which pierces the string-course. Beautifully restored after a fire in 1960, the church has symmetry and economy of decoration. It also shows that relatively cheaply built churches could, with the genius of an architect like Lane, achieve real distinction.

With the succeeding phase of the Gothic Revival came a number of crucial changes. The first was ideological: the High Victorian churches were originally promoted by men soaked in the ideals of the High Church movement and were intended to restore the ecclesiastical atmosphere of the Catholic past. Secondly the 'Decorated' Gothic of the fourteenth century was preferred to the Perpendicular, and churches lost their slender, almost crystalline, appearance and became more material and more ornamented, inside and out. Thirdly, with the triumph of the Camden ideas, considerable scholarship and architectural research (of varying quality) was invested in purity: the churches built, and those restored, were to be exactly faithful to the techniques and decoration of the medieval originals. Lastly, after an earlier preoccupation with English traditions of building, the High Victorian Revivalists came to study and incorporate elements of continental European Gothic. Out of this came some very distinguished churches, the work of learned architects who struggled, under the ever-critical eyes of the school of ecclesiologists, to perfect the details.

All Saints', Margaret Street, in the West End of London, is a good place to start, not just because of the fineness of the church itself, but because it was the structure of which the Ecclesiological Society most approved. It may therefore be taken as the model of their style, praised even by Ruskin. The architect was William Butterfield, whose career had begun when he was apprenticed to a builder, and so he knew about structural technique from actual experience. His first church was in 1844; All Saints', Margaret Street, was built from 1849 to 1859, and between the two undertakings Butterfield gained valuable experience with his work on the college of St Augustine in Canterbury. All Saints' replaced an earlier, eighteenth-century Dissenting chapel, which had been taken over by a group of Anglican High Churchmen, and on the rather cramped site Butterfield raised his church. It is most notable for its rich decoration and for structural polychrome. This last feature was assisted by the use of brick, to which the very earliest of the ecclesiologists would have been opposed with all their usual vehemence. Butterfield used coloured bricks mixed with interior marble.

St Luke's, Chelsea, London, was among the most serious of the early Gothic Revival churches. Designed by James Savage and built between 1820 and 1824, it has an interior vault supported by authentic flying buttresses.

Above: the chapel of Keble College, Oxford (1873–76), one of the masterpieces of William Butterfield, whose speciality – polychrome brickwork – was seen as a way of developing Gothic beyond the point where it had been cut short by the Renaissance.

272

At All Saints', Margaret Street, London
(right), begun in 1849, Butterfield
achieved the model 'ecclesiological'
church, richly adorned with sculpture and
with every surface covered with
polychrome decoration. The pulpit and
chancel screen show Butterfield's typically
robust geometry and unrestrained
enjoyment of colour.

*Sedilia at St James-the-Less, London
(above), by G. E. Street (1858–61). With
its brightly coloured tiles and free use of
patterning, it is another highly personal
adaptation of Early Gothic.*

After this, brick was no longer thought of as the resort of those with economy
of cost primarily in mind, and it became, indeed, a major ingredient of High
Victorian church building. The use of structural polychrome came from the
Continent. The foundation there had really been laid by Jacques-Ignace Hittorff
and his discovery (aided by the Englishman Thomas Donaldson) that classical
Greek buildings had been coloured. That was in the 1820s; before that time most
architects had supposed that all classical buildings were as they by then appeared,
in their natural fabric colour. The discovery of polychrome design by the Gothic
Revivalists produced a number of distinguished mid-Victorian churches in the
style: Keble College Chapel in Oxford, Rugby School Chapel, and St James-the-
Less in Vauxhall Bridge Road, London. The last, of red and black banded brick
in an Italianate Gothic, with a dramatic tower, was designed by George Edmund
Street and built between 1858 and 1861. Street had travelled extensively to other
European countries and in 1855 had published work on the brick and marble
architecture of Italy. He was a particularly religious man, who dwelt frequently
on the connexion between true Christianity and the appropriate architectural
styles.

Pugin's combined home, monastery and parish church: St Augustine's, Ramsgate, built between 1845 and 1850. The intended spire, shown here, was never built.

St Finbarr's Cathedral, Cork, Ireland (1865–76), by William Burges, in his favourite early French Gothic style.

Augustus Welby Pugin's insistence on this sort of connexion, raised by him to exact dogma, is well known. In his seminal propagandist publication on behalf of the Gothic (or as he would have said, *Christian*) style, *Contrasts*, which appeared at his own expense in 1836, Pugin exclaimed: 'From Christianity has arisen an architecture so glorious, so sublime, so perfect, that all the productions of ancient paganism sink, when compared before it, to a level with the false and corrupt systems from which they originated.' The same thesis appeared in his *Apology for the Revival of Christian Architecture* (1843) and was implicit in every building which he designed or built. Pugin contended, simply, that Gothic was not a mere style but the very embodiment of religious truth. Buildings, he supposed, had quasi-sacramental qualities; they disclosed the interior values of the age and then in turn helped to inspire men with the beliefs germane to their structure and decoration. Gothic was the form of Christianity, and to recover it in the nineteenth century was to restore the spirituality and authenticity of medieval Christendom, as he imagined them to have been. Pugin's conversion to Catholicism, in 1834, was itself evidence of his indebtedness to these convictions. A good and noble age produced good and noble buildings; Ruskin was later to spell out even more emphatically the individual implication that good men were needed to construct good buildings, that there was an exact relationship between morality and spirituality on the one hand and successful and satisfying craftsmanship on the other. These ideas helped to produce the Arts and Crafts artistic mentality and Guild Socialism.

Pugin's buildings, however, were never political or even social statements: they were quintessentially religious. At Ramsgate, then a fashionable resort, he built himself a church and a house which, precisely because he was working for himself and not for a patron or a body of ecclesiastical trustees, can be taken to exemplify everything in which he believed. St Augustine's, begun in 1845 and completed in 1850, has a banded exterior of knapped flint and Whitby stone which became coloured differently by an accident of weathering. Originally the exterior was intended to echo the local traditional Kentish building style. The square, rather squat, tower was meant to have had a steeple, a landmark for sailors at sea: Pugin was obsessed by the sea and by marine pursuits. The structure consists of a short nave and chancel, a single south aisle, and transept. It is, to say the least, unusual. The roofs are made of wood. The effect is really one of some austerity, broken only by the stone bands. It is not, therefore, from the structure but from the decoration that St Augustine's derives its exceptional richness, and its striking array of colours. Pugin died in 1852 and the south transept is his chantry chapel, with an effigy in stone, dressed in a kind of Gothic medieval smock, set upon an altar tomb of veined alabaster.

Pugin's understanding of Gothic was English in sentiment and style. Increasingly, however, the influence of foreign Gothic styles began to penetrate the consciousness of the progenitors of the High Victorian phase of the Gothic Revival. Just as Street progressively turned to Italian and French models, after working first in English, so others looked overseas. William Burges designed churches exclusively in foreign styles, and particularly in the French Gothic of the thirteenth century. At its most grandiose this was demonstrated in his cathedral of St Finbarr in Cork, Ireland, built between 1865 and 1876. Like most French Gothic it aspires to soaring height, with tall towers and spires. There is a richly carved west front, with rose windows. Mention has already been made of the importation of structural polychrome from overseas; other foreign features were the design of towers and large gables. An example of high quality, which combines both in characteristically French Gothic, is St Stephen's Methodist

Church, Cliftonville, Kent, by Drewe and Bower, and completed in 1878. Built in ragstone and on a Greek cross plan, the church is something of a local landmark because of the prominence of the tower. It is a noble square-shaped structure with a pitched gable roof.

John Loughborough Pearson was another who assisted the spread of continental influences: in his case it was the use of the stone vault. Very few Gothic Revival churches had had stone vaults before his work; now they became characteristic of his churches. When Truro became the seat of an Anglican diocese in 1876, it turned to Pearson for a cathedral, and the result, begun in 1879 and completed in 1910, was in an Early English Gothic style but with decidedly French towers and spires. Pearson was very precise and accurate about the interior decoration, in thirteenth-century taste, but the effect is sometimes fussy. Externally, however, the cathedral manages to contrive the soaring qualities of the French Gothic masterpieces. Height, too, was achieved in Lancing College Chapel in Sussex, whose tall buttressed shape, with the now completed great rose window at the west end, is a remarkable and successful version of French Gothic. At Giles Gilbert Scott's Liverpool Anglican Cathedral, started in 1904 and only just completed, it is height which is intended to elicit the appreciation of the worshipper, but this enormous building is English rather than continental in its style, and it is massive rather than slender in its impact.

The style of Gothic Revival which extended to the rest of the English-speaking world was often English rather than French. George Bodley, the first pupil of Sir George Gilbert Scott, designed the Episcopal cathedral for Washington D.C. in 1906 – built (and still being built) after his death the following year. It has striking resemblances to Canterbury Cathedral, especially in the appearance of the central tower. Bodley's buildings were nearly all in the English 'Decorated' style. His interiors, especially, were English: repositories of the genius of Pre-Raphaelite art and design. American architects had themselves shown remarkable confidence in their adaptation of the ideals of the English Gothic Revival. Trinity Church in New York City, completed in 1846, clearly showed the influence of Pugin on its designer, Richard Upjohn; although, as in Upjohn's other buildings, there is also a strong German Gothic presence. American English Gothic rather specialized in crenellated square towers set beside the west end of churches – as in All Saints, Pasadena in California, or Trinity Episcopal Church in Lawrence, Kansas. England was alone among European countries in regarding the west end of a church as the usual place to site a tower, and as the Gothic Revival developed, the idea of a flanking tower at the west end became more and more popular. It was this convention which was transmitted overseas so successfully.

The Gothic Revivalists quarrelled among themselves about the problem of the restoration of old churches. The purists, in their desire to remove falsity and to make buildings correspond as closely as possible, and as homogeneously as possible, to their original medieval ideal, were often great destroyers of other styles or of the Gothic variants of which they chanced to disapprove. Most churches which survived to the nineteenth century were a mixture of styles, the accretion of centuries patched up from time to time but rarely rationalized or harmonized. The Revivalists often swept the accumulated historical deposits away, so that the authentic churches of the medieval period, as they now appear, are virtually all nineteenth-century reconstructions. Some impression of Gothic churches before restoration may be received from paintings or prints. The old church at Chingford in Essex, for example, was used in Arthur Hughes's melancholy but moving *Home from Sea* – a Pre-Raphaelite picture of undoubted

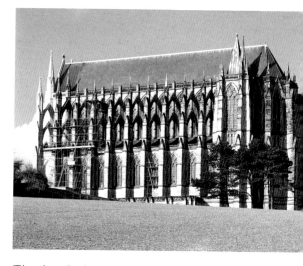

The chapel of Lancing College, Sussex, rises over the South Downs like a rural cathedral. It was begun in 1868 to the designs of R. H. Carpenter, and achieves slender grace in the French Gothic manner.

The Victorians not only built thousands of new churches, they restored almost all the old ones, so that it is now hard to find a medieval church that is completely authentic. The churches had, however, often reached a state of dilapidation that made basic repairs necessary. Arthur Hughes's *Home from Sea (detail)* shows Chingford old church, in Essex, as it was in 1862.

The openwork spires of Cologne Cathedral (far left), though designed in the Middle Ages, were not built until the 1840s. They provoked a rush of imitations. Heinrich von Ferstel's Votivkirche, in Vienna, (left) of 1857–79 is particularly slender and spiky. Ste-Clotilde, Paris, (below left) of 1846–57 looks back to the French thirteenth century and comes closer to its models. The architect was Franz-Christian Gau.

Victorian sentimentality (painted in 1862) which also shows the exterior of an ancient church before the restorers started work on it. A boy sailor laments the death of his mother by prostrating himself on her grave; behind him the decaying walls of the church are beginning to crumble beneath the encroaching vegetation.

As it happens, the restorers' own interiors have rarely remained untouched by twentieth-century reactions to Victorian taste, and it is only in the last couple of decades that the Gothic Revivalists' work is itself being restored, often out of respect for Pre-Raphaelite art. Holy Trinity Church in the Rocks district of Sydney, Australia, has a rather ordinary pinnacled exterior, but it preserves a perfect nineteenth-century interior. This building is the work of Henry Ginn and Edmund Blacket; it was a garrison church for the soldiers stationed in Sydney harbour. Those who believe the restorers' enterprises were too destructive have usually pointed to Lord Grimthorpe's reconstruction of St Albans Cathedral in England as their worst-case scenario realized in practice. The restorers, as Lord Clark long ago reminded us, were concerned with *restoration* not *preservation*, and this was shown very obviously in Sir George Gilbert Scott's work on English cathedrals. Scott saw himself as the popularizer of the Gothic Revival, as an advocate less concerned with the learned debates of the ecclesiologists than with giving Pugin's idealism practical expression. Though he also supposed he was something of a conservative restorer, the churches and cathedrals he saved from further ruination were in fact transformed in the process.

The rest of the world embraced the Gothic Revival with less ardour than England did. Rival styles, especially classicism, retained their attractions. Both France and Germany were inclined to regard the original Gothic style as their own, and hence claimed to be its legitimate heirs. Italy resisted its charms, as it had those of Gothic itself. Spain remained totally unmoved. But the rest of the English-speaking world, and most notably the United States, showed a degree of enthusiasm which indeed grew keener as the original movement in England began to wane.

An event that caught the imagination of architects on the Continent was the completion in the 1840s of Cologne Cathedral, a building which had stood as an unfinished shell for hundreds of years, and of which the original designs had recently been discovered just at a time to appeal to German national pride. Its pair of openwork spires were new and exciting. Soon they began to rise in other countries – in Paris at Ste-Clotilde by Franz-Christian Gau (1846–57); in Vienna at the Votivenkirche by Heinrich von Ferstel (1857–79); and in New York at St Patrick's Catholic Cathedral by James Renwick (1858–88). After this, however, the Gothic Revival progeny of Germany is somewhat disappointing. It is symptomatic that Schinkel's only Gothic church, the Werdersche Kirche in Berlin, was also prepared by its architect in classical dress, indicating a lack of commitment to Gothic of which no English designer would have been guilty. And for one of the major Neo-Gothic churches, the Nikolaikirche in Hamburg, the authorities turned to an Englishman, Sir George Gilbert Scott.

France possessed the most learned champion of the Gothic Revival, Eugène Viollet-le-Duc. Most of his enormous energy went into restoration, and he was adept at supplying features, and even whole façades, that were either ruined or had been left unfinished in the Middle Ages. His own buildings are less impressive; churches such as those at Aillant-sur-Tholon or St Denis, interesting from an architectural point of view, make little appeal to the emotions. In an architectural world dominated by the teachings of the Ecole des Beaux Arts, Viollet was virtually on his own. Of the other architects working in Gothic in France, Jean-Baptiste Lassu, who built St-Nicholas at Nantes in 1843, is probably the most notable. The rest tended to rebel against historical restraints and to launch out into ambitious attempts to combine styles, like Bossan's church at Lyons, previously mentioned, or Vaudoyer's unprecedented and unimitated cathedral at Marseilles, which is a sort of history of architecture in stone. A similar act of self-expression produced the most unmissable of Parisian churches, the gleaming white marble, Neo-Byzantine Sacré-Coeur by Paul Abadie.

It is to America that we must turn in order to recover the true line of the Gothic Revival; that is, the development of a manner of building which, while retaining the spirit and formal language of Gothic, left the way open for original invention and creative talent. It was in such terms that the English architects had seen their role: to build what the Gothic style *would* have produced had it not ended at the Renaissance. Architects in America, moreover, were presented with opportunities that hardly ever arose in Europe: to build cathedral-size churches for rich congregations. In England the only two Neo-Gothic cathedrals are Truro and Liverpool. In America that number could be multiplied many times.

During the first half of the nineteenth century American architects followed the delicate, Rococo Gothic style that had been popular before Pugin. The Unitarian church of Charleston by F. D. Lee (1852) has arcades of light shafts, Perpendicular windows and plaster pendant vaults imitating those of Henry VIII's Chapel at Westminster. Renwick's St Patrick's, begun in 1858, is already fully mature and built with a lavishness of materials and decoration (foliage carving on the capitals, elaborate – though not stone – bosses on the rib vault) that must have been overwhelming when it was completed in 1888.

The Protestant cathedral of St John the Divine in New York was in some sense a reply to the Catholic St Patrick's. Begun in 1893 on a vast scale, it has suffered a series of setbacks and delays and is still unfinished. In 1911 it was taken over by Ralph Adams Cram, America's leading Neo-Gothic architect, who changed the previous Romanesque style to Gothic. In spite of these alterations, its gaunt strength is immensely impressive.

Viollet-le-Duc's 'ideal cathedral'. For most Neo-Gothic architects, the thirteenth century was the high-water mark of church building. Viollet's sketch is based on Laon (p. 166), adding the towers and spires that were never built – two at the west end, two beside each transept and the largest over the crossing.

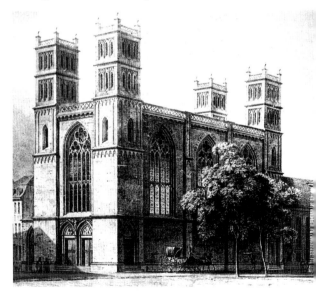

Karl Friedrich Schinkel, whose fantasy of a Gothic cathedral is illustrated in pl. 61, never built anything so romantic. His Werdersche Kirche in Berlin, of 1821–31, seems like a classical design uncomfortably clothed in Gothic dress.

Trinity Church, New York, designed by Richard Upjohn, was among the city's first Gothic Revival churches. It was built between 1844 and 1846.

The cathedral of Bryn Athyn, Pennsylvania (1913–29) is more conventional in style, though it too went through a number of revisions. Much more unusual is the church of St Vincent Ferrer, New York, by Bertram Goodhue, designed in 1916. This combines features from the Gothic of several European countries into a stimulating and inventive unity. Its stained glass is particularly admired. In Minneapolis, the Hennepin Avenue Methodist Church, designed by Hewitt and Brown of Minneapolis, and started in 1914, was intended to echo the central octagon of Ely Cathedral in England. This was successfully achieved; with the addition of an extremely slender spire the whole church expresses a delicate blend of French and English Gothic styles. Another church in New York, the Riverside Church by Collens and Pelton, of 1926, relies more on French than English precedent. With its superb central tower dominating a prominent site, it is one of New York's most easily visible landmarks. Inside, its wide nave is spanned by simple quadripartite vaults, again on the French model.

The last great enterprise of the Gothic Revival in America, or in the world, was the Episcopal Cathedral of Philadelphia. Quite deliberately, it set out to be the largest Gothic cathedral ever attempted, but it was begun at a bad time (1932) and had proceeded only as far as the Lady Chapel when funds ran out and work came to a standstill. It remains a fragment, an unrealized dream.

The Gothic Revival was not confined to the grandiose. On a much smaller scale, English Decorated Gothic – as exemplified by the parish church at Stoke Poges in Buckinghamshire – is said to have inspired the 'Little Church of the Flowers' at Forest Lawn Memorial Park in Glendale, California. This extraordinary cemetery, the vision of Hubert Eaton, who died in 1966, contained a number of chapels, each one intended to illustrate a particular theme. The 'Little Church of the Flowers', designed like the others for funerals, has, because of its atmosphere of instant serenity, become popular for weddings too: a happy fulfilment of the founder's conviction that cemeteries should be places for the living as well as for the dead.

The Episcopal Cathedral of Philadelphia: this model shows what would have been the most ambitious Gothic church ever built. Work began in 1932 but was stopped by the Depression and never resumed. After the Second World War the whole dream of a revived Middle Ages seemed to evaporate. The modern Church looks for a different image.

Opposite: another descendant of Cologne Cathedral – James Renwick's Catholic Cathedral of St Patrick, New York, built between 1858 and 1888. Once it soared above the neighbouring streets. Now one can look down on it from a position that the architect can hardly have imagined.

10 In the modern world: the new community

FOR THE FIRST FORTY YEARS of the twentieth century, church building experienced no radical break with the past. Even the trauma of the First World War made no significant impact either on the established Churches as institutions or on their buildings. Europe and America were still the heartlands of Christianity and the areas from which Christian leadership was expected. Architecturally there were experiments in new styles, such as Expressionism in Germany or Art Nouveau in Austria or Spain, but on the whole there was continuity rather than revolution. Fewer Neo-Gothic churches were begun, but those under construction went on being built.

The Second World War, on the other hand, seems in retrospect to mark a decisive break at almost every level. From the 1950s onwards Christianity has no longer been Euro-centred. The Churches of Africa and South America, faced with burning political and moral issues, have taken their places in the ideological front line. In the West, the established Churches, the Roman Catholic in particular, have embarked on a programme of *aggiornamento* ('bringing up to date'), shedding their hierarchic, conservative, custom-bound image and adopting one that is modern, egalitarian, controversial and involved with the world's problems. These attitudes were formalized in the Second Vatican Council of 1962–67, whose liturgical changes, for instance the forward-facing altar, modified the layout of existing churches and conditioned the design of new ones.

These developments in Church discipline and theology coincided with parallel developments in architecture. By 1945 the Modern Movement had decisively rejected the past. Henceforth, until the late 1980s, no self-respecting architect would build in a historical style. It was a mood that suited the new disposition of the Churches. Both patrons and designers were looking for fresh, untried solutions and the result has been a bewildering variety about which it is impossible to generalize.

One kind of polarity, however, is as observable now as it was in the early Middle Ages: between those who (like Abbot Suger) believe in using every resource of art and imagery to glorify God, and those who (like St Bernard) believe that the Church is essentially the community of the faithful and that any building will do. As the twentieth century draws to its close, the future role of architecture in the Christian faith can be a subject of only the most hazardous speculation.

For captions to colour plates 72–80, see p. 289

75

76

Colour plates 72–80

72 *The Anglican cathedral of Liverpool is among the last major Gothic Revival buildings in the world. During the nineteenth century Liverpool had grown into a major city. The Catholics made it the seat of a bishop in 1850, the Anglicans in 1880. Both communities were ambitious to build cathedrals worthy of their status (see pp. 291, 296). For the Anglican cathedral a competition was held in 1901, which was won by Giles Gilbert Scott, then aged twenty-one. His design, which was modified as work progressed, contained a number of highly original features, though still in the spirit of Gothic. One was the bridge spanning the nave, a version of the medieval choir-screen or pulpitum, but allowing views through into the crossing and choir beyond. Another was the doubling of the transepts, with the space between them given to an immensely tall lantern tower.*

73 *Stained glass window by Louis Comfort Tiffany in the Wade Memorial Chapel, Cleveland, Ohio. Made at the turn of the century, it represents the 'Consummation of the Divine Promise in the Passing of the Goal from the Earthly Abode to the Heavenly Home'. Tiffany produces an almost mystical effect by means of colour and light, combining explicit religious imagery with the natural forms of bushes and flowers that he had made so much his own.*

74 *Antonio Gaudí's extraordinary church of the Sagrada Familia (the Holy Family) in Barcelona was taken over by him in 1884 and is still unfinished. Gaudí invented and promoted a very personal form of Art Nouveau, which he saw as a logical continuation of Gothic (see p. 302), but brought to it an organic feeling that makes his church close to living things – trees, tendrils or sea-shells. The four spires seen here rise above the south transept front.*

75 *Le Corbusier's pilgrimage chapel at Ronchamp, in the mountains of central France, of 1950–55, is a deliberate essay in the architecture of mysticism. Traditional forms of church building have been completely abandoned. Curved surfaces, irregular shapes, leaning walls and an apparently random distribution of windows give both the exterior and interior a strangely evocative power.*

76 *In the late 1940s Henri Matisse decorated the chapel of the Dominican nuns at Vence, southern France. His cool, depersonalized figures represent the non-worldly tradition of Christian worship, the tradition of the Cistercians, the Puritans and the Quakers.*

77 *S. Giovanni Battista, outside Florence, stands on the Autostrada del Sol and was built between 1960 and 1963. The architect, Giovanni Michelucci, put forward an elaborate theoretical programme to explain his novel forms – 'a tent, symbolizing the transient passage not only of the passing motorist but also of the Christian on his way from this world to the next'.*

78 *The 'Crystal Cathedral' in Los Angeles, by Philip Johnson, is a church conceived for the age of mass evangelism. It is star-shaped and made entirely of glass on a steel frame. All the resources of modern technology are brought to bear. The preacher, plus an orchestra, soloist and chorus are on the left. Facing them are television cameras, while microphones relay the service to another congregation in the car-park who can see inside when vast glass doors are swung open.*

79 *Oscar Niemeyer's cathedral, begun in the 1950s, for Brasilia, the new capital of Brazil, was among the first to exploit modern materials to create churches without precedent in the past. Rising like a flower from beneath the earth (see p. 294), its vault of concrete ribs and glass opens to the real sky as Baroque domes opened to a fictitious one.*

80 *Open-air service on the Feast of the Assumption at a wayside shrine at Kalwaria Pacłaska, in southern Poland. This is one of the major pilgrimages in Eastern Europe, attended annually by about fifty thousand people, many of whom sleep in the fields. There is a whole circuit of churches, chapels and shrines stretching across fifty miles, at each of which parties stop and pray over a three-day period. Such ceremonies could be paralleled in many parts of the world and are probably growing in popularity – a sign of the regionalism and encouragement of local observance that mark Churches of all denominations today. They may also indicate a diminishing interest in the architectural setting of worship and a shift of emphasis from buildings to communities and the individuals that compose them.*

In the modern world

As the twentieth century draws to its close, it becomes clear that, from the point of view of the history of the Christian Church, the era will be remembered as the one in which the centre of gravity shifted from Europe and North America to the Developing World – largely to the Southern Hemisphere. It seems likely that by the end of the century, a sizeable majority of Christian believers will come from the southern part of the globe, and there is very little reason to suppose – despite some occasional flickerings in the dying embers – that the progressively secularized churches of the Western world will suddenly revive. Even in North America, where Christianity has shown an extraordinary vigour in the twentieth century, there must be a suspicion that the secularizing materialism simultaneously espoused by its numerous adherents will eventually produce the same decline which the European churches have experienced.

The twentieth century is the great age of Christian expansion; yet in the Developing World where adoption of the faith is occurring, and especially in the centre and the south of Africa, there are no real signs that distinctive church buildings are being conceived. There has been, in the determination to rid the Church of an outdated 'missionary' image, a rush to use ethnic symbols in versions of local structural styles. But these attempts at localization tend to derive from a kind of Western 'Arts and Crafts' impulse, transposed to the Developing World and there cultivated by the more self-conscious, educated, and most Westernized leaders of Christian opinion. The really vibrant Christianity has actually been characterized by a desire to copy the hierarchical European churches, at least in some patterns of ecclesiastical authority and symbolism, and to put up church buildings in styles which, where they are not plainly utilitarian on grounds of cost, suggest the more ornate of the traditional European styles. This has been particularly a characteristic of the tremendously vital independent Black Churches and sects of southern Africa, as the Swedish sociologist Benkt Sundkler has noticed.

One feature of modern Christian worship has, above all others, helped to dictate the plan of churches: the emphasis on community. Only within Orthodoxy has the purity of the liturgy, as unfolding the timeless truths of the faith, continued to supply the essential design of a church structure. Set amidst increasingly articulate and educated societies whose citizens, in varying degrees of effectiveness according to their local political cultures, are able to select their own values, the Catholic and Protestant Churches have tried to reinterpret their existence around shared religious experience rather than around dogma or the performance of rites in which the priest or ecclesiastical official, and not the lay believers, have a dominant role. Churches are no longer the place where mysteries are celebrated, or where the Word is dispensed. They are halls for the assembly of the 'People of God'. Not since before the Reformation have churches been intended for such a variety of uses: they are places not for shared worship only, but for liturgical dance, for discussions, and for a whole range of social and teaching functions. The world has come into the church again, and although this

Pope John XXIII summoned the Second Vatican Council in 1962 but did not live to see the end of it. To commemorate it the sculptor Giacomo Manzù made a pair of bronze doors for St Peter's with figured panels. This one shows the Pope welcoming the Black African Cardinal Rugambwa.

Opposite: the Catholic cathedral of Liverpool was begun in 1933 to designs by Sir Edwin Lutyens (see p. 296). When the Second World War began in 1939 the crypt had been built (seen here at the bottom of the photograph) but only the platform for the main building. After the War tastes had changed and money was in short supply. Sir Frederick Gibberd was asked to design a new cathedral, which has a centralized plan, crowned by a spectacular lantern of glass. In the background to the left can be seen the tower of the Anglican cathedral.

291

is all still a little self-conscious and identifiable in social class terms, it presages what the leaders of Western religious opinion see as a great new attempt, based on authentic scriptural foundations, to engage society in a fruitful interrelationship of the sacred and the secular. With this vision, and obviously related to it, has gone an emphasis on the social priorities of Christianity. There is, in contemporary Christianity, an impatience with truth when it is represented in the language of dogma or exact doctrine, and a desire to see an overflowing of Christian insights, as new wine bursts old wine skins, where this can be of immediate service to the material, as well as to the spiritual, condition of the peoples of the earth.

This new sense of 'community' within Christianity is, by an accident of building design and the use of modern materials by recent architects, capable of expression in very demonstrable ways in actual church structures. Chancels have tended to disappear, and altars have been placed at the centre of a church, or where they are unencumbered. The 'triumphalist' forms, both of altars and of their surrounds, have also gone. In the Catholic Church this act has been associated with the Second Vatican Council and the religious *aggiornamento* (or 'bringing up to date') it expressed. The popularity of 'collegial' understandings of ecclesiastical authority, in which the laity as well as the clergy are conceived as equal in the ability to discern truth, is also more obviously expressed in open-plan churches than in the traditional Greek or Latin cross arrangements where the clergy in the sanctuary were physically and symbolically separated. The contemporary enthusiasm for ecumenism – understood as the prelude to an eventual organic reunion of the Churches – has often been anticipated in practice by shared worship across the denominational lines, and this has been enormously assisted in practice when church buildings have few distinctive features which suggest different liturgical use. Probably at no time in the Church's history have so many people been able to participate in the choice of a style for a new church building. Wide choice and broad participation do not, however, inhibit the achievement of excellence, and the twentieth century has so far seen the construction of some churches of breathtaking splendour.

The most visible change has been the use of reinforced concrete in construction. Modern experiments in concrete began with François Coignet in the 1850s. Concrete allows great weight to be held up and large expanses of wall to be filled with glass – and fulfils, therefore, the aspirations of the medieval Gothic builders to produce diaphanous buildings of soaring height and support structures of apparent lightness. In the 1870s Viollet-le-Duc had advocated the use of iron to give buildings a less substantial structural appearance. In the twentieth century these two innovative ideas have come together, with mixed results, in a large number of churches in which concrete roofs and canopies are held in place with slender iron or steel supports.

Sometimes, however, concrete has been used to produce a pervasive massivity, as in Frank Lloyd Wright's Unity Temple, a Chicago Unitarian church of 1906. There enormously solid walls, without windows, and roofs made of great concrete slabs, enclose a galleried space of sombre contemplative qualities. Far, too, from the use of concrete to produce light structures, are the thousands of functional churches, put together from concrete panels, and favoured where speed or financial considerations have been motivating factors for local Church authorities. At the simplest level, examples can be found in buildings like the Botshabelo Dutch Reformed Church at Diepkloof in Soweto, the huge Black city adjacent to Johannesburg in South Africa. This austere concrete box, set beside a dirt road, was assembled in 1959 and intended as a youth centre for Blacks. In

At Oak Park, near Chicago, Frank Lloyd Wright built one of his few churches, the Unity Temple, of 1906. Abstract and coolly rational in its planning, it is given richness by its decoration: wall panels, light-fittings and stained glass.

1964 it became a church. Both within and without it is undecorated, partly in recognition of Calvinist orthodoxy, but partly, also, because of the sheer poverty of the worshippers. The concrete floor is at least suitable for dancing – a part of Church life, for Black Calvinism is expressed in the vigorous exuberance of traditional ethnic custom. The only ornamental feature is an embroidered cloth over the minister's reading-desk, which bears, in the Sotho language, the words 'Modimo O Lerabo' ('God is Love'). It is a place of pathos and of spiritual confidence. There are churches like this all over the Developing World, of all denominations and with varying degrees of permanence.

Simple concrete structures, on a rather more ambitious scale, have sometimes incorporated brick or stone walls and the use of other materials, with very satisfying results. Thus the Parrochia di Don Bosco in Viareggio in Tuscany, Italy, is a tall church which, while self-consciously contemporary, suggests traditional Tuscan ecclesiastical vernacular, especially in the gabled west end, where narrow lancet windows are set between modern concrete pilasters. Another example of the successful use of mixed materials, which again represents vast numbers of others throughout the world, is the Catholic church of Our Lady, Star of the Sea, in Condado, Puerto Rico. This is a straightforward, rectilinear box, whose ornament comes entirely from interior decoration. Churches built for newly established populations, at the extremity of parish boundaries, often look like this.

The advantage of concrete as a building material is not really its durability, for it stains easily and cracks readily, but its simulation of plasticity. It is a material which allows dramatic shapes. As a result, a series of round churches have been constructed in modern times to which it has been possible to attribute religious symbolism. In fact, there are also many secular buildings – concert halls and exhibition centres especially – whose external appearance is very similar. This should not matter. If Christianity offers the best of the works of men, and if the insights of believers penetrate the earthly veil which divides the sacred and the secular, then a common building style can scarcely be regarded as a disturbing feature. The concrete and glass circular churches of today are not *martyria*, as

In 1967 a new church (on the right) was opened in Mexico City to house the miraculous image of Our Lady of Guadeloupe (see p. 222). Its rounded plan ensures an unobstructed view.

The cathedral of Brasilia (see pl. 79) suggests the Crown of Thorns. Niemeyer's is one of the simplest, yet one of the most effective, of all modern church designs: a ring of mutually supporting concrete struts filled in with glass.

round churches were in the past; they are, on the contrary, typically celebrations of Christ, the structure intended to suggest the crown of Christ the King, or the symbol of his Passion, the Crown of Thorns. The best known of these great buildings is undoubtedly the cathedral of Brasilia, the new capital of Brazil, designed by Oscar Niemeyer and Joachim Cardozo. Gigantic curved fins of concrete rise to 131 feet and enclose draped walls of clear glass. It is the Crown of Thorns, transfigured with light and pointing upwards to the celestial world; inside sculpted angels hang suspended from the converging fins, suggesting the welcoming hosts of the city of eternity.

At Nazareth in Israel the new basilica of the Annunciation, by Antonio Barluzzi (begun in 1960), is a two-tiered, approximately rectangular building of concrete, but the roof and dome, also of concrete, are symbolical uses of rounded design. The cupola is raised over 160 feet above the ground. It, and the drum of the dome, in the form of an open loggia, are dressed in stone, interlaced to give a kind of filigree effect, and intended to suggest both the opening of a lily (representing the attribute of the Virgin as the Lily of Purity) and the Crown of Heaven.

Another great church which uses a circular concrete design with symbolical purpose is the new basilica of Our Lady of Guadeloupe in Mexico City, opened in 1976 to replace the Baroque church which had before then housed the miraculous serape of St Juan Diego. It is a pilgrim church on an irregular rounded plan intended to allow an unobstructed view of the image of the Virgin to the thousands who each day crowd into the enormous building. The slightly elliptical roof is hung on concrete ribs radiating from a central box-like cupola and cross, the effect not unlike an enormous petrified tent, and suggesting the pavilioned or canopied cover of a great treasure – which indeed it is.

The Catholic cathedral of Christ the King in Liverpool, England, is a round structure whose roof and tower are associated by local people with the upended cathode-ray tube of a television set. The effect is also one of concrete basket-work. The original design of the cathedral, in 1933, was by Sir Edwin Lutyens, and

Opposite: the church of Notre-Dame at Royan, in France, by Guillaume Gillet, built between 1954 and 1959. Here the architect puts reinforced concrete to bold and harmonious use. The vertical fins are V-shaped in plan and rise straight from the floor to the ceiling. Between them windows equally tall flood the interior with light – an effect that has been compared to Gothic.

envisaged a series of barrel vaults and triumphal arches rising to a huge circular dome, all in a Neo-classical polychromed style. The only part of the colossal project to be completed was the crypt, of brick vaults. The modern cathedral which now sits on top of it was conceived by Sir Frederick Gibberd, and represents the necessary decision of the ecclesiastical authorities to scale down the cost. The building, completed in 1967, suggests the crown of Christ. It is a classic of concrete and glass construction, the glass cylinder of the tower illuminating the space below, in which the high altar is placed centrally and so is suited to the liturgical uses which have followed the Second Vatican Council. The glass is by John Piper and Patrick Reyntiens; the continuous sequence of colours has a jewelled effect which both recalls the medieval use of coloured lights to

Sir Edwin Lutyens's Liverpool Cathedral would have been the last great progeny of the classical tradition, a church worthy to be compared to St Peter's. It is based on a series of ratios expressed as large and small arches related as in a triumphal arch. But with its spare use of the orders, its brick construction and its relatively subdued light, there would also have been an element of Byzantine mystery. Apart from the crypt, this model is all that remains to suggest the effect it would have had.

suggest a sacred reliquary and also represents the unity of the divine presence. At night, the light from inside the cathedral shines out like a beacon over the city. The cathedral was designed with contemporary needs in mind, and there are two high-level television galleries.

Glass in modern churches has been used very ambitiously and, as in Liverpool's Catholic Cathedral, sometimes very successfully. The medievalism of the Pre-Raphaelite glass of the nineteenth century has had twentieth-century emulators as well. Charles Connick in America, for example, undertook numerous commissions, especially in the 1930s, which were all in traditionalist 'Gothic' styles. The clarity and harmony of his work, though not always achieving the highest distinction, is admirable: for example, his clerestory window at St Patrick's Cathedral in New York City, completed in 1940, is a marvellous essay in blue glass. In Ireland there are many examples of the work of Evie Hone. Though in a modern mode, the style continues to have echoes and hints of medieval glass, both because of the brilliance of the colours and because of the postures of the figures. The window of 'The Ascension' at St Mary's Catholic Church in Kingscourt, County Cavan, for example, shows Christ in

prayer as he rises above the heads of the disciples – their faces upturned and somehow wooden, just as in a medieval representation.

Some of the most astonishing of all modern glass is to be found in Sir Basil Spence's Coventry Cathedral in England, built between 1956 and 1962 contiguous to the ruins of the Perpendicular church which had served as the cathedral until its destruction during the Second World War. John Hutton's engraved west window depicts the figures of saints and angels. The window forms a huge screen between the cathedral and the outside world, and the transparent figures suggest the unity of that world and the celestial beings who watch over it and pray with it. But the most extraordinary glass here is in John Piper's baptistry window, a heavenly flood intended to show the light of the Holy Spirit penetrating the lives of men. It is the more dramatic since the other windows of the nave are narrow lancets set at an angle so that their light is cast towards the altar, though they are themselves hidden from view at the entrance to the building. The glass in the basilica of the Agony in the Garden of Gethsemane, in Jerusalem, is purple and violet. The church itself, by Barluzzi, is a Neo-Byzantine structure, completed in 1924, but the glass is used in an emphatically modern way

Coventry Cathedral, designed by Sir Basil Spence in 1951 and built between 1956 and 1962, sought to re-interpret many aspects of traditional church architecture in a way that was relevant to the post-War world. Epstein's bronze figure of St Michael tramples upon a defeated Lucifer; next to him is the huge baptistry window with glass by John Piper; and beyond that the series of tall nave windows which illuminate the interior but are mysteriously invisible from the entrance.

to create a particular atmosphere. The mood is sombre and pensive, calling the worshipper to join the Saviour in the suffering of his Passion; the dark colour leaves the church in semi-darkness, like the night of Christ's betrayal.

The modern use of structural glass ultimately derives from the secular vision of the German architect, Bruno Taut. He supposed glass would have ideological consequences; that men would be renewed and society purified. These socialist aspirations were promoted by Taut in the first two decades of the century. The use of glass for churches has actually derived from less ambitious motivation. Some modern churches have been entirely of glass. This has occasionally been a response to particular needs: at Knock in County Mayo, Ireland, the glass octagon is intended to shelter the priests saying Mass for the huge assemblage of pilgrims. Appearances of the Virgin here in 1879 have made the place a major shrine, visited by the Pope, and the centre of numerous retreats and religious festivals. The glass chapel, which enables the Mass to be seen by the crowds, is surmounted by a cupola whose circular 'windows' are in fact loud-speakers. The largest glass church in the world is unquestionably the Crystal Cathedral at Anaheim in California. This astonishing edifice, in the shape of a star, serves the needs of America's 'electronic church': it was designed for television transmissions, the scenographic arena for the evangelists whose regular exhortations into millions of homes has become one of the most powerful and effective contemporary conveyances of popular religiosity. The external effect of the building is massive rather than crystalline – huge elevations of shimmering light reflected from the surfaces, cliffs of glass offering an impression of greater height than the building actually attains.

The Crystal Cathedral illustrates another characteristic of some of the more successful churches of this century: the extraordinary sculptural shapes and visual images produced by different ways of using materials.

Sometimes, as in the Crystal Cathedral, this serves to dissolve the solid walls of the building altogether, uniting inner and outer space. Such an effect is achieved on a far more intimate scale at the Thorncrown Chapel, Eureka Springs, designed by E. Fay Jones in 1980. Jones was a pupil of Frank Lloyd Wright and here movingly applies Wright's philosophy of nature and natural materials to a religious end, the structure almost disappearing into the countryside.

Frank Lloyd Wright's Annie Pfeiffer Memorial Chapel at Florida Southern College (below) was designed thirty years after his Unity Temple, in 1941, when he was over seventy. His style had radically changed. An irregular space, lit by abruptly sloping windows, is tied together by a balcony focused on the pulpit.

St Louis Priory, Saint Louis, Missouri (right), was designed by Gyo Obata as two concentric and superimposed rings of parabolic shells, the whole covered by a flat, domed ceiling. The parabolic arches form the windows on the upper level, and on the ground floor twenty private chapels.

Two American experiments in church design. Right: the Air Force Academy Cadet Chapel (1956–62) by Skidmore, Owings and Merrill (Walter A. Netsch Jnr, architect) at Colorado Springs, Colorado, of reinforced concrete and aluminium. It combines sanctuaries for Protestants, Catholics and Jews. Below: the Thorncrown Chapel, Eureka Springs, Arkansas, by E. Fay Jones (1980) is no more than a covered lattice of wood and steel, the interstices filled with glass. It is a nondenominational chapel for meditation and pilgrimage.

Marcel Breuer's church of St John's Abbey at Collegeville, Minnesota, is almost at the opposite extreme. The construction is overwhelming in its solidity and heaviness. Its most prominent feature is the bell-tower, a vast concrete 'banner' over 100 feet high with two rectangular holes in it, one containing a cross, the other a row of bells: a unique and unforgettable image.

Other modern churches in the USA offer a bewildering variety of new forms, some clearly expressive of ecclesiastical tradition, so that churches are recognizably churches, others totally without parallel in the past. Frank Lloyd Wright's Annie Pfeiffer Memorial Chapel at Lakeland, Florida (1941), and Gyo Obata's St Louis Priory at Saint Louis, Missouri (1962), are examples of the latter. The first is composed of jagged, rectangular shapes, a gaunt tower punched with lozenges over a two-tier auditorium composed of equally angular lines. The second, on the contrary, is all curves, a series of wave-like arches one above the other forming large windows lighting a round central space. From a technical point of view, the Air Force Academy Cadet Chapel at Colorado Springs (1956–62) by Walter Netsch of Skidmore, Owings and Merrill, is perhaps even more remarkable. It is made up of aluminium fins set between concrete buttresses and rising above the roof, as one critic put it, 'like a person's hands pressed together in prayer'.

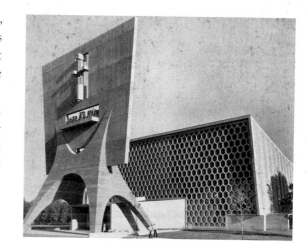

Bell-tower of St John's Abbey, Collegeville, Minnesota, by Marcel Breuer, 1961. The church itself, in contrast to this Expressionist composition, is severely rectangular.

Tokyo Cathedral (1967–69) by Kenzo Tange (right) is perhaps the most revolutionary church design of the whole century. It consists essentially of the four arms of a cross (nave, transepts, chancel), but with the vaults replaced by glass and the end of each arm also totally glazed. The side walls are huge expanses of concrete pulled out to form a kite-shaped ground-plan and sloping like the sides of a tent.

Philip Johnson's 'Roofless Church' at New Harmony, Indiana, of 1960 is in some sense misnamed. One could equally well call it a church that is nothing but a roof. It is simply a single 'embracing' space.

That even Philip Johnson, too, can achieve effects of repose and meditation quite unlike his Crystal Cathedral is proved by his Roofless Church (1960) at New Harmony, Indiana. It is simply a canopy, rising as if buoyed up from inside and anchored to concrete plinths. In Johnson's own words, a great church 'contains, cuddles, exalts or stimulates the person in that space'.

Sometimes, then, these highly contemporary designs disclose Christian symbolism in a modern interpretation; sometimes they are attempts to match the timeless truths with local or national culture. Thus a structure like Tokyo Cathedral, by Kenzo Tange (who also designed the Olympic swimming pool at Yoyogi), or the Anglican Church of the Resurrection at Hiroshima, also in Japan, achieve striking appearance at the same time as religious meaning. It was a fearful irony that the nuclear bombs released on Hiroshima and Nagasaki by a Christian nation destroyed the largest concentrations of Christians in Japan. At Hiroshima the Resurrection Church has a tower whose rounded glass cupola, like a cylinder lying on its side, suggests both strength and shelter, transcendence and final hope for the suffering creation.

Le Corbusier's celebrated chapel of Notre-Dame-du-Haut at Ronchamp in France is sculptural in a very obvious sense. It is a pilgrim church, built between

1950 and 1955, and intended to create a monumental presence which would inspire visitors. Despite its size, it holds only fifty worshippers, and an external pulpit allows oration to those outside. Set on grass, with trees in the background, the church is like an unexpected fungus on a garden lawn, a cumbersome fantasy whose attraction is immediate and visual rather than intellectual or spiritual.

The delightful church of S. Giovanni Battista on the Italian Autostrada del Sol, near Prato in Tuscany, however, achieves monumentality and symbolism with ease. It was designed in 1960 by Giovanni Michelucci (whose railway station in Florence is also admired by many). The green roof seems draped in folds which descend to rough white walls of stone. Concrete piers lean inwards. The effect is to suggest a journey; the church is like a road winding upwards. It was, indeed, designed for the use of travellers on the motorway.

The ultimate expression of sculptured form must surely be the 'Cathedral of Salt' at Zipaquirá in Colombia. A vast church has been excavated within a salt mine, with capacity for 8,000 people. It is 450 feet below ground, and the roof of the chamber rises to 80 feet. The 'cathedral', which took ten years to build, is in fact also a place of burial, with side-galleries, behind iron grilles, for the stacking

German architects had experimented with Expressionist churches before the War, a style of sharp angles, ridged surfaces, wedge-shaped openings and crystalline forms, and they carried it further in the 1950s and 1960s. The church of St Josef at Neuss-Wecklingen in the Ruhr, of 1966–67, is by F. Schaller and S. Polónyi.

The interior of Gaudí's Sagrada Familia, Barcelona (see pl. 74), carries the parallel with organic growth even further than the exterior. This is a reconstruction of the architect's model for the nave; it has yet to be built. The structural principles are close to Gothic, but Gaudí rationalized the system of thrusts and counter-thrusts by making the piers lean inwards and sprout branches, like trees.

The cathedral of the Holy Family, Nairobi (1960–63), an adaptation of the vocabulary of modern architecture to an African setting.

of coffins. The awesome and mysterious beauty of the main chamber is therefore tinged with faintly macabre associations, not lessened by the echoes and the weird luminosity of the reflections of candlelight from the compacted salt crystalline walls. The church is fittingly dedicated to Our Lady of the Rosary, patron of the miners who once worked down there.

With all the emphasis on the use of concrete construction in modern churches, it is easy to overlook the often extremely effective use of stone. This has been particularly successful where the stone has local significance. The Catholic cathedral of the Holy Family in Nairobi, for example, combines stone with glass and concrete to create an atmosphere which, while thoroughly 'modern', is at the same time redolent of Kenyan culture. The cathedral was built between 1960 and 1963. At Peterhouse School in Marondera, Zimbabwe, the splendid chapel, built in 1958 to accommodate 600 boys and parents, has east- and west-end walls of local undressed stone. The result, as was doubtless intended, is a satisfactory harmony of the Christian presence with the surrounding landscape of the area: this part of Zimbabwe is characterized by boulder outcrops, and the name of the school itself, which honours St Peter – the Rock – is therefore also expressed in the very structure of the building.

Churches have been built in all the available styles of the twentieth century, including, of course, the revivals of past styles. There are even examples which reflect obviously decorative and 'artistic' architectural and aesthetic fashions. The most representative of these – though there is really nothing else like it – is surely Gaudí's great and unfinished expiatory church of the Sagrada Familia in Barcelona, the capital of Catalonia in Spain. Gaudí was originally a Gothic Revivalist; his visionary buildings in a distinctive mutation of Art Nouveau decorative styles constitute one of the major architectural pleasures of Barcelona. His use of coloured tile and ceramic fragments in decoration – first pioneered in Paris by Hector Guimard – give his structures a jewelled brilliance which recalls the fantasy buildings of children's storybooks. The great church of the Holy Family occupies a square site on which a cruciform Gothic church was being built, from 1882. When Gaudí took over the work, in 1884, he abandoned the

previous designs altogether. Until his death in 1926 – he was killed just outside the church when he stepped into the path of an oncoming tram – he was absorbed by what he regarded, correctly, as his greatest project. By 1887 the crypt was complete. Then he began the *chevet*, still in a version of recognizable Gothic. By 1903, when he had completed the Nativity façade of the south transept, it became clear that Gaudí was building in a quite new style. As work proceeded on the transept itself, up until 1930, the public were astonished at the extraordinary gables and helicoidal towers (now so familiar a part of the Barcelona skyline) that went up. In 1952 work was resumed, according to Gaudí's original design, on the Passion transept, and more recently the nave itself has been started. It is, in a way, a pity that the church will be finished, for the tapering spires, like basket-work cones, create an outstandingly dramatic impact as they are: free-standing and sharply defined. The organic and molten appearance of the decoration clearly derive from Gothic; the riotous interlacing and bold use of forms from Art Nouveau. As a testimony to Gaudí's faith, this unique church will always attract admiration. It is unlikely, to say the least, to inspire, as its designer hoped it would, a generation of new cathedrals in the same architectural genre.

If Art Nouveau churches were rare, so also were churches in the Art Deco style – whose streamlined appearance was more suited to the houses, cinemas and dance-halls of the 1930s than to places of worship. But one extremely successful version of the style can be seen at Turner's Cross in Cork city, Ireland. The Catholic church of Christ the King is actually the work of two Americans. The architect was Barry Byrne of Chicago, and the sculptor of the figure of Christ, which is the leading feature of the church's western exterior, was John Storrs. The base of the tower contains two entrance doorways with the statue of Christ between them, his arms raised in a gesture both of blessing and of welcome as the worshippers pass each side of his body to enter the church. The symbolism is obvious and successful. Inside, the altar stands in front of the choir and this, together with the absence of internal roof supports, allows an unimpeded view of the central rites to the congregation. In this sense the church anticipated by three decades the liturgical requirements of the Second Vatican Council.

A late version of Art Deco is to be found in an unexpected place. In 1915 a Black South African prophet called Engenas Lekganyane took himself into the Cloud Mountains of the north-western Transvaal, beyond Pietersburg, and there received a series of visions. The result was the foundation of one of the largest of the independent Black Churches – the Zion Christian Church. Lekganyane died in 1948; by then the Church had established a permanent settlement called, after the Temple Mount in Jerusalem (of which it was considered a direct descendant), Moria. The central building in the settlement is a rather wistfully 'modern' church: a long stuccoed hall, with a low oval gable, and a square-shaped tower which is the most Art Deco feature of all. Its plain lines produce a good contrast with the curved roof, and the overall effect is one of surprising grace for a building obviously intended to be utilitarian. The great success of the Zion Christian Church means that on some days as many as 60,000 pilgrims make their way here, in fleets of buses, to attend the services in the church and the mystic purification rites in other parts of the steep valley in which it is situated.

If we ask for a distinctive 'church style' of architecture in the twentieth century, we shall be disappointed. It is, indeed, difficult to speak of a distinctive architectural style of any sort in the modern world, when, even more than in the nineteenth century, builders have had an enormous variety from which to choose. There has been, it is true, a growing internationalism, in the sense that the continuation of building in traditional styles, and experiments in modern

The west door of the church of Christ the King, in Cork, Ireland, is an Art Deco transformation of a type of Romanesque portal in which the figure of Christ occupies the trumeau. The architect was Barry Byrne of Chicago, the sculptor another American, John Storrs.

building techniques used to create quite different sorts of structures from those of the past, have shown a fairly even distribution across the nations of the earth.

These factors have had their effect on churches, too. There is now no way of detecting the denomination of a church from its external appearance – except for the Orthodox churches which have continued to be constructed, especially in Greece and North America, according to Byzantine formulae. The denominations themselves have demonstrated great and increasing internal pluralism, and an allied disposition to echo the cultural forms of the particular secular societies in which they are set. The Catholic Church, too, has seen a resurgence of localism, with the recognition that centralized authority is not as absolute and unchallengeable as the nineteenth century would have asserted. The Orthodox churches, never particularly indebted to internationalist impulses anyway, since their traditional self-governing units were based upon national entities, have mostly found themselves cut off behind the Iron Curtain. The Protestant bodies, who were always known for institutional devolution and individualist theology, have richly enhanced these characteristics in the twentieth century.

And so the emphasis seems to be returning from the large, centralized body to the small, less organized, more intimate group of believers, and above all to the communal experience of those seeking salvation and the knowledge of God. Men and women still evidently experience the need for places where the transcendent can be rendered in the materials of the earth, and where memorials of faith can transform the commonplaces of the present into expectations of eternity.

Stanley Spencer's great picture of the Resurrection of soldiers at the Oratory of All Souls at Burghclere in Berkshire, painted in 1928, brings out the immediacy of the supernatural in the experience of ordinary people in a way hardly attempted before. Spencer had served in Macedonia himself in the Great War and had therefore seen the circumstances of military life at the front. His memories were now transformed into tableaux of an extraordinary spiritual intensity which are also somehow disturbing. In the distance, Christ receives the crosses, which resemble the crosses of war cemeteries, from resurrecting soldiers. All around them the slaughtered army horses, too, raise their heads in curious experience of unexpected life. A heap of crosses in the foreground symbolizes the random waste of life that has occurred and which yet speaks of sacrifice. Ordinary men, caught up in events over which they have no control, are suddenly called to Resurrection and clasp the hands of their comrades. The informal spirituality of the pictures, and the numinous atmosphere they create in the chapel of All Souls, say all that needs to be said about the persistence of church building in the modern world.

Glossary

ambulatory: aisle encircling the choir

apse: a part of a building that is semicircular in plan

arcade: a series of arches on piers or columns

baldacchino: canopy supported on four uprights, usually over an altar

barrel vault: a continuous arched stone roof or ceiling. See vault

bar tracery: see tracery

basilica: a building that consists of a central space between two arcades or colonnades surmounted by a wall with windows, and flanked by lower side aisles

bay: one unit of a basilican building, from one pier to the next

blind arcading: arcading set against a wall

boss: large carved stone set at the meeting-point of vaulting ribs

campanile: bell-tower of an Italian church, usually free-standing

cashel: a circular bank of earth and stone containing dwellings in a rocky area

catacomb: system of underground passages used for burials

chancel: part of church containing the altar

chevet: apsidal east end of a church with chapels opening off an ambulatory

chevron: zig-zag design

choir: part of church next to the altar containing choir-stalls

clerestory: upper part of a church containing windows

clochan: dry-stone cells

coffered ceiling (or coffering): wooden ceiling divided into recessed panels

colonnade: a row of columns

colonnette: a miniature column or shaft

conch: semi-dome over an apse

corbel: a stone bracket

crocket: Gothic decorative motif, like a stylized curled leaf ending in a bud

crossing: area in the centre of a church where nave, transepts and eastern arm meet

cupola: a small dome

dog-tooth: Gothic ornament consisting of four small leaf or petal shapes forming a raised square

east end: conventionally the end where the altar is situated

edicule: classical frame round a window or other opening, consisting of columns or pilasters surmounted by a pediment

elevation: the vertical dimension of a building, as distinct from the plan, which is horizontal

entablature: continuous horizontal element that runs above a classical order

exonarthex: a subsidiary narthex outside the narthex proper

flying buttress: a half-arch of masonry on the exterior of a Gothic building counteracting the thrust of a vault

gesso: thin plaster laid as preparation for painting

Greek cross: a cross with four equal arms

groin vault: see vault

hammerbeam roof: an arched wooden roof resting on the ends of beams or brackets projecting from the wall in order to reduce the span to be covered

iconostasis: screen displaying icons, dividing the priest's area from the congregation in Orthodox churches

kellia: hermits' dwellings

lancet: a long, thin pointed window in Gothic architecture

lantern tower: tower whose windows are open to the interior

Latin cross: cross with one arm longer than the other three

lavra: Greek Orthodox monastery

lunette: semi-circular space between an arch and its flat lintel

narthex: a porch stretching across the whole width of a church façade

ogee: an arch formed by two curves in opposite directions

Pantocrator: lit. 'Ruler of All', an attribute of Christ

pareclesion: chapel of a Byzantine church

pediment: the triangular gable at the end of the roof of a classical building

pendant vault: see vault

pendentive: the concave triangular space between the arches supporting a dome and its circular base

pier: compound support acting as a column or pillar in medieval architecture

pilaster: flattened version of a classical column

plate tracery: see tracery

porticus: separate chapels or chambers opening off the nave

pulpitum: a solid stone screen separating the nave from the choir

quadripartite: see vault

rath: a circular bank of earth and stone containing dwellings

reticulated tracery: tracery like a net

retrochoir: an extension of the church behind the choir

rib vault: see vault

rood: sculpture of Christ on the cross. Rood screen: screen separating the nave from the chancel, surmounted by the rood. Rood loft: the top part of a rood screen if there is room to walk on it

rotunda: a circular building

sacristy: office of the sacrist where vestments and church plate are kept

sarcophagus: a stone coffin

sexpartite: see vault

sketae: small dependencies of large monasteries in the Orthodox tradition

spandrel: triangular space between two arches

stoa: in Greek architecture, a covered way

string-course: a horizontal moulding running across or along a building

suppedaneum: Russian- or Byzantine-style foot-rest

tesserae: small pieces of stone or glass used in mosaic

tierceron: see vault

tracery: stone frame to hold glass in a window. In bar tracery the opening is filled with thin curving ribs. In plate tracery holes are punched in solid masonry

transept: part of church at right angles to the nave and choir and normally projecting beyond them

triforium: middle unit of three-storey elevation, between arcade and clerestory

trumeau: pier in the middle of an entrance

tympanum: semi-circular space between the lintel and arch of a doorway

vault: a stone ceiling or roof. Barrel or tunnel vault: a continuous arched surface. Groin vault: vault formed by the intersection of two tunnel vaults at right angles. Rib vault: vault in which the groins, or edges, are outlined by stone ribs. Quadripartite vault: vault in which the ribs form a simple cross, dividing the bay into four. Sexpartite vault: vault in which there is an extra pair of ribs dividing the bay into six. Ridge-rib: a rib running longitudinally along the crown of a vault. Tierceron: a rib running from the wall to the ridge-rib. Lierne: a short rib between two other ribs. Fan vault: vault formed by sections in the form of inverted cones. Pendant vault: vault in which the bosses carry downward-pointing projections

west end: conventionally, the end opposite the altar, with the main entrance

Sources of illustrations

Colour plates are identified by **bold** numerals and black-and-white illustrations by the page numbers on which they appear. As an aid to identification, the following abbreviations are used: *a* above, *b* bottom, *l* left, *r* right.

By gracious permission of Her Majesty the Queen 13, **57**;
Aberdeen Art Gallery 146;
Helen Adant **76**;
Frank Aleksandrowicz 298 *r*;
Alinari, Rome 32, 65, 164, 185, 187 *ar&br*, 190, 192, 193 *r*, 194 *l&r*, 214 *bl*, 216 *bl&br*, 217 *l*;
J. Allan Cash 297;
Appetiti 219 *a*;
Masao Arai, Tokyo 300 *r*;
Archives Photographiques, Paris 86, 131 *r*, 150 *r*, 153 *l*, 167 *l*;
James Austin **75**, 129, 167 *r*;
Austrian National Tourist Office 276 *ar*;
Barcelona, Gaudí Society 302 *l*;
Damian Bayon 223, 224 *l*, 226 *a&b*, 227 *a*, 268;
Roloff Beny **5**, 24;
Berlin, Kaiser Friedrich Museum 33;
Staatliche Museen Berlin (West), Preussischer Kulturbesitz, Nationalgalerie. Photo Jörg P. Anders **61**;
Raccolta delle Stampe Archivi Bertarelli, Milan 214 *r*;
Osvaldo Böhm, Venice 66, 213 *l*;
Cambridge, Director of Aerial Photography, University of Cambridge 87 *b*, 99 *b*, 102;
Camera Press 52;
Richard Cheek **67**;
Peter Chèze-Brown 122 *b*, 159 *r*;
Colour Library International 173 *ar*, 186;
Country Life 296;
Courtesy of the Byzantine Institute Inc 54 *a*, 55, 62 *a*;
Christie's, London 83;
Cyprus Museum 57;
De Antonis **12**;
Jean Dieuzaide **28**, **29**, 125;
Dublin, Commissioners of Public Works 97; National Library of Ireland 240 *a*, 271 *b*; Courtesy Board Trinity College 100 *r*;
Istituto Editoriale Electa 213 *ar*;
E.J. Farmer 244 *l*, 246 *a*;
The Fine Art Society, London **19**;
David Finn 117 *r*;
A. Franz, New York 60 *r*;
Henry Fuerman 293;
Yukio Futagawa 294 *r*, 298 *l*, 299 *ar*;
Gabinetto Fotografico Nazionale, Rome 82;
G. Gerster/Hillelson **1**;
Vadim Gippenreiter **15**;
Giraudon **22**, **56**, **70**, 153 *r*, 156 *al*, 162 *r*, 213 *br*, 238;

Werner Guttmann 250;
Sonia Halliday **23**, **65**, 63 *r*;
Lee A. Hanley 299 *br*;
Hans Hartz 240 *b*;
Ian Hausbrand/Camera Press **80**;
André Held **3**, **14**, **16**, **21**;
Hirmer Verlag **44**, **48**, **49**, 18, 28 *a*, 51, 52, 53, 54 *r*, 56, 63 *l*, 166, 168 *r*, 214 *al*;
Frank Horlbeck 20, 60 *l*, 89 *a*;
Angelo Hornak **59**;
Hans Hüber 27;
Martin Hürlimann 128 *r*, 134 *b*, 156 *ar*, 160 *al&ar*, 228;
Greg Hursley/Hursley/Lark/Hursley 299 *l*;
Impartial Reporter, Enniskillen 103;
Irish Tourist Board 87 *a*, 119 *br*, 130 *a*;
A.F. Kersting **25**, **31**, **37**, 58 *b*, 67, 84, 85, 96, 117 *l*, 123 *a*, 124 *al&br*, 132 *l*, 134 *a*, 154, 158, 160 *b*, 161 *bl&br*, 171 *b*, 172, 173 *al*, 174, 175 *l&ar*, 215, 217 *ar*, 218 *a*, 220 *r*, 230 *r*, 241 *r*, 243 *r*, 249 *b*, 251 *br*, 272 *a*, 274 *b*, 275 *a*, 302 *r*;
Balthazar Korab 300 *l*;
Richard Lannoy 35;
Robert Lautman Photography 248 *l*;
Dr V.N. Lasarew, Moscow 69 *b*;
Eric Lessing **11**;
Lingard Gallery 266;
London, British Architectural Library 22, 25 *b*, 27, 38, 191, 218 *b*, 219 *b*; British Museum 188, 193 *l*; Congregation of the Brompton Oratory **68**; Conway Library, Courtauld Institute of Art 131 *al*, 168 *l*, 175 *br*, 212, 220 *l*, (Photo Anthony Blunt) 225 *l*, (Photo G.A. Martin) 225 *r*, 276 *b*; Museum of London 195; National Gallery **35**, **42**, 147; National Monuments Record 94, 120 *a*, 155, 239, 242, 245 *l*, 247 *a*, 269 *a*, 272 *b*, 273 *r*; Royal Commission on the Historical Monuments of England 150 *l*, 243 *l*, 273 *l*; Royal Institute of British Architects 66; Courtesy of Sir John Soane's Museum 62, 251 *l*; Victoria and Albert Museum 274 *a*; Derek Lowman 294 *l*;
Marburg 89 *b*, 115, 118, 119 *ar*, 131 *bl*, 156 *b*, 157 *bl&r*, 165, 276 *al*;
R.A. Markus 33 *b*;
Mas **34**, **50**, **51**;
Georgina Masson 26, 28 *b*, 29, 216 *a*;
Leonard von Matt 19;
Mexican National Tourist Council 224 *b*;
Middle East Archive **6**, **8**;
George Mott 119 *l*, 249 *a*, 303;
National Trust Photographic Library/A.C. Cooper 305;
Werner Neumeister 25, 182;
S. Newbery 241 *l*;
New York, the J. Clarence Davies Collection, Museum of the City of New York 278 *l*;
Oxford, Ashmolean Museum 275 *b*;
Paris, Direction Generale du Tourisme

295; Institut de France 183; Monuments Historiques 63;
Canon Parsons/Architectural Association Slide Library, London 173 *br*;
Yanni Petsopoulos/Barbara Heller **18**;
Philadelphia, Courtesy of St Mary's-at-the-Cathedral 278 *r*;
Nicholas A.J. Philpot **53**, **54**, **79**;
Rosmarie Pierer 61 *l*;
Courtesy S. Polonyi 301;
Paolo Portoghesi 211;
Josephine Powell 58 *l*, 59 *l&r*;
Rockefeller Centre Inc, New York 279;
Réné Roland **74**;
Rome, Pontificia Commissione di Archeologia Sacra 30 *a&b*;
Jean Roubier 116, 123 *b*, 126, 130 *br*, 169;
Sandak Inc, Stamford, CT, USA 248 *r*;
Scala **2**, **4**, **9**, **17**, **30**, **31**, **38**, **40**, **41**, **43**, **45**, **46**, **47**, **55**, **60**, **77**, 149;
Collection Georg Schäfer 267;
Gordon H. Schenk **78**;
Helga Schmidt-Glassner 124 *ar*, 128 *l*, 130 *bl*, 151, 170, 230 *l*;
Tony Schneiders 221, 231;
Daniel Schwartz **10**;
Ronald Sheridan 20 *l*;
Schwerin, Staatliche Museen 210;
Edwin Smith 61 *r*, 64, 70 *b*, 98, 99 *r*, 100 *l*, 101, 114, 120 *b*, 121 *l&r*, 127 *l&r*, 132 *a&b*, 133, 157 *al*, 159 *l*, 163, 171 *al&ar*, 189, 229, 244 *ar&br*, 245 *br*, 247 *b*, 251 *a*, 270, 271;
H. Snoek-Westwood 290;
Dr Franz Stoedtner 277 *b*;
Wim Swaan/Camera Press **7**, **36**;
N. Tombazi 70 *a*, 91, 92;
G. Tomisch 54 *b*;
Ulm, Münsterbauamt 149 *l*;
VAAP 68 *a*;
Vatican, Biblioteca Apostolica Vaticana 24; St Peter's 291;
Vienna, Kupferstichkabinett, Akademie der bildenden Künste 148;
Rolf Vogel 135;
Washington, the Catholic University of America. Photo Nick Crettier 71; Library of Congress 245 *ar*;
Jeremy Whitaker **71**;
Tim Woodcock **32**, **39**;
Woodmansterne **37**, **64**.

Index

312